The *Sams Teach Yourself in 24 Hours* Series

Sams Teach Yourself in 24 Hours books provide quick-and-easy answers in a proven step-by-step approach that works for you. In just 24 sessions of one hour or less, you will tackle every task you need to get the results you want. Let our experienced authors present the most accurate information to get you reliable answers—fast!

Lotus SmartSuite Millennium Edition

SAMS

Faithe Wempen

SAMS
Teach Yourself

Lotus
SmartSuite
Millennium Edition

in 24 Hours

SAMS

A Division of Macmillan Computer Publishing
201 West 103rd St., Indianapolis, Indiana 46290 USA

EXECUTIVE EDITOR
Jim Minatel

ACQUISITIONS EDITOR
Jill Byus

DEVELOPMENT EDITOR
Rick Kughen

TECHNICAL EDITOR
Don Roche

MANAGING EDITOR
Thomas F. Hayes

PRODUCTION EDITOR
Linda Seifert

COPY EDITOR
Cliff Shubs

INDEXER
Larry Sweazy

PRODUCTION
Laura A. Knox
Daniela Raderstorf
Pamela Woolf

COVER DESIGNER
Aren Howell

BOOK DESIGNER
Gary Adair

Overview

Contents

Dedication

To Margaret

Acknowledgments

What a joy it is to work with the team of professionals at Sams. Thanks to Jill Byus, acquisitions editor, for thinking of me for this project and for her help in the contract negotiation phase. Rick Kughen did an excellent job with development, and Don Roche went one step beyond the normal technical editing to offer some great content suggestions. I also want to thank the copy editor, Cliff Shubs, and the project editor, Linda Seifert, for cleaning up my wording, and the oft-underappreciated production team for their hard work in layout and proofreading.

—**Faithe Wempen**

About the Author

FAITHE WEMPEN, M.A., operates Your Computer Friend, a computer training and troubleshooting business in Indianapolis that specializes in helping beginning users with their PCs. Her eclectic writing credits include 22 computer books, including *Microsoft Office 97 Professional 6-in-1*, *Using Microsoft Home Essentials*, and *The 10 Minute Guide to Access*, plus articles, essays, training manuals, and OEM documentation. Her hobbies include surfing the Internet, doing cross-stitch, being an active member of Broadway United Methodist Church in Indianapolis, vacationing in Las Vegas, and raising Shetland Sheepdogs.

Tell Us What You Think!

As the reader of this book, you are our most important critic and commentator. We value your opinion and want to know what we're doing right, what we could do better, what areas you'd like to see us publish in, and any other words of wisdom you're willing to pass our way.

As the executive editor for the General Desktop Applications team at Macmillan Computer Publishing, I welcome your comments. You can fax, email, or write me directly to let me know what you did or didn't like about this book—as well as what we can do to make our books stronger.

Please note that I cannot help you with technical problems related to the topic of this book, and that due to the high volume of mail I receive, I might not be able to reply to every message.

When you write, please be sure to include this book's title and author as well as your name and phone or fax number. I will carefully review your comments and share them with the author and editors who worked on the book.

Fax: 317-817-7070

Email: pcs@mcp.com

Mail: Executive Editor Jim Minatel
         General Desktop Applications
         Macmillan Computer Publishing
         201 West 103rd Street
         Indianapolis, IN 46290 USA

Introduction

SmartSuite is the number-two selling integrated office suite in the world, with millions of users. (It's second only to Microsoft Office, a larger, more expensive product.)

Why is SmartSuite so popular? There are several reasons. One is that it's not a huge, mutant monster program, with hundreds of features that most people will never use. SmartSuite is just the right size, with just the right features for the average business-person or home user. Another reason—let's be honest here—is the price. SmartSuite is priced well below the competitor. It's a great value.

Whatever the reason you chose SmartSuite, congratulations on your choice! I think you'll find that SmartSuite is easy, fun, and powerful enough for almost any task.

Who Should Read This Book

This book is for people who have had some experience with Windows and with comput-ing, but who may not have worked much with SmartSuite to date. I won't hold your hand too tightly in this book; we'll move at a brisk pace. We have to, after all, to get through this entire suite of applications in 24 hours!

Anyone who wants to create basic business documents, worksheets, and databases in SmartSuite will find their needs met in this book. I won't try to make you a techno-expert, but I will make sure that you have all the skills you need to venture off on your own and explore some of the more advanced features later, after your 24-hour "cram period" is over.

What This Book Will Do For You

Believe it or not, with this book, you really can learn to use the entire SmartSuite group of applications in only 24 hours!

How is this possible? It's because of the consistency built into SmartSuite. When you learn how to perform an action in one SmartSuite application, you've learned how to do it in all. For example, no matter which application you're working with, there is always a Save command located on the File menu. You always print by clicking the Print SmartIcon. You always change your preferences with the User Setup command. See what I mean? In this book, the skills you learn will build on one another, with no boring repe-tition. You'll accomplish more than you ever dreamed, in less time than you ever imag-ined possible.

Conventions Used in This Book

Each hour begins with a list of the things you'll learn, and ends with a summary and question-and-answer session, so you can review your new skills.

In addition, these special boxed elements appear along the way:

Notes clarify concepts and procedures, and provide extra information.

Tips offer shortcuts and solutions, and suggest ways to use the program features for greater productivity.

Cautions point out possible pitfalls. Reading them will save you from making critical mistakes.

New Term New terms are introduced with this special designation.

Part I
Introducing SmartSuite

Hour

HOUR 1

Welcome to SmartSuite

SmartSuite isn't your run-of-the-mill integrated package of software. Sure enough, it's got all the basic tools you need for home and business, such as a word processor, spreadsheet, and database. But it also has some unexpected—and very cool—extras that make it special, such as desktop filing drawers and support for voice commands. Even if you're a die-hard user of another suite (and *I* was before writing this book!), you may find yourself falling in love with SmartSuite's user-friendly personality.

In this first hour, I'll take you on a tour (that's a *one*-hour tour, not three, for you *Gilligan* fans) of SmartSuite's components, so you can get a feel for what's in store. Along the way, I'll try to show you not only what features SmartSuite offers, but examples of projects you can actually create with SmartSuite.

The highlights of this hour include:

- What tools you get with SmartSuite
- How the SmartCenter provides easy access
- What you can create with each component

- How the components work together
- Where to turn for help

What Have We Here?

SmartSuite includes everything you need to create correspondence, forms, reports, calendars, posters, and almost any other kind of printed document you can imagine. It also provides the tools you need to manage your schedule, keep track of data (such as addresses or an inventory), and create dazzling business presentations. Here's a rundown of the players:

- **SmartCenter**. A central starting point that ties all the other components together.
- **Word Pro**. A word processor, for typing and editing text.
- **1-2-3**. A spreadsheet, for entering and calculating numbers.
- **Approach**. A database, for organizing and searching for information.
- **Freelance**. A presentation program, for creating slides and handouts for meetings.
- **Organizer**. A Personal Information Manager (PIM), for organizing your contacts and your schedule.
- **ScreenCam**. A recorder that records "movies" of onscreen activities.
- **FastSite**. A Web site organizer, for preparing Web pages for publication on the Internet.

Don't worry if you are not quite certain about any of the preceding items; you'll learn about each of the components as you go along in this book.

The SmartCenter Desktop Drawers

SmartCenter is a filing system—and more. It consists of a series of drawers that appears at the top of your screen. Click a drawer to open it, as shown in Figure 1.1. Drawers stay open until you close them by clicking their Close (X) button.

FIGURE 1.1.

A SmartCenter drawer, complete with several folders.

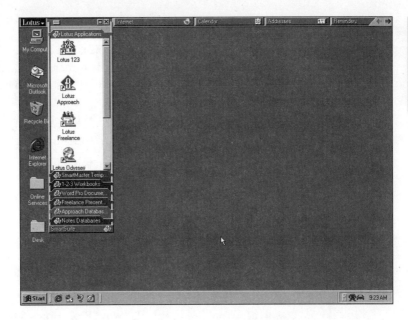

| NEW TERM | *Folders:* Inside a drawer, you'll find colored tabs called *folders*. They're sort of like drawers-within-drawers. You can open a folder by clicking its tab.

If the folder contains icons (for example, for programs or documents), you can activate them by double-clicking them. Figure 1.1 shows the drawer and folder that contains the icons that start the various SmartSuite components. Drawers can also contain Web pages, as you'll learn in Hour 2. When you open one of these drawers, if you are not currently connected to the Internet, a connection box appears. After you connect, the Web page appears in SmartSuite's own Web browser.

Project Possibilities with SmartSuite

Take a few moments in this first hour to dream. What would you like to be able to create? To organize? To present to the world? Then take a look at the following descriptions of SmartSuite components, to see where your dreams fit in.

Word Pro Projects

Word Pro, the word processor, is great for any project that involves a lot of text. This component is designed specifically to handle whole paragraphs and pages of stuff, like the newsletter shown in Figure 1.2. For that reason, you'll want to use it for:

- Booklets
- Business cards
- Business plans
- Calendars
- Catalogs
- Journals
- Faxes
- Indexes
- Invoices

- Letters
- Mailing labels
- Memos
- Newsletters
- Outlines
- Reports
- Resumes
- Term papers
- Web pages

You'll learn how to use Word Pro in Part II, "Word Pro," Hours 5 through 10.

FIGURE 1.2.

This newsletter was created with Word Pro.

1-2-3 Projects

With 1-2-3, you can write formulas that calculate numbers, and explore what-if possibilities by changing the numbers involved. Sounds kind of boring when described generally like that, eh? But you'd be surprised how many situations this is handy for. For example, Figure 1.3 shows 1-2-3 being used to calculate loan payments. You can find out exactly how much per month a $170,000 house will cost as opposed to a $100,000 one, for example. You can also use 1-2-3 for:

- Expense reports
- Financial records
- Grade books
- Invoices
- Loan amortization
- Personal budgeting

- Purchase orders
- Sales plans
- Score cards
- Sports averages
- Tax records
- Time sheets

Part III, "1-2-3," of this book, Hours 11 through 15, indicates what you need to know to create your own projects in 1-2-3.

FIGURE 1.3.

With 1-2-3, you can find out how much house (or car) you can afford.

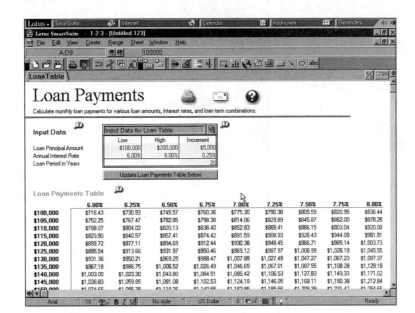

Approach Projects

Approach's database tools are perfect for organizing a lot of data. One type of data that almost everyone must keep track of is an address and telephone list, like the one shown in Figure 1.4. Other data you can manage with Approach includes:

- Art collections
- Music and video collections
- Business contacts
- Contracts
- Employees
- Trade shows

- Mailing lists
- Household inventories
- Products
- Recipes
- Investments
- Exercise logs

Part IV, "Approach," Hours 16 through 19, showcases Approach and the features you can use to create your own database projects.

FIGURE 1.4.

A name and address list is a simple database.

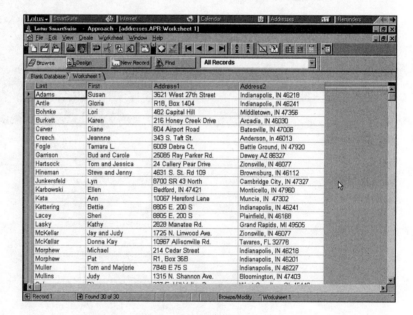

Freelance Projects

Freelance is a boon to anyone who has to make business presentations. It enables you to create beautiful, consistent slides for any speech or sales pitch. Figure 1.5 shows a slide from a show that introduces employees to their new health insurance options. Some other presentations you can create include:

- Business plans
- Motivational speeches
- Industry analyses
- Proposals
- Marketing plans
- Meeting agendas

- New product rollouts
- Sales plans
- Sales reports
- Brainstorming sessions
- New employee orientations
- Training classes

Hour 20 is jam-packed with information about creating your own presentations in Freelance.

FIGURE 1.5.

This slide is being created in Freelance for an employee insurance meeting.

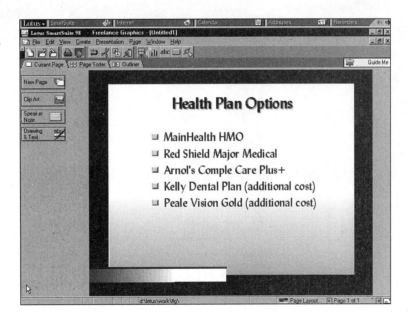

Organizer Projects

Organizer is more single-minded than the other SmartSuite applications. The other applications are flexible and general, but Organizer is sharply focused on one goal—managing your personal information. Its components that work seamlessly together toward this goal include:

- Address and telephone book
- Calendar with event scheduling and reminders
- Anniversary (annual event) listing
- Event planner
- Notes area

Figure 1.6 shows a page from the Calendar portion of Organizer, with several appointments scheduled.

FIGURE 1.6.

Use Organizer to plan each day and track the things you need to do.

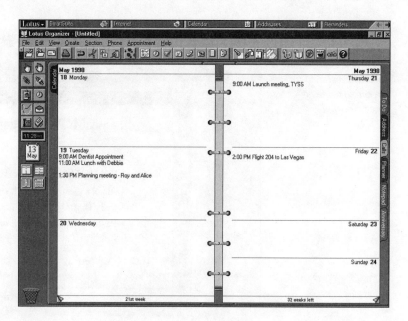

In Hour 21, you'll learn how to work with each of these Organizer tools to keep your daily life neatly organized.

How the Components Work Together

It's no accident that the SmartSuite components are sold as a set. Each is a powerful tool in its own right, but the group soars when you use the components together. You'll learn about intercomponent data sharing in Hour 22.

As with any Windows-based program, you can cut-and-paste information from one SmartSuite component to another. For example, you can copy a graph from 1-2-3 into the report you are writing in Word Pro, as in Figure 1.7.

FIGURE 1.7.

A Word Pro report can contain data from any other SmartSuite tool, such as this graph from 1-2-3.

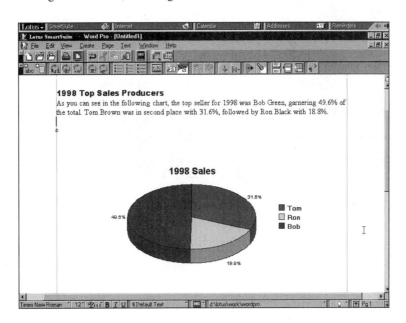

Here are some other ways the SmartSuite components work together:

- Copy notes from an Organizer notes page into a Word Pro document.
- Create an OLE link from a 1-2-3 spreadsheet to a Freelance presentation, to make sure you always have the most current figures in your presentation.

NEW TERM *OLE:* OLE stands for Object Linking and Embedding, a type of link that is automatically updated with the latest data every time the source changes.

- Paste cells from a 1-2-3 spreadsheet into an Approach data table.
- Import data from Approach or Organizer into a 1-2-3 spreadsheet.
- Perform mail merges, as you'll learn in Hour 23, by pulling data from Organizer, 1-2-3, or Approach into Word Pro.

Getting Help in SmartSuite

Help is available almost everywhere you turn in SmartSuite. You're never without a help-ing hand to guide you.

Help Within an Application

Each SmartSuite component has a Help menu. Just click the word "Help" on the menu bar at the top of the window, and then click the menu item you want. You'll find the fol-lowing types of help in each application:

- **Ask the Expert**. This opens a window where you can type your question in plain English. For example, if you want to know about printing, you can type **How do I print?** and click the Ask button. Figure 1.8 shows the results you get from that question.

FIGURE 1.8.

The "Expert" answers your questions, or pro-vides a list of possible solutions from which to choose.

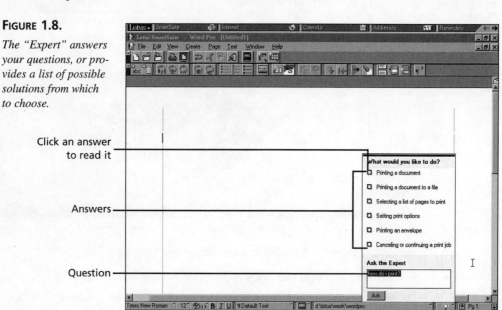

- **Help Topics**. The more traditional Help system is available through this command. With it, you can browse through the help system's Contents, look up terms in an Index, or use Find to locate all help topics that contain a certain word or phrase. See Figure 1.9.

Almost all Windows-based programs use the same kind of Help system that you'll find under Help, Help Topics. If you have used other programs' Help systems before, you'll feel right at home.

FIGURE 1.9.

The Contents tab of the Help Topics window is organized by "book," as in most other Windows programs.

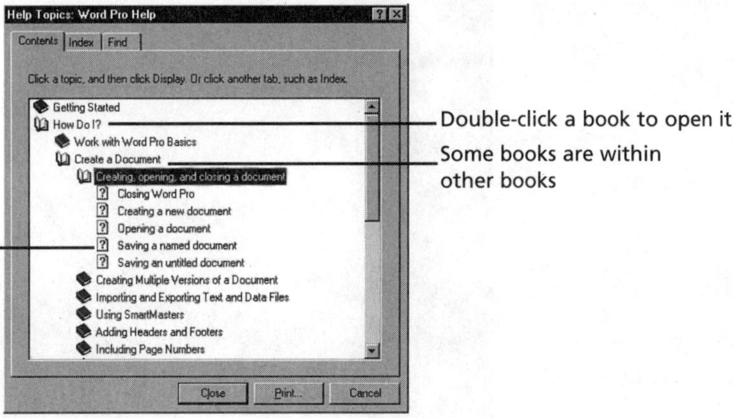

Double-click a book to open it

Some books are within other books

Double-click a help document to read it

- **Lotus Internet Support**. This command opens a submenu of Web pages that offer more help with the application. If you are connected to the Internet, you can choose any of them to jump directly to that Web page.

If you do not have an Internet connection, consult your local Yellow Pages to find an Internet service provider (ISP) in your area. The provider provides you with an ID and password, along with instructions for setting up your connection.

Help from the SmartCenter

The SmartCenter offers a direct connection to the Lotus Web site, along with access to a special SmartSuite Help file. (You'll learn more about using SmartCenter during the next hour's session.)

The SmartCenter Help drawer is called Suite Help. You may not be able to see it by default, depending on your screen resolution. But it's there. Just click the right arrow button at the far right end of the SmartCenter bar to scroll the Suite Help drawer into view (see Figure 1.10). Then open it by clicking it, and check out the various Help folders. Some of them lead to Web pages; others contain icons that run Help programs.

Click these arrows to scroll the drawers——

FIGURE 1.10.

The Lotus Online folder points to helpful Web pages that pertain to SmartSuite.

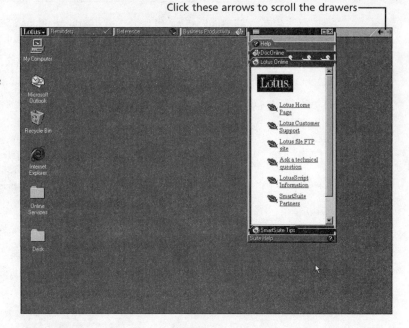

Reading the DocOnline User Manual

SmartSuite comes with a 600-page user manual, but you won't find it in the cardboard box. That's because it's not printed—it's in electronic format. The manual is not terribly convenient to use, but if you have a question that can't be answered by the Help system, it can be an effective solution. (Of course, your first, best reference is this book you're holding in your hands right now! You should not need the online user manual for the majority of your work.)

NEW TERM   *PDF:* The user manual files are in PDF format, a special file format that you can read with a program called Adobe Acrobat Reader. (This program comes free with SmartSuite, and is automatically installed when you install SmartSuite).

PDF files are often used to create user manuals because they enable readers on different kinds of systems to view and print a fully formatted page without having to have the actual fonts needed installed on their system.

To Do: Using the Online User Manual

▼To Do

To read the manual, open it from the Start menu:

1. Click the Start button, and then point to Programs, Lotus SmartSuite, Lotus DocOnline. A submenu appears of the Help documents available.

2. Click the document you want to view. Unless you are a programmer or an advanced user, the one you want is **Exploring SmartSuite 98**.

3. When the document opens in Acrobat Reader, you see the chapters in the navigation pane on the left. Click the chapter you want to read. See Figure 1.11.

FIGURE 1.11.

Use Adobe Acrobat Reader to peruse the user manual.

Click a chapter to read

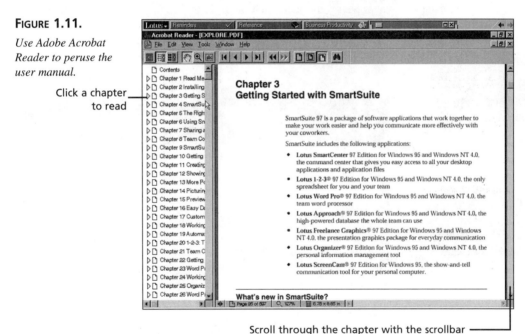

Scroll through the chapter with the scrollbar

4. When you are finished reading the user manual, choose File, Exit to close the reader.

▲

While you are reading the manual, you can take some shortcuts in finding the information you want:

- Click the arrow button next to a chapter name to open a list of the headings in that chapter. You can then click a heading to jump directly to it. See Figure 1.12.

- If you can't quite read the titles of the chapters, drag the divider line between the two panes to the right to increase the width of the list's window.

- To find all mentions of a specific word or phrase, click the Find button on the toolbar (it looks like binoculars). Then type the word or phrase and click Find to locate the first instance of it. Click Find again to go to the next instance, and so on.

- Zoom the view in and out by opening the View menu and choosing a view (such as Actual Size, Fit Page, or Fit Width). Or, click the Zoom In tool on the toolbar (looks like a magnifying class) and then click the document to zoom in. To zoom out, right-click the document and choose Go Back from the shortcut menu that appears.

- Print the current page by choosing File, Print. Click the Current Page button in the dialog box that appears, and then click the Print button to print it. (You can also print the entire document from the Print dialog box, but I don't recommend it, unless you have a lot of paper and ink that you need to waste.)

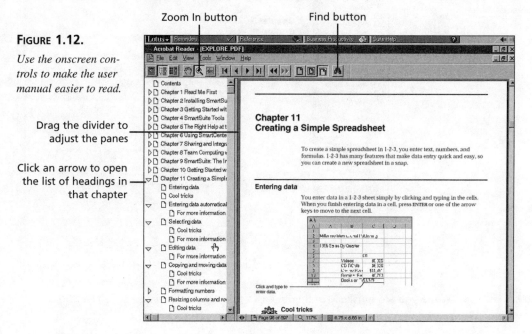

FIGURE 1.12.

Use the onscreen controls to make the user manual easier to read.

Drag the divider to adjust the panes

Click an arrow to open the list of headings in that chapter

Summary

This hour introduced SmartSuite by giving you a sample of the types of projects you can create with each component. You also learned about the Help system that SmartSuite uses to make your learning experience painless.

The next hour explains the SmartCenter, which is that strip of green boxes at the top of your screen. You'll learn how to manage its drawers and folders to make the most of your SmartSuite applications.

Q&A

Q All I need to do right now is type a few letters in the word processor. Should I take the time to learn these other programs too?

A If you are interested only in Word Pro right now, it's perfectly okay to focus all your attention there. You can always come back and learn about the other applications when you need them. However, you likely will find that many skills you learn in one SmartSuite application transfer nicely to the other applications.

Q Some of the projects listed in this hour sound like they are difficult. As a beginner, will I be able to do them?

A This shouldn't be a problem, because you won't have to start from scratch. Each SmartSuite application comes with templates called SmartMasters that provide a giant headstart for creating most of the projects I've told you about in this chapter. In most SmartMaster templates, the text is preformatted,—the columns laid out— all you have to do is fill in the information. You'll learn more about them in Hour 4.

Q Why is my SmartCenter bar missing?

A SmartCenter may be turned off. To turn it on, choose Start, Programs, Lotus SmartSuite, Lotus SmartCenter.

Q I use America Online (AOL) as my Internet connection. Can I use SmartSuite's Online Help with it?

A You can use the Internet connection, but not the AOL software. Start your AOL session, and then minimize its window. As long as you are connected to AOL, SmartSuite can go through that connection to the Internet.

Q I am experienced with Microsoft Office products. How can I find out what menu commands and toolbar buttons correspond to those I'm familiar with?

A SmartSuite offers a special feature to help with this. Choose Help, Microsoft {product} for Windows Menu Help. (The product name depends on what SmartSuite application you are using.) Click a menu, and then select a menu item. A Help topic appears that explains how to do that activity in Word Pro.

Hour 2

Managing Your Desktop with SmartCenter

After you install SmartSuite, the very first part of it you encounter is the SmartCenter. It's a row of green buttons running across the top of your screen. Don't let that unassuming appearance fool you, though—the SmartCenter is a powerful tool that can help you keep organized.

The most obvious feature of the SmartCenter is that it helps you launch SmartSuite applications. That's just the tip of the iceberg of its functionality, though, as you'll see in this hour's session.

The highlights of this hour include:

- Starting and stopping the SmartCenter
- Working with folders and drawers
- Adding drawer content
- Creating your own drawers
- Customizing the SmartCenter

Turning SmartCenter On (or Off)

When you install SmartSuite, the installation program places several utilities in your Startup folder, so that those utilities start each time Windows does. One of these utilities is the SmartCenter.

> The other two utilities that SmartSuite setup places in the Startup folder are Lotus SuiteStart, which places icons for each of the SmartSuite applications in your system tray (down by the clock in the bottom-right corner), and Lotus QuickStart, which makes SmartSuite applications start up quickly.

If you need to turn off the SmartCenter temporarily, click the Lotus button on the SmartCenter and then choose Exit SmartCenter from the menu that appears. To restart it again, choose Start, Programs, Lotus SmartSuite, Lotus SmartCenter.

To Do: Preventing SmartCenter from Launching at Startup

If you want to prevent SmartCenter from starting when you start Windows in the future, remove it from your Startup folder. To do so, follow these steps:

1. Right-click on the Start menu and choose Open from the shortcut menu.
2. In the window that appears, double-click the Programs icon.
3. In the window that appears, double-click the Startup icon.
4. Click on the Lotus SmartCenter icon, and press the Delete key on your keyboard.
5. When asked if you are sure you want to send the icon to the Recycle Bin, click Yes.
6. Test your work by restarting the PC (Start, Shut Down, Restart).

> Don't be afraid in step 5 when it says you are deleting the program. You are not really deleting the SmartCenter application; you're just deleting the shortcut to it that was in the StartUp folder. The original is still safe.

Understanding Folders and Drawers

Each of the green rectangles on the SmartCenter is a *drawer*. A drawer resembles a drop-down menu in that when you click on it, its content "drops down." However, unlike a menu, a drawer stays open until you close it. You can close a window in any of these ways:

- Click its Close (X) button
- Click its name (at the bottom of its window)
- Click the solid bar at the top of the drawer (where the name would appear if the drawer were closed).

Also unlike menus, you can have more than one drawer open at once. Figure 2.1 shows the SmartSuite and Calendar drawers open.

FIGURE 2.1.

SmartSuite drawers drop open when you click on them and stay open until you close them.

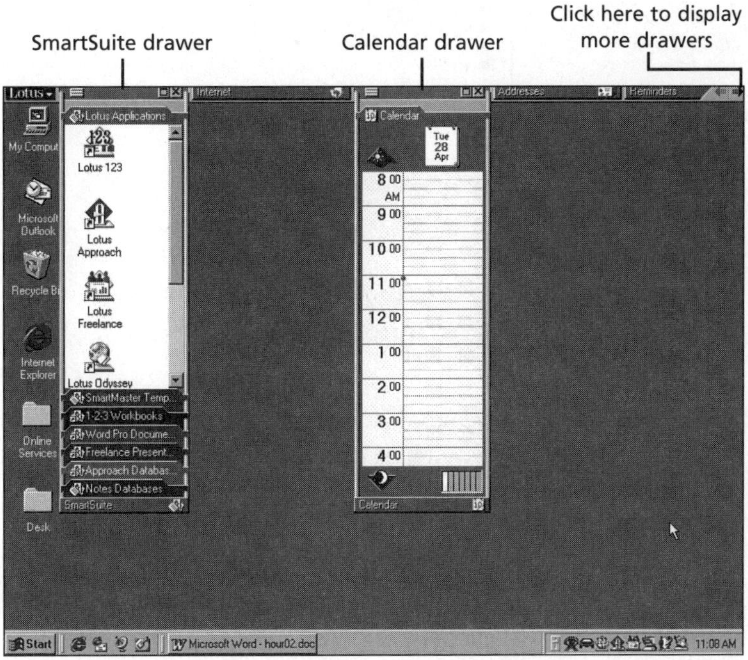

Some drawers contain icons for programs you can start or documents you can open. The SmartSuite drawer is like that. Notice in Figure 2.1 that icons appear in the SmartSuite drawer for Lotus 1-2-3, Lotus Approach, and so on. Other folders are special-purpose, displaying their own unique content. The Calendar drawer is an example. It displays your daily calendar, pulled from your Organizer file.

All the drawers may not fit across the top of your screen at once. To see the other drawers that are not currently displayed, click the right-pointing arrow at the right end of the SmartCenter bar (see Figure 2.1). Then, to scroll back to the originally displayed drawers, click the left-pointing arrow next to it.

Within some drawers are multiple folders. Notice in Figure 2.1 that the SmartSuite drawer is displaying the Lotus Applications folder. It also has other drawers that contain SmartMaster Templates and documents you have created with each of the SmartSuite programs. To switch to a different folder, click on its tab. Figure 2.2 shows the SmartSuite drawer with the Word Pro Documents folder displayed.

FIGURE 2.2.

Click on a tab in a drawer to display a different folder.

Folder tabs

Some drawer content relies on Internet access. If you try to open such a drawer or such a folder within a drawer, a box appears prompting you to start your Internet connection if it is not already running.

If you do not want to connect to the Internet now, first close the drawer, *then* close the Internet connection window. If you try to close the connection window first, it will keep reopening itself as long as the drawer is open, and you won't be able to exit from it.

Working with the Default Drawers

SmartSuite provides a nice array of default drawers. You can use most of these productively without any customization. They are:

- *SmartSuite*. Contains several folders that provide access to SmartSuite applications and documents. There is a separate folder for the applications and for each type of SmartSuite document. A folder also exists for Notes data, in case you use Lotus Notes.

NEW TERM *Lotus Notes* is a groupware product used by many companies to help employees work together, using email, scheduling calendars, and so forth. It is not included with SmartSuite, but many companies that use SmartSuite also use Notes.

- *Internet*. Contains several folders, each of which contains either a Web page or a series of links to Web pages. You can customize these links, as explained in "Setting Up Internet Drawers" later in this chapter.
- *Calendar*. Accesses a daily view of your calendar from Lotus Organizer.
- *Addresses*. Accesses your address book from Lotus Organizer.
- *Reminders*. Contains folders where you can input and read reminders for your business and personal life.
- *Reference*. Provides quick access to a dictionary and thesaurus.
- *Business Productivity*. Contains several folders, organized by industry, of shortcuts to various SmartMaster templates that help with business tasks such as creating business cards and newsletters.
- *Suite Help*. Contains links to information, both locally and on the Internet, that can help you use SmartSuite better. See Hour 1's session for details.

NEW TERM *SmartMaster* templates are head-starts for creating various kinds of documents, spreadsheets, databases, and so on. Hour 4 explains SmartMasters in more detail.

Customizing Your Drawers and Folders

You aren't stuck with the default sizes, shapes, and colors for your drawers and folders. Heck, you aren't even stuck with the default content! In this section, you'll learn how to dress up a drawer and change its content.

Changing a Drawer's Size

When a drawer is open, it is like any other window. You can make it wider or narrower by dragging its right border with your mouse (see Figure 2.3). Whatever size you set will continue after the drawer is closed. You can also maximize its window by clicking its Maximize button (or right-clicking and choosing Maximize Drawer). If you maximize a drawer and then close it, it'll be maximized the next time you open it again.

Changing a Drawer's Name and Handle

To rename a drawer or change its handle, right-click the drawer and choose Drawer Properties from the shortcut menu. The Drawer Properties dialog box appears (see Figure 2.4). Change the name if desired or choose a different icon from the Drawer Handle drop-down list. Then click OK.

Maximize button

FIGURE 2.3.

Resize a drawer by dragging its right border or maximize it with the Maximize button.

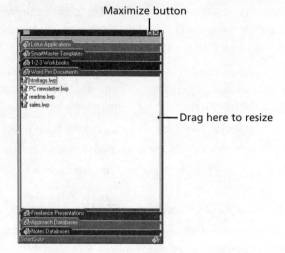

Drag here to resize

NEW TERM The *drawer handle* is the icon that appears on the drawer's name bar when it is closed.

FIGURE 2.4.

Change the drawer name or handle if desired.

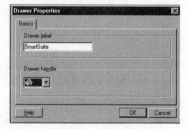

Setting Folder Properties

Each folder has its own set of options you can set. When a drawer is open and a folder is displayed, right-click the folder tab and choose Folder Properties to display its Properties dialog box.

This dialog box has two tabs. On the Basics tab, you can choose a folder label, icon, and color. On the Display tab you can choose to display small or large icons and set the sort order for folder items (for example, by name or by type).

To Do: Setting SmartCenter Drawer Color

Don't like the green drawers? You can't change the color of individual drawers, but you can change all drawers collectively. To do so, follow these steps:

1. Click the Lotus button and choose SmartCenter Properties from the menu. The SmartCenter Properties dialog box opens.

2. Click the Appearance tab. A selection of drawer colors and patterns appears. See Figure 2.5.

FIGURE 2.5.

Choose a different color for the drawers if you want.

3. Click the color and pattern you want and then click OK.

Take note of the resolution designation next to each pattern in Figure 2.5. Some say 16/256 color, while others are High Color. Unless you are running Windows in High Color video mode, stick with one of the 16/256 color choices.

To enable High Color video mode, right-click on the Windows desktop and choose Properties from the shortcut menu. Click the Settings tab and change the Color Palette setting to High Color (or True Color, if available).

Setting Other SmartCenter Properties

While you are in the SmartCenter Properties dialog box (Figure 2.5), you might want to check out some of the other settings on the other tabs:

• On the Basics tab, you can choose Bottom of Screen to make the SmartCenter bar appear at the bottom. Watch out, however: If you have Windows' Taskbar set to AutoHide, the two bars may interfere with one another.

- On the Effects tab, choose a sound that Windows should make when a drawer opens and set how quickly a drawer will open.
- On the Browser tab, choose whether SmartCenter will use its own Web browser or the default one for your system (probably Internet Explorer) when displaying Web content.

Setting Up Internet Drawer

Some of the folders in the Internet drawer require some setup to be made useful. For example, the Weather folder requires you to choose your city so it can provide your local weather conditions. The Stock Quotes folder requires that you enter which stocks you want to track.

To set up an Internet folder, click the icon on its tab and choose Folder Properties from the menu that appears. A Folder Properties dialog box appears. The exact options that appear in the box depend on which folder you are customizing; the one for Stock Quotes appears in Figure 2.6. Make your selections (for example, in Figure 2.6, click the Add button to add a stock symbol), and then click OK. From then on, the chosen content will appear each time you access that folder.

FIGURE 2.6.

Set up the Internet content that you want to retrieve from the folder.

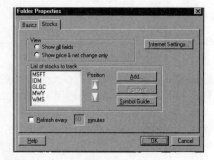

Creating New Folders

You can create your own folders within any drawer, and that folder can hold any kind of information you want.

To Do: Creating A New Folder

1. Open the drawer to which you want to add a folder.
2. Right-click the drawer's handle (the icon at the top) and choose New Folder from the shortcut menu. The New Folder dialog box appears.

3. Choose the folder content type you want (see Figure 2.7). Choices include File, Internet URL, Calendar, and more. Click Next to move to step 4.

4. Choose a folder label, folder color, and icon. Then click Next to move to step 5.

5. Complete any additional steps as prompted. The steps (and the number of them) vary depending on the content type you chose in step 3.

6. Click Done to complete your folder.

FIGURE 2.7.

Choose the content type for the folder. Different content types have different setup options.

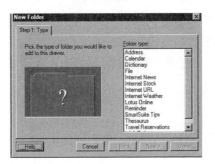

Creating New Drawers

You can create new drawers on the SmartCenter whenever you deem it appropriate. The number of drawers you can have has no limit; however, remember that you may have to use the scroll arrows on the right end of the SmartCenter bar to see some of the drawers.

 Don't be too eager to create new drawers because drawers take up on-screen space. Consider instead whether a new folder within an existing drawer might satisfy your needs.

To create a new drawer, click the Lotus button and choose New Drawer from the menu. Assign a label (a name) and choose a drawer handle (an icon). Then click OK. The new drawer is added to the right end of the SmartCenter bar.

 If you use a few drawers more than the others, you might want to move them to the left side of the SmartCenter bar for easy access. To move a drawer, drag it (click and hold) where you want it. Easy, eh?

Working with the SmartCenter Browser

When working with Internet content from the SmartCenter, the SmartCenter Browser may open (depending on the way the content has been set up). It works much like other Web browsers you may have used before. Figure 2.8 points out the controls you'll need.

> If you prefer to use your own default Windows browser, such as Microsoft Internet Explorer or Netscape Communicator, choose it from the SmartCenter Properties dialog box as explained in "Setting Other SmartCenter Properties" earlier in this chapter. When you open items from the Favorites folder on the Internet drawer, they open in your default Windows browser anyway, regardless of this setting.

FIGURE 2.8.

The SmartCenter Browser displays Internet content.

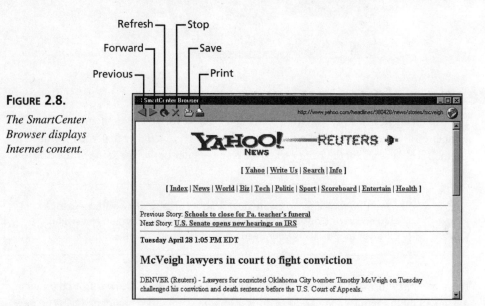

The Previous button takes you to the last page you visited. After you have used Previous, Forward returns you to the page you were looking at before. Refresh reloads the current page, whereas Stop halts an in-progress page load. Save saves the content of the window to a file on your hard disk, and Print prints it.

Summary

This hour introduced you to the SmartCenter bar and showed you how it can help you launch programs quickly and gain access to your calendar, addresses, and the Internet. You also learned how to customize the SmartCenter and how to improve the Internet drawer's offerings by tailoring the information provided for your location and interest.

In the next hour, we'll begin looking at the most popular SmartSuite component, Word Pro.

2

Q&A

Q What are those little yellow ducks doing gliding across one of my folders?

A When you are working with a folder that contains Internet content, and you are connected to the Internet, the moving yellow ducks appear to remind you of that fact. You can ignore them. (No, you can't shoot them.)

Q I ve created a new folder in my SmartSuite drawer, and I want to put some files in it for quick access. How do I do that?

A When you create a new folder for files, a corresponding folder is created in your SmartSuite folder on your hard disk (C:\Lotus\Work\SmartCtr\SmartSuite). You should not add "real" files to it, but rather shortcuts to files. To do this, right-click on the new folder and choose Explorer to open Windows Explorer. In Windows Explorer, right-drag a file into your new folder. When you drop it, a shortcut menu appears. Choose Create Shortcut Here.

Q How can I display more than one day in the Calendar drawer?

A See the little bar at the bottom of the Calendar drawer that looks like a group of piano keys? It looks like a single "key" (the leftmost one) is highlighted. Drag to select multiple bars corresponding to the number of days you want to see at once.

Q How do I add addresses to the Addresses drawer?

A Click the words "Add Name" at the top of the list to display a dialog box containing fields to fill in. Click on each field and type to replace its placeholder. When you are finished, click OK to add that name to your address list.

Q Can I use the Addresses drawer if I don t have Outlook installed?

A Yes. If Outlook is not installed, the Addresses drawer saves its address information in a text file.

Q How do I change which address book s names are displayed in the Addresses drawer?

A Right-click the open drawer and choose Folder Properties. A dialog box appears. Choose the file type and the name of the file from the Name & Address tab.

HOUR 3

Working with a SmartSuite Component

Remember the first time you tried to ride a bicycle? Mastering the balancing act took every bit of concentration and skill you could muster. It eventually became second nature, and when the time came for you to learn to ride bigger two-wheeled vehicles, such as a multispeed racing bike or a motorcycle, you had no trouble keeping it upright.

SmartSuite components are like bikes in that once you've mastered one of them, the others are easy to pick up. The best way to learn about SmartSuite is to pick one application, such as Word Pro, and learn its basics. Because all SmartSuite applications have common features, the other components will be a breeze.

In this hour, I'm going to show you the common features that SmartSuite applications share. You can follow along using Word Pro, 1-2-3, Freelance, or Approach. Pick the SmartSuite application that you have the most immediate need to learn and use it when working through this hour. Then for reinforcement, hop over to a second (or third) SmartSuite application and try the new skills there as well.

Highlights of this hour include:

- Starting a program
- Working with SmartMaster templates
- What all programs have in common
- Moving and copying data
- Printing your work
- Exiting a program

Starting a Program

There are several ways to start a SmartSuite program from within Windows. Some methods are SmartSuite-specific, whereas others work with any Windows-based program. Experiment with them to see which you prefer!

To Do: Starting a Program Through SmartCenter

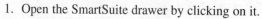

If you are using the SmartCenter (explained in the preceding chapter), you can take advantage of its SmartSuite drawer to start programs.

1. Open the SmartSuite drawer by clicking on it.
2. If needed, click the Lotus Applications tab to display that folder.
3. Locate the icon for the SmartSuite application you want to run. You may need to scroll down using the scrollbar.
4. Double-click the icon to run the program.

To Do: Starting a Program with the Start Menu

Another way to start a program is from the Start menu. The Start menu in Windows starts all kinds of programs, not just SmartSuite ones. To use it, open it, find the folder (submenu) for the program you want to use and click on the line that starts the program. To start a SmartSuite application:

1. Click the Start button, point to Programs, and then to Lotus SmartSuite.
2. Click the program name that you want (for example, Lotus Word Pro) from the menu that appears. The program starts.

Starting a Program and Opening a Data File

Sometimes you want to start a program in order to open an existing data file that you have created. When this is the case, you can accomplish both tasks at once with any of these shortcut methods.

NEW TERM *Data file:* A *data file* is a computer file that contains something you have created—the text, numbers, or graphics that you have input. Other kinds of files include program files (which run the programs) and system files (which keep your PC running). Data files are sometimes called *documents*.

- Open the SmartSuite drawer in the SmartCenter and click on the folder tab for the kind of data file you want to open (for example, Word Pro Documents). Then double-click the document you want to open. This works only for documents that you have saved in the default Word Pro location. (More on saving later in this hour.)

- Click the Start button and point to Documents. The last 15 data files you have opened (in all programs) appear. If the one you want to open is there, click it to open it in its native program.

- Open the Windows Explorer window (Start, Programs, Windows Explorer) and navigate to the folder that contains the data file. When you find it, double-click it to open it in its native program. This works for all data files, but you must be familiar with using Windows Explorer.

NEW TERM *File Associations:* Windows knows which data files were created in which programs because of *file associations*. The three-letter extension at the end of a file name (such as .lwp for Lotus Word Pro) is a code that tells Windows which application to use. Other extensions include .apr for Approach, .123 for 1-2-3, .or4 for Organizer, and .prz for Freelance.

Common Features

One of the most useful common features in SmartSuite programs is the Help system, which you learned about in Hour 1. With a consistent Help system throughout all applications, you never need to wonder where to turn.

SmartSuite programs offer several other common features too, all designed for consistency and ease of use.

The Welcome To... Window

When a SmartSuite program starts, the first thing you see is a "Welcome to" window. (The name after "Welcome to" changes depending on the program.) It prompts you to choose a template for a new document or open an existing document.

The Welcome to window appears only when you start up. You won't see it again until you exit from the program and restart it. You don't need it, however—you can accomplish everything it offers with menu commands. To start a new document, use File, New. To open an existing one, use File, Open.

The Welcome to window has two tabs—one for creating new data files and one for opening existing ones. On the Create New tab, you can choose from a variety of SmartMaster templates, or you can choose to start a plain, blank document (or database, spreadsheet, or presentation). On the Open an Existing tab, you can choose from recently used files or click a button to browse your entire hard disk for a file. You'll learn more about creating and opening files in Hour 4.

For now, you'll just want a plain, blank document to practice on, so click the button for that. Its exact name and location depend on the application:

- Word Pro. Click the Create a Plain Document button.
- 1-2-3. Click the Create a Blank Workbook button.
- Freelance. Click the Create a Blank Presentation button.
- Approach. Click the Create a New File Using a SmartMaster tab and then choose Blank Database from the list and click OK.

Common Menu Commands

Like most Windows-based programs, SmartSuite programs provide drop-down menus, and they use consistent commands whenever possible. For example, there is always a File menu, and it always contains commands for saving, opening, and printing. An Edit menu always exists and contains commands for cutting, copying, and pasting. Figure 3.1 compares the File menus from Word Pro, 1-2-3, and Approach. Although each program offers its own special commands, each one also offers the same basic, familiar commands that are applicable to any type of data file.

Common Toolbar Buttons

Toolbars are those rows of buttons across the top of the application window. Each button provides a shortcut to a common menu command. For example, the scissors button is a shortcut for the Cut command on the Edit menu. If you aren't sure what a button is for, point the mouse at it for a couple of seconds; a balloon pops up providing its name.

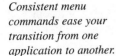

FIGURE 3.1.

Consistent menu commands ease your transition from one application to another.

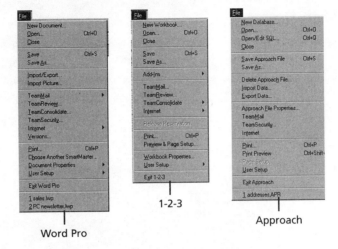

Word Pro

1-2-3

Approach

Although each program is different and therefore requires different buttons, some buttons appear in almost every application. Table 3.1 shows a sampling of them.

TABLE 3.1. APPLICATION BUTTONS

Button	Name	Purpose
	New	Opens the New dialog box so you can create a new data file based on a SmartMaster template.
	Open	Opens the Open dialog box so you can select an existing data file to open.
	Save	Opens the Save dialog box so you can save your work.
	Print	Opens the Print dialog box so you can print your work.
	Print Preview	Opens a Print Preview window so you can check your layout before printing. This is called Zoom to a Full Page in Word Pro.
	Undo	Reverses your last action, if possible.
	Cut	Moves the selected data to the Clipboard.
	Copy	Copies the selected data to the Clipboard.
	Paste	Pastes the Clipboard content into the data file in the cursor location.

Dialog Boxes

A dialog box is a window that requests additional information when you issue a command. For example, when you issue the Print command (either by clicking the Print button on the toolbar or choosing Print from the File menu), the Print dialog box appears.

All dialog boxes use the same types of controls. After you're familiar with them, you can use any dialog box with confidence. Figure 3.2 points out some of the common controls you'll find.

FIGURE 3.2.

Dialog box controls.

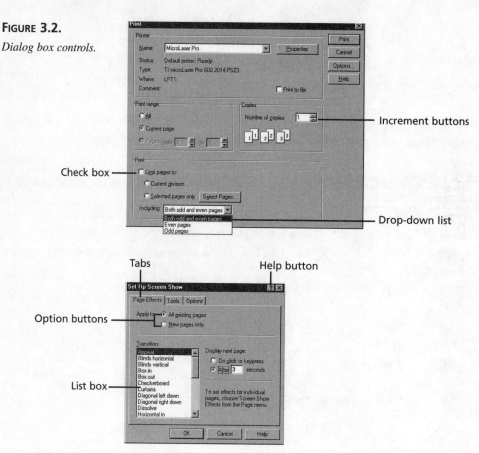

Dialog box elements you will encounter include:

Drop-down lists. Click the down-pointing arrow next to the list box to open the list and click on your selection.

Check boxes. Click in the square box to select or deselect the option. Each check box is independent.

Increment buttons. Click the up or down arrow button to increment or decrement the number in the box. Or you can type the number into the box.

Option buttons. Click on a round button to select it. Option buttons work in sets so that when you choose one, the previously chosen one is deselected.

Tabs. Click on a tab to see a different set of controls.

Help button. Click on the button and then on the dialog box control that you need help with.

Some dialog boxes control *properties*, which are formatting attributes. These dialog boxes are called Property Sheets, and they are unique to SmartSuite. Read about them in the following section.

InfoBoxes

InfoBoxes control the formatting, or properties, of text, graphics, or specific locations (such as fields or cells). The content of an InfoBox may vary, but its organization is consistent.

For example, whenever you have text that can be formatted, that text has a Text Properties InfoBox. To view it, select the text and then press Alt+Enter, or right-click it and choose Text Properties. The InfoBox for text, shown in Figure 3.3, includes controls for size, font, color, alignment, and other attributes. It is the same whether you are formatting text in Word Pro, 1-2-3, or some other SmartSuite application. There are also InfoBoxes for graphics, for page layout, and for headers and footers, to name just a few examples.

Drag the sheet around by its title bar as needed

FIGURE 3.3.

InfoBoxes, like this one for text, are common in every SmartSuite application.

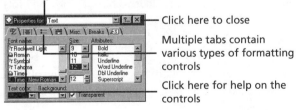

Click here to close

Multiple tabs contain various types of formatting controls

Click here for help on the controls

Entering Data

NEW TERM   *Data:* Data is anything that you enter or import into the program yourself. It can include text, slides, database records, graphics, numbers, charts, tables—anything you create.

The sole purpose of SmartSuite is to let you enter, manipulate, and save different kinds of data. In almost all cases, you enter data using this basic procedure:

1. You position a cursor or insertion point where you want the data.

2. You type, draw, or otherwise input the data.

The exact procedure for entering data differs depending on what application you are working with and what kind of data you want to enter.

- In Word Pro, you enter text and numbers by typing them. They appear at the *insertion point*, a flashing vertical line. You can move the insertion point by clicking the mouse or by using the arrow keys on your keyboard.

- In 1-2-3, you enter text, numbers, and formulas into cells. You choose which cell by moving the *cell cursor*, a dark outline that appears around one cell at a time. Then type your data, pressing Enter when finished. You can move the cell cursor by clicking on a cell or by using the arrow keys.

- In Freelance, the way you work depends on which view you are working with. In Outliner view, you type text on a lined "paper," as you would in a word processor. In Current Page view, you click on a placeholder to open a box where you can type.

- In Approach, your entry strategy also depends on the view. In Database (form) view, you enter bits of data into boxed fields. In Worksheet view, you enter data into cells, just like in 1-2-3.

- In Organizer, you click where you want to enter text and then type it. You can enter calendar entries, to-do items, address book entries, and lots more.

Editing Data

Editing means changing your data in some way. It can involve changing the actual letters and numbers that comprise it, moving it around, or formatting it to make it more attractive and understandable.

The general procedure for editing data in a SmartSuite application is this:

1. You select the data you want to edit.

2. You issue a command or perform an action that affects it.

That first step is very important, but many beginners frequently forget it, and then wonder why their commands won't take effect. Remember: an application doesn't know what data you want to work with unless you select it first. Selected data appears highlighted (white on a black background), as you can see in Figure 3.4.

Selected range of cells in 1-2-3

FIGURE 3.4.

Selected text in Word Pro and 1-2-3.

Selected paragraph in Word Pro

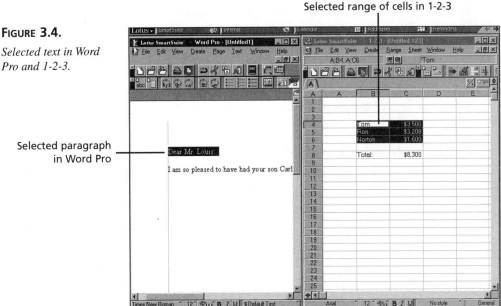

There are several ways to select in a SmartSuite application. Here are two of the most common and universal:

- Drag over the data with the mouse while holding down the left mouse button
- Hold down the Shift key on the keyboard and then press the arrow keys to extend the selection.

You'll learn other selection methods specific to each application in the upcoming hours.

NEW TERM   *Range:* In 1-2-3, when you select multiple cells, it's called a *range*.

Moving and Copying Data

SmartSuite applications provide two ways to move and copy data: cut-and-paste and drag-and-drop. Cut-and-paste is handiest when moving or copying between different documents (and different applications). Drag-and-drop works especially well when moving or copying within the same document (for example, when rearranging paragraphs in a report).

Cut-and-Paste with the Windows Clipboard

Almost all Windows-based programs, including all the SmartSuite applications, provide access to the Windows Clipboard. The *Clipboard* is a holding area that all programs share collectively. You place data on the Clipboard by selecting it and then issuing the Cut or Copy command. The difference between the two? Cut removes the original and places it on the Clipboard; Copy copies the original, leaving it intact in the document.

Because all programs share a single Clipboard, you can cut or copy data from one application and paste it into another. For example, you can copy a graph in 1-2-3 and paste it into a Word Pro letter.

To Do: Copying or Cutting Text to the Clipboard

1. Select the data. You can select anything from a single character to an entire document.
2. Open the Edit menu and choose Copy or Cut, or click the Copy button or Cut button on the toolbar.

To Do: Pasting Copy from the Clipboard

1. Move the insertion point or cell cursor where you want the pasted data to be.
2. Open the Edit menu and choose Paste, or click the Paste button on the toolbar.

You can paste the Clipboard content as many times as you like. The content remains on the Clipboard until you cut or copy something else.

There are shortcut keys for the Cut, Copy, and Paste commands that many users prefer:

Ctrl+X for Cut

Ctrl+C for Copy

Ctrl+V for Paste

> You can place only one selection on the Clipboard. When you cut or copy something else, whatever was on the Clipboard disappears. Before issuing the Cut or Copy command, make sure that you do not have some unpasted data on the Clipboard that you need to keep.

Drag-and-Drop

Drag-and-drop is an easy way to move and copy data from one spot to another. It works best when the original location and the destination are near one another (for instance, on the same page in the same data file). I frequently use it to rearrange paragraphs in Word Pro and to move a group of cells in 1-2-3 down a few rows.

> Drag-and-drop can be used to move and copy between different data files too, but both files must be visible on the screen at the same time, and the jockeying involved to set up that arrangement usually makes it not worth the trouble.

3

To Do: Dragging and Dropping Data

1. Select the data to be moved or copied.

2. Position the mouse pointer over the selection so that the mouse pointer turns into a hand. For Word Pro text or a graphic, you can position it anywhere over the selection; for a 1-2-3 range of cells, you must position it over an edge.

3. If you are copying (rather than moving), hold down the Ctrl key and keep it down until step 5.

4. Click and hold the left mouse button and drag the selection where you want it.

   - In Word Pro (or when dragging text in Outlining view of Freelance), a red insertion point appears on your mouse pointer, showing where the selection will go.

   - In 1-2-3, a dotted outline the same size and shape as the selected range appears (see Figure 3.5).

5. When the outline is in the right place, release the mouse button.

> In Word Pro and most other programs, when you drag-and-drop something, any existing text in that spot moves over to make room for the new. In 1-2-3, however, if you drag some cells on top of other cells, the new content replaces the old. (A warning box appears first, which prevents you from doing it unintentionally.) If needed, insert new rows or columns to make room before you move or copy. See Hour 11 for details.

FIGURE 3.5.

Drag your selection where you want it to go.

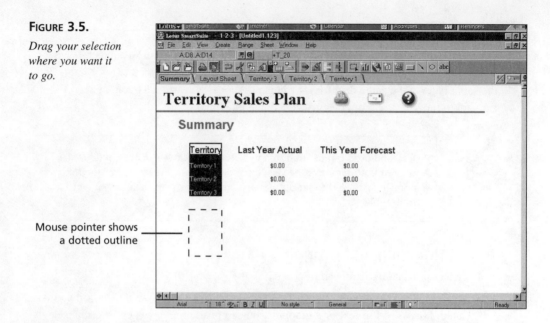

Mouse pointer shows a dotted outline

Printing Your Work

As you saw earlier in this hour, all SmartSuite programs include a Print command on the File menu (and a Print button on the toolbar). Choose either of these to open the Print dialog box.

The exact options in the Print dialog box depend on the application, but you will generally find the following (as shown in Figure 3.6):

- *Print To*. Use this drop-down list to choose a different printer if you have more than one.

- *Pages*. This section enables you to choose a page range to print if your data file has more than one page.

- *Number of Copies*. If you need more than one copy, indicate the number in this box.

- *Print*. Depending on the application, there may be a Print section where you can choose what part of the data file to print. In 1-2-3, for example, you can choose a single sheet, the selected range, or the entire multisheet workbook.

FIGURE 3.6.

This Print dialog box is from 1-2-3, but it is much the same for all SmartSuite programs.

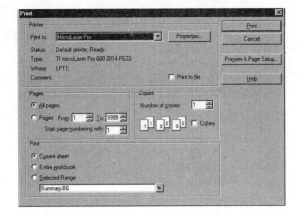

3

You can print in either Portrait (tall) or Landscape (wide) page orientations. The method for changing the page orientation differs depending on the application:

- Word Pro. Choose File, Document Properties, Print Setup. There are Portrait and Landscape option buttons in the dialog box that appears.

- 1-2-3. Choose File, Preview & Page Setup. The Page Setup Properties sheet appears. Choose an orientation with the buttons in the Orientation section on the Margins, Orientation, & Placement tab.

- Approach. You can choose an orientation only for reports; everything else prints out in its default orientation. To change the report orientation, view the report onscreen, and then choose File, Page Setup. Choose an orientation in the dialog box that appears.

- Freelance. Choose File, Page Setup, and choose an orientation from the dialog box that appears.

Exiting a Program

To exit any program, choose File, Exit or press Alt+F4. If you have entered or edited any data, a box appears asking whether you want to save your work. Click Yes or No as appropriate. (If you choose Yes, a Save As dialog box appears. See Hour 4 for details on saving.)

Summary

This chapter led you through some important basic skills that you will need later as you tackle the individual SmartSuite applications. You learned how to start and exit programs, enter and edit data, and print your work. You also learned about the common menu commands, toolbar buttons, and property sheets that give SmartSuite applications an overall consistency that makes learning easier.

But what good is entering data if you can't save it? That's why in the next hour we'll look at some file-management techniques that all SmartSuite applications have in common. By following along, you'll learn how to save, open, and close data files like a pro.

Q&A

Q I never use that Welcome To window. Is there a way I can prevent it from appearing each time I start?

A To disable it, choose File, User Setup, {application} Preferences. The Preferences dialog box that appears contains a command for turning it off. The exact location of the command varies depending on the application. In Word Pro, you click the Enable tab and click to remove the checkmark next to Welcome Dialog. In 1-2-3, you click Show Welcome Dialog on the Other Options list.

Q When I move or copy with drag-and-drop, does the data go through the Clipboard?

A No. Drag-and-drop bypasses the Windows Clipboard. After a drag-and-drop operation, the Clipboard still contains the last data that was cut or copied with the cut-and-paste method.

Q Is there a way to print using the default settings without going through the Print dialog box?

A No. The Print dialog box appears each time. If you want to use the default print settings, you can simply press Enter to accept them and go on.

HOUR 4

Managing SmartSuite Files

In the last hour, you learned some basics for working with data in SmartSuite programs. But what do you do with that data? If you're smart, you save it so that it'll be available when you need it later. This hour deals with data files—how to save them, open them, start new ones, and get rid of old ones that you no longer want.

Highlights in this hour include:

- Creating new files
- Working with SmartMaster templates
- Saving your work
- Closing a file without exiting the program
- Opening saved files
- Deleting unwanted files

Starting a New File

When you start a SmartSuite application, the Welcome To box appears, as you learned last hour. From this box, you can do any of the following:

- Start a new data file based on a SmartMaster template
- Start a new, blank data file
- Open an existing file

We'll look into that third possibility later in this hour; first let's focus on the two ways of starting a new file.

If the Welcome To box is not onscreen—no problem. Choose File, New to open the New dialog box, which contains the same options for creating a new file. (The command is slightly different in each application; in Word Pro, for example, it is File, New Document.) The one for Word Pro appears in Figure 4.1. Then jump to the appropriate section below, depending on which kind of new document you want.

FIGURE 4.1.

In each application, the New dialog box (File, New) enables you to start a new document.

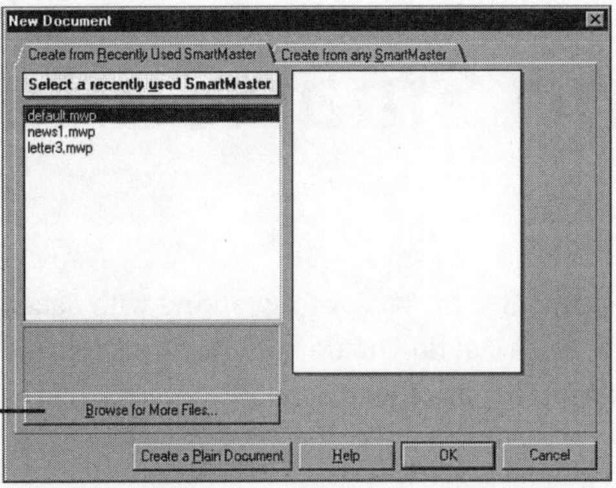

Click here to see the full list of SmartMasters (Word Pro only)

Starting with a SmartMaster Template

The easiest way to create a new file is to base it on one of SmartSuite's SmartMaster templates. As I explained in Hour 1, these templates provide wonderful shortcuts for professional results.

SmartMasters work approximately the same in all SmartSuite applications, but there are small variations. The "easy" one is 1-2-3, which is quite straightforward in its handling of templates. Each of the other applications, however, has one or more "quirks," as explained in the following sections.

SmartMasters in 1-2-3

In 1-2-3, the SmartMaster templates are listed right there in the Welcome To (or New) dialog box. Simply pick the one you want and click OK to start your new document. Figure 4.2 shows the list in 1-2-3.

FIGURE 4.2.

In 1-2-3, just click the SmartMaster you want and then click OK.

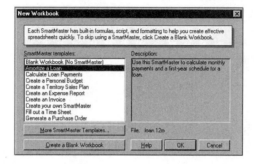

SmartMasters in Word Pro

In Word Pro, only a few recently used templates appear in the Welcome To or New dialog box (see Figure 4.1). To see the complete list of templates, try the following:

- If you are in the Welcome To box, click the Browse for More Files button. This opens the New dialog box with the Create from Any SmartMaster tab showing (see Figure 4.3).

- If you are already in the New Document dialog box, click the Create from Any SmartMaster tab.

> The Browse for More Files button in the Welcome To box is different from the button of the same name in the New dialog box. In the Welcome To box, it takes you to the New box's Create from Any SmartMaster tab. In the New box, it takes you to a Browse dialog box where you can locate other templates on your hard drive.

The complete array of SmartMasters for Word Pro is broken down into categories, as you can see in Figure 4.3. Choose a category from the top list (for example, Letter) and then choose a design from the bottom list (for example, Letter1). The Sample area to the right shows what the selected design will look like. When you are satisfied, click OK to start the document.

FIGURE 4.3.

After clicking Browse for More Files, you see the entire list of Word Pro SmartMasters.

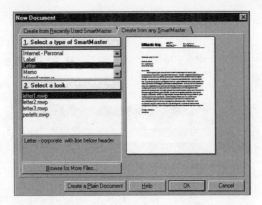

SmartMasters in Approach

In the Welcome To box for Approach, the default tab is Open an Existing Approach File if you have any existing files. To start a new file, you must click on the other tab, Create a New File Using a SmartMaster. (If you are starting from the New dialog box, this isn't an issue.)

On the Create a New File Using a SmartMaster tab, you'll notice a drop-down list of SmartMaster Types. The default is Applications, which are the more complex, multifile databases. Most home users will want to change this to Templates to see the list of templates instead, as shown in Figure 4.4. Then choose a template from the list and click OK to accept it.

FIGURE 4.4.

In Approach, most users will want to work with Templates rather than Applications.

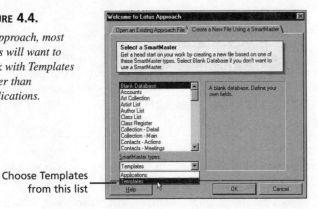

Choose Templates from this list

The other quirk in Approach is that when you first create a file, it asks you to specify a database filename for saving. (In all other programs, your work is not saved until you issue the Save command, which you'll learn about later this hour.) It saves your data in that file automatically as you work.

When prompted, type a name in the File Name text box and click the Create button (see Figure 4.5).

FIGURE 4.5.

Specify a filename when Approach asks for it. It's all part of creating a new Approach file.

 The file that Approach prompts you to create upfront is a dBASE database file, with a .dbf extension. Note that this is *not* an Approach file. The .dbf file is the table that holds your raw data. Later, when you save your work in Approach, you will create an Approach file (.apr extension), which contains all your Approach settings, reports, queries, and so on, and which references the .dbf file that you create now.

SmartMasters in Freelance

In Freelance, you have two SmartMaster lists, as shown in Figure 4.6. The top one selects the sample content. For example, you can choose Business Plan, Market Research, and so on. The bottom list selects the color scheme and layout. You can use any combination of the two, or you can make either or both "blank."

Starting a Blank Data File

Some people like to "do it yourself," rather than relying on a template. If you want to start a completely empty data file in a Smartsuite application, you can do so.

FIGURE 4.6.

In Freelance you can choose the content SmartMaster and the design SmartMaster separately.

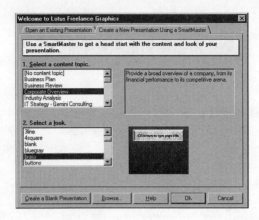

Beginners should not attempt to start from scratch in either Approach or Freelance, at least until they have created a few projects with SmartMaster templates and are familiar with the program. In these programs, it is difficult for a beginner to get professional-quality results without a template.

In both the Welcome To dialog box and the New dialog box, there is a button for creating a plain, blank file. Its name varies depending on the application; in 1-2-3 the button is called Create a Blank Workbook (see Figure 4.2), whereas in Word Pro it's called Create a Plain Document (see Figure 4.3). Just click it.

The exception to this procedure is Approach. In Approach, there is no such button in the New dialog box. Instead, you must choose Blank Database from the list of SmartMasters and then click OK. You're also prompted for a filename for the database (as in Figure 4.5) and then prompted to start creating fields for the database. (We'll get into that procedure in Hour 16.)

Saving Your Work

You must save, or you will lose your changes. If you do not save, the application prompts you to do so when you attempt to exit the program or close the file.

Approach automatically saves the data you type in, such as your addresses, inventory and so on, in a special format known as dBase. Approach does this without being told to save. You do, however, need to save the layouts and forms that you create with Approach. If you lose power or Approach locks up before you save, you will lose any changes you made to your layouts. Your data, however, will be fine because it is saved automatically as you type it.

To save your work, choose File, Save or click the Save button on the toolbar. The first time you save a file, the Save As dialog box appears, so you can specify a filename and location (see Figure 4.7). Subsequent times, the Save command simply updates the copy of the file already on disk and does not prompt for information.

FIGURE 4.7.

This dialog box from Word Pro is typical of the Save As boxes in all SmartSuite applications.

If you want to save an already saved file with a different name, location, or file type, use the File, Save As command. This reopens the Save As dialog box so you can save another copy under a different name or in a different location.

Changing the Save Location

Most people want to use the default saving locations for all SmartSuite programs. When you do so, the files remain available from the SmartSuite drawer in SmartCenter (as you learned in Hour 2). However, people who create many documents may want to organize them into different folders and even different drives. To change the folder or drive, use the controls shown in Table 4.1.

TABLE 4.1. DIALOG BOX CONTROLS FOR CHANGING THE FOLDER OR DRIVE

Control	Name	Purpose
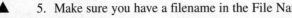	Save In drop-down list	Select a different drive or folder if needed
	Up One Level button	Move up one level in the folder structure
	Create New Folder button	Create a new folder
	List button	View the list of filenames
	Details button	View details for each file (date, size, and so on)

For example, suppose you wanted to save a file on your A: drive (your floppy drive). You would place a disk in that drive and open the Save In drop-down list and choose 3 1/2 Floppy (A:) from the list.

For another example, suppose you want to save a file in a new folder on your hard disk called Projects.

To Do: Saving a File in a New Folder

1. Click the Up One Level button until your hard disk (probably C:) appears in the Save In box. Or open the Save In drop-down list and choose the drive directly.
2. Click the Create New Folder button. A new folder appears.
3. Type a name for the folder (for example, Projects) and press Enter.
4. Double-click on the folder to open it.
5. Make sure you have a filename in the File Name box, and then click Save.

To save another file to that same folder, perform steps 1, 4, and 5.

If you want to change the default location for files in a SmartSuite application, choose File, User Setup, {*application*} Preferences. This opens the setup options for the program.

The exact location of the setting varies.

- In Word Pro, click the Locations tab and specify a different folder for Documents.
- In 1-2-3, click the File Locations tab and enter a different folder under Workbook files.

- In Approach, click the Default Directories button and change the Default Working Directory.
- In Freelance, click the File Locations button and change the folder in the Presentations field.

Saving a Different File Type

Sometimes, you may have to give a file to someone who does not use SmartSuite. (Believe it or not, not everyone does.) A lot of people use a competing product called Microsoft Office, for example. Luckily, most SmartSuite applications enable you to save in a different format so you can share files with anyone who uses one or more of the Office products or a variety of other programs.

In the Save As dialog box, open the Save As Type drop-down list and choose the format you need. Most popular word processing, spreadsheet, and presentation formats are included.

If you can't find the format you need, consider a "generic" format, one that most other programs can recognize. For word processing, RTF (rich text format) is a standard. For spreadsheets, tab-delimited text files work well. As a last resort, you can always save in Text-Only format, which loses the formatting but preserves the verbiage.

4

Once again, Approach is the exception. On the Save as type drop-down list, you won't find other database programs listed; your only choices are some Internet formats and variations on plain-text. However, with Approach, you don't need to use Save As to save your data in an exportable format. Your data is already saved in that that dBASE (.dbf) file that you created when you started the database, and dBASE files will import into almost any database program. Simply share that .dbf file.

Opening a Saved File

You can open a saved file from the Welcome To dialog box if it is still open. Just click the Open an Existing Document tab in Word Pro (or the corresponding tab in one of the other applications) and click on the file you want. The files listed there are the ones stored in your default Word Pro folder; to see others, click the Browse for More Files button (see Figure 4.8).

To open a saved file, choose File, Open or click the Open button on the toolbar. The Open dialog box appears. (This is the same box as the one you get when you click Browse for More Files from the Welcome To dialog box.) Click the file you want and then the Open button to open it.

FIGURE 4.8.

From the Welcome To box, you can easily choose an existing file from the list.

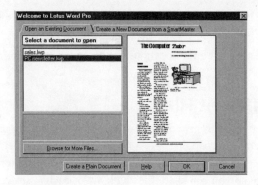

You can change the folder, if needed, to find files in other folders. Use the same procedures you learned in "Changing the Save Location" earlier in this chapter.

If you want to open a file that was created in a different program, most SmartSuite applications can accommodate you. Simply open the Files Of Type drop-down list and choose the file format you want to open. For example, Word Pro can open files from Microsoft Word, WordPerfect, WordStar, and other word processors.

All SmartSuite applications (except Organizer) allow you to have more than one file open at a time. You can switch among the open files with the Window menu. When you open files, files that were already open remain so. To close a file, use the procedure outlined in the following section.

Closing a File

When you exit an application, all open data files are closed. You can also close a data file without exiting if you are finished with it.

To close a file, choose File, Close, or click the Close (X) button for the document window. If your changes are not saved, you'll be prompted to save them; click Yes to do so.

Deleting a File

As with any other files in Windows, you can delete SmartSuite data files from Windows Explorer. Just highlight the files you want to delete and then press the Delete key.

However, there's a more convenient method. You can delete files from within a SmartSuite application.

1. Open the Open dialog box (File, Open).

2. Select the file you want to delete.

3. Press the Delete key on the keyboard. A warning box appears.

4. Click Yes to delete the file.

5. Click Cancel to close the Open dialog box.

 When you delete a file using the above steps, the file is not immediately destroyed. It is instead moved to the Recycle Bin, which you can access from your Windows desktop. To retrieve a file from the Recycle Bin, double-click the Recycle Bin icon to open it. Then select the file and choose File, Restore.

Summary

This hour taught you about file management in SmartSuite. You learned how to create new files, both blank ones and based on SmartSuite templates. You also learned how to save your work, how to open saved documents, and how to close and delete files. Congratulations, you have completed the first phase of your training! In the next few hours, you begin phase two—Word Pro.

Q&A

Q I need to share a file with a friend who is working in a format that SmartSuite doesn't list in the Save As Type box. Is there any way to do this, short of saving in text-only format?

A If you can't find the format you want (for example, some obscure old word processing format), you may be able to find a format that a person using that program can also open. For example, perhaps you don't have ClarisWorks as a choice, but you do have WordPerfect 5.1 on your list, which is a file format that ClarisWorks can import. Ask your friend to open his Open dialog box and look at the available file types in his Files of Type drop-down list. (The names of the dialog box and its controls may vary somewhat depending on the program.) Try to find a match between what he can open and what you can save as. As a last resort, you can always save in text-only format, which will retain the text but not the formatting.

Q Why does Approach prompt me for a filename when I first create a new database and then again later as I am exiting the program? Haven't I already specified a name?

A Approach creates two separate files. The data file is in .dbf format. That's the one you create upfront. It holds your data. The other one, the Approach file (.apr), holds all your other settings—forms, tables, queries, and so on. This is the one that you're prompted to create when you exit. They need not have the same name. The .dbf file is automatically saved each time you add or edit data. The .apr file is not saved unless you issue the Save command.

Q I made a mistake and started with the wrong SmartMaster template. Can I change the template being used without starting a whole new document?

A Yes, in some programs. In Word Pro, choose File, Choose Another SmartMaster. In Freelance, you can change the look but not the content. To do so, choose Presentation, Choose a Different SmartMaster Look. You can't change the template on-the-fly in Approach or 1-2-3.

PART II
Word Pro

Hour

HOUR 5

Word Pro Basics

Of all the applications in SmartSuite, Word Pro is the most popular. That's because Word Pro helps you write, and almost everyone needs to do that. Whether you're an accountant or a plumber, there's always a letter to be written or a report to type up.

In this hour, we'll ease into Word Pro, and you'll pick up some skills that will carry you through in upcoming hours, like how to edit your work and check your spelling and grammar.

Highlights of this hour include:

- Learning about the status bar controls
- Typing and editing text
- Working with different views
- Finding and replacing
- Inserting page breaks
- Running a spelling check
- The grammar checker and other proofreading tools

Using the Word Pro Status Bar Controls

By now you probably have a good working knowledge of the standard SmartSuite program interface. There are windows and menus, toolbars and work areas. I won't belabor that stuff here, but take a close look at the status bar, the thin row of buttons at the bottom of the screen (see Figure 5.1). It's filled with buttons, sort of like a toolbar. Some of these buttons open pop-up lists when you click them, as in Figure 5.1. Others apply certain formatting or open dialog boxes.

FIGURE 5.1.

Word Pro's status bar offers a variety of extra controls.

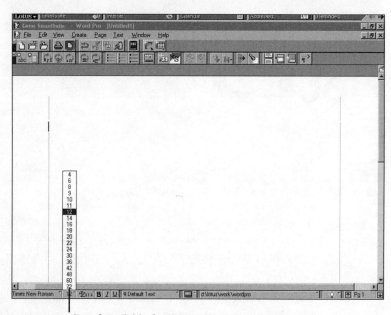

This button pops up a list of available font sizes

Table 5.1 shows each element and explains what it does. Take the time now to learn about these status bar controls because they will save you time later!

TABLE 5.1. WORD PRO STATUS BAR CONTROLS

Control	Function
Times New Roman	Opens a list of available fonts.
12	Opens a list of available sizes for the chosen font.
Zııı	Opens a list of available colors for the chosen font.

Control	Function
B	Makes selected text bold.
I	Makes selected text italic.
U	Makes selected text underlined.
¶ Default Text	Opens a list of available styles from the template.
[nbc]	Shows misspelled words.
d:\lotus\work\wordpro	Opens a list of miscellaneous information that can appear on the Status button.
[💡]	Opens Ask the Expert help.
[⬆]	Scrolls to the previous page in a multipage document.
Pg 1	Opens the Go To dialog box so you can go to a specific page or marked location.
[⬇]	Scrolls to the next page in a multipage document.

5

Don't worry if you don't quite understand all the buttons on the status bar right now. By the time you finish with the Word Pro part of this book, you'll know how to use each of them with confidence.

One cool, not-so-obvious feature of the status bar is the Status button. By default it shows the location where the file you are working on is stored, but you can make it show any of a variety of other tidbits of information instead, such as the date and time, the cursor position, or which version of the document you are working with. Just click on it to open its list and choose what you want.

Typing Text

When you start Word Pro, you choose between opening an existing document and starting a new one (either plain or based on a SmartMaster). For the sake of practice, let's forget about SmartMasters right now and focus on a plain old (er, *new*) document.

Remember, to get a new, plain document, click the Create a Plain Document button in either the Welcome To or the New dialog box.

Then what? Just start typing. The insertion point (that flashing vertical line) moves with you as you type so that whatever you type appears immediately to its left. To start a new paragraph, press Enter. (Do not press Enter to start a new line in the same paragraph; the lines wrap automatically when you get to the right edge of the page.)

For practice, type a whole paragraph right now. Don't worry about your spelling accuracy. If you don't have anything in mind to type, type a paragraph from this book!

Editing Text

Although typing text is a simple affair, editing that text provides lots of possibilities!

Inserting Text

Remember, whatever you type appears to the left of the insertion point, and the insertion point moves over to make room for it. Therefore, if you want to insert some text in the midst of other text, you move the insertion point to that spot. Then type. The other text moves over to make room for it.

NEW TERM *Typing modes:* Word Pro has two typing modes, *insert* and *type over*. Insert is the default, in which old text moves over to make room for new. In type over mode, new text types "over" old text, replacing it.

If you type new text and the old text doesn't move over, you probably have accidentally turned on *type over mode*. Press the Insert key on the keyboard to toggle back to *insert mode*.

 If you have a hard time staying away from the Insert key and find yourself frequently turning on type over mode accidentally, you might want to change the Status button on the status bar to display the mode (either Type Over or Insert).

Correcting Simple Mistakes

Typing errors can be corrected in two way. One is to move the insertion point (with the arrow keys or by clicking the mouse where you want it) and then use the Backspace key to remove whatever is to its left. You can then retype. This method works well for small errors, such as transposing two letters or typing an extra vowel.

 An alternative: If you press the Delete key, rather than Backspace, the insertion point moves to the right and removes whatever character was to the right of it.

The other method is to select the text you want to fix (by dragging across it with the left mouse button held down) and type the correction. Whatever you type replaces whatever was selected. If you press Backspace or Delete after making a selection, that entire selection is deleted.

 If you make a mistake in editing, click the Undo SmartIcon or choose Edit, Undo.

Selecting Text

As you learned in Hour 3, you can select text by dragging across it with the mouse. You can also select text in any of the ways shown in Table 5.2.

TABLE 5.2. SELECTING TEXT

To select	Do this
Word	Double-click on it or choose Text, Select, Word
Sentence	Ctrl+click on it or choose Text, Select, Sentence.
Paragraph	Ctrl+double-click on it or choose Text, Select, Paragraph

5

Moving and Copying Text

The skills you learned for moving and copying in Hour 3 will serve you well in Word Pro. You can move or copy text with either the drag-and-drop or the cut-and-paste method.

You can also use a couple of keyboard shortcuts to move selected paragraphs. Ctrl+Up arrow moves a paragraph up in the document, and Ctrl+Down arrow moves it down.

Changing the View

As you are writing and editing your text, you might want to adjust some of the onscreen viewing options to make your work experience more pleasant. These settings are largely a matter of personal preference; some people swear by one setting, while others can't function unless using a different one. Try them out and make up your own mind.

Viewing Modes

Word Pro offers four viewing modes, any of which you can choose from the View menu:

- **Layout**. The default. You can see the page margins for the page you are working on, and all graphics and multicolumn layouts appear as they will when printed. See Figure 5.2.

- **Draft**. Text appears at the very top of the work area, with no indication of the margins that will be used for printing. The layout and graphic elements do not display at all. See Figure 5.3.

- **Outline**. Each paragraph appears with an outline symbol next to it and is indented to indicate which level in the outline it represents. A special toolbar also appears, with outlining buttons.

- **Page Sorter**. Each page appears as a thumbnail of itself, in zoomed-out view, so you can see multiple pages at once.

FIGURE 5.2.

In Layout view, you see all graphics, frames, and multicolumn layouts.

FIGURE 5.3.

In Draft view, you focus exclusively on the text.

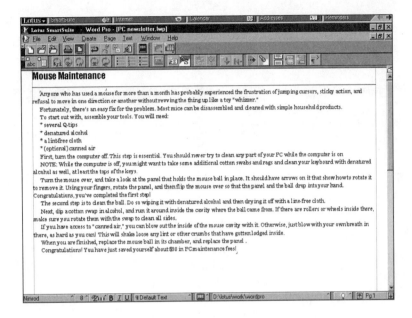

The newsletter in Figures 5.2 and 5.3 may look complicated, but it was easy to produce using the Newsletter SmartMaster. You can easily make one just like it by starting with the SmartMaster and adding some text and formatting. You'll learn about text in this chapter and formatting in the next couple of chapters.

5

For regular typing and editing, use either Layout or Draft view. Most people prefer Layout. Draft view has an advantage of displaying each page's text more quickly because it does not have to fuss with graphic placement, but this is an issue only if you are working with an extremely complex document with many graphics or on an extremely slow computer. Outline view is useful chiefly when creating outlines. (No surprise there.) It is not suitable for regular editing. Nor is Page Sorter, which is useful primarily for checking page layout (to avoid awkward paragraph breaks).

Zooming In and Out

The "zoom" is the magnification of what you see onscreen. It doesn't have any effect on the printout; it's strictly "for your eyes only." The default zoom is 100%. To zoom in so that things are bigger, you increase the zoom percentage (say, to 150% or 200%). The drawback is that you may have to use the scroll bars quite a bit to move around. You won't see much of the document onscreen at a time. To zoom out so that things are

smaller, decrease the zoom (for example, to 75% or 50%). When you zoom out, you can
see more of the page without scrolling, but text or graphics may be too tiny to work with.
Figure 5.4 shows two windows—one zoomed in to 200% and one zoomed out to 75%.

FIGURE 5.4.

On the left, a zoomed-in view; on the right, zoomed-out.

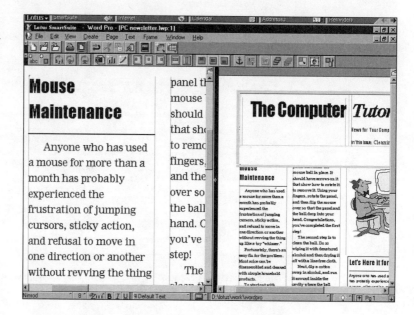

To zoom, open the View menu and choose one of the Zoom options:

- Zoom to Full Page sets the zoom to the correct setting in order to view the entire
  page onscreen at once. The exact number varies depending on your screen resolution.
- Zoom to 100% restores your view to 100% zoom, the default.
- Zoom to opens a submenu of other zooming choices. Popular choices here include
  Margin Width, which sets the zoom so that the entire document, margin-to-margin,
  fits onscreen, and Page Width, which sets the zoom so that you can see both the
  right and left page edges.

Splitting the View

Take a closer look at Figure 5.4. There are two separate viewing panes, but only one document open. This was accomplished by creating a split view. Split views are great
because they let you be in two places at once within the same document For example,
suppose you have a list at the beginning of a document that you want to refer to, but you
also need to work on page 10. In one pane you can have your list and in the other the
page you need to work on. Each pane can display a different page, a different zoom, and
a different view (draft, layout, or whatever).

To split, choose one of the split views from the View menu: Split Left/Right or Split Top/Bottom. You can even split an already-split view—just click inside the window you want to split further and issue another Split command. You can also drag the splitter bar between the two panes to resize them so that one pane takes up more room than the other.

To get rid of the splits, choose View, Clear All Splits.

To clear a single split, rather than all splits, drag the splitter bar in the direction of the little gray arrow on it. When you drag it as far as it will go, the split disappears. Make sure you drag in the direction of the little arrow; if you drag in the other direction, the splitter bar remains.

Showing Hidden Characters

There are many characters in a Word Pro file that don't print. For example, each time you press Enter to begin a new paragraph, an end-of-paragraph character is inserted. And every time you press Tab, a tab character appears.

Normally you don't see these onscreen because Word Pro doesn't want to confuse you, but sometimes it's helpful to see them—for example, if you are trying to proofread to make sure you haven't included extra tab stops in a manuscript.

To turn on their display, click the Show/Hide Tabs and Returns button on the toolbar. (It's the rightmost button on the second row.) Click it again to turn them off.

Word Pro also offers a very powerful means of precisely controlling which hidden characters appear. Choose View, Set View Preferences to open an InfoBox containing the Show options (see Figure 5.5). Choose from the assortment of check boxes to specify exactly what will appear onscreen. Then open the Show Marks drop-down list and click to place or remove the check mark next to each specific item to show or hide, including Tabs, Returns, Page Breaks, Column Breaks, or (to make it simpler) choose All or None.

Other tabs in the View Preferences InfoBox configure Zoom, Outline, and Clean Screen views precisely. Clean Screen is a view where all the tools are gone and you have just one large expanse of work area for typing.

5

FIGURE 5.5.

Use the View Preferences InfoBox to precisely configure your view.

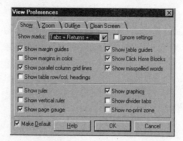

Finding and Replacing Text

If you write nothing but short memos, you may never need the Find command. However, if you have multipage documents, you might find it handy to have Word Pro search for a particular word or phrase for you, rather than trying to browse through yourself. For example, suppose you know that you are prone to using "your" when you really mean "you're." You could try to proofread your work to catch all instances of "your" and check them, but it's much easier (and more accurate) to have Word Pro perform the search.

The other half of the Find operation is Replace. Replacing is optional. Sometimes you just want to find occurrences; other times you need to replace them with something else. For example, suppose you are writing a proposal for Acme Corporation, and you are creating it by making changes to an old proposal you did for Smith Construction. You could find all instances of Smith Corporation and replace them with Acme Corporation.

Finding and replacing is a skill that will carry over into other SmartSuite applications. Approach, 1-2-3, and Freelance all have the same Find and Replace command on the Edit menu.

To Do: Performing a Search in a Document

1. Choose Edit, Find & Replace Text, or press Ctrl+F. Extra tools appear at the top of your document.

2. Type the text you want to find in the Find text box. (You can open the text box's drop-down list to select text from previous Find operations, if you have any.) See Figure 5.6.

3. (Optional) If you want to replace the text string with another, enter the replacement text in the Replace With text box. (It too has a drop-down list for choosing previous entries.)

FIGURE 5.6.

These Find & Replace controls appear as an extra toolbar at the top of your document.

4. Open the drop-down list to the left of the Replace With box and choose how you want to find. The default is Whole Words Only, but you can also choose Words Starting With, Words Ending With, or Words Containing (which finds any words that contain the search string, such as the letter string "the" in *theme* or *other*.

5. Click the Find button to find the first instance. Word Pro jumps to and highlights it in the document.

6. To replace it, click the Replace button. Or, to find another without replacing anything, click the Find button again. When no more instances occur, Word Pro will tell you so.

You can use the Replace All button to replace all instances at once, but be careful; this can make changes that you did not intend. For example, if you are replacing "cold" with "malady," it could change the word "scold" to "smalady."

You can continue to edit the document normally as you are using Find and Replace. That way, if you uncover any more changes you want to make as you are finding/replacing, you can stop and make them without disrupting the Find/Replace operation.

5

7. When you are finished, click Done to close the Find and Replace tools.

That's the basic procedure. You can modify it to your precise specifications in these ways:

- Click the right or left arrow buttons to specify in which direction from the insertion point the search will run. The right-pointing arrow runs the search backward (toward the beginning of the document); the left-pointing one (the default) runs the search forward.

- Click the Options button to open a dialog box with additional find/replace options, shown in Figure 5.7. These include Match Case, which finds only text with the same case (upper or lower).

Choose how much of the document to search

FIGURE 5.7.

Set additional find and replace options in this dialog box.

Refer to this list of nonprinting charac-ters to search for

Click this button to search for certain formatting

The list of special characters shown in Figure 5.7 is for reference only. Selecting one from the list doesn't do anything. Open the list, make a note of the code you want to use, and then close the Options dialog box and type your code in either the Find or Replace With box. For example, note that the reference indicates * Any Characters. That means I can type S^* and find all the words in the document that begin with the letter S.

Inserting a Page Break

When you fill up one page, Word Pro automatically goes on to the next page. To end a page early, click the Insert Page Break button on the toolbar or press Ctrl+Enter.

The page break is a hidden character. To get rid of it, delete it like any other character: move the insertion point below it and press Backspace or move the insertion point above it and press Delete.

Using the Spelling Checker

Word Pro comes with its own dictionary, and as you type, it looks up each word. If one of the words you type doesn't match a dictionary entry, Word Pro makes a note of that fact.

You can check the misspelled words that it found by clicking the Spelling button on the status bar (it's the one that looks like the ABC book). A little menu appears with only one option on it—Show Misspelled Words. Click it, and all the misspelled words appear highlighted in light blue. You can easily correct them manually.

To Do: Using the Spell Checker on a Single Word

To Do ▼

1. With Show Misspelled Words turned on (as explained above), click to place the insertion point within a misspelled word.

2. Click the Spelling button on the status bar again. This time, a menu appears listing possible spelling corrections, along with some other options. See Figure 5.8.

FIGURE 5.8.

When a word is not in the dictionary, Word Pro offers several suggestions for correction.

Insertion point in shaded misspelled word ———

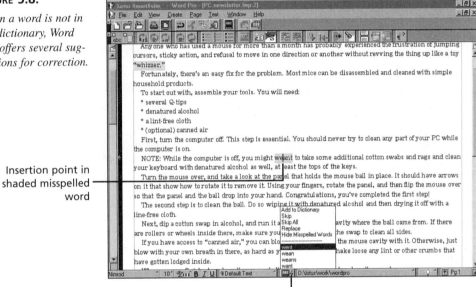

Click here to open the menu

▲ 3. Click on the correct spelling for the word.

The preceding explained how to check individual words, but you can also run a full spell check on the entire document.

To Do: Using the Spell Checker on an Entire Document

To Do ▼

1. Click the Spelling button on the toolbar (at the top of the Word Pro window) or press Ctrl+F2. Spelling tools appear at the top of the work area (see Figure 5.9).

2. (Optional) Click the Options button and set any spell-check options you want. (You can also edit your custom dictionary from here.)

3. Do any of the following to correct the error:

   • Click on the correct word on the list and then click the Replace button to replace this occurrence or Replace All to replace all occurrences in the document.

▼

5

- Click Skip to skip this occurrence or Skip All to ignore this word from now on in this document.

- Click Add to User Dictionary to add this word to your dictionary so it will not be marked as misspelled in other documents (or this one either!).

> Remember, if the word is not in the dictionary, WordPro thinks it's spelled incorrectly. Client names, company names, and others may come up misspelled when they are not. Simply add them into the dictionary, and they will never be flagged as misspelled again.

4. When you have checked all the words in the document, a dialog box asks whether you would like to close the Spell Check bar. Click Yes.

FIGURE 5.9.

The Spell Check bar offers tools that let you check the entire document for spelling errors.

> Word Pro also offers a grammar checker, which you can reach from the Edit, Proofing Tools menu. The Grammar Check controls operate just like those for the Spell Check.
>
> There is also a Thesaurus, which provides synonyms you can use to make your writing more varied and colorful. It's also available from the Edit, Proofing Tools menu.

Summary

In this hour, you learned how to type, edit, and check your text in Word Pro, and how to work with Word Pro's special onscreen controls and features. That doesn't sound like a lot, but you've now built a very solid foundation in Word Pro on which you'll build in the next several chapters.

In the next hour, you'll learn how to format your text using different fonts, colors, and other attributes.

Q&A

Q **Help! I typed text by pressing Enter at the end of each line. Now when I try to edit the paragraph, the lines break in weird places.**

A You need to remove all those extra end-of-paragraph markers so the lines will wrap normally. To do so, click the Show/Hide Tabs & Returns button on the toolbar so that the paragraph symbols are visible. Position the insertion point in front of each one and press the Delete key to get rid of it.

Q **What are some of the special character strings I can enter when using Find & Replace?**

A Each one begins with ^, which is a special designation meaning "the following is a code, not regular text." They include ^* for any string of characters, ^? for any one character, ^t for a Tab, and ^r for a return (a paragraph break). You can see a complete list in the Special Characters Help drop-down list in the Find & Replace Text Options dialog box.

Q **Can I use Find and Replace to change formatting?**

A Yes. Open the Find & Replace box (Edit, Find & Replace Text). Enter ^* in both the Find and the Replace With text boxes. Then click the Options button. In the dialog box that appears, click the AZ button in the Find area. In the InfoBox that appears, specify the formatting to find and then close the InfoBox. Repeat with the AZ button in the Replace area to specify the desired new formatting. Close the dialog box and begin your Find and Replace operation normally.

Q **I accidentally added a misspelled word to my dictionary. How do I remove it?**

A Click the Options button in the Spell Check bar to open the Spell Check Options dialog box. Click the Edit Dictionary button. Select the word from the dictionary list and click the Remove button.

5

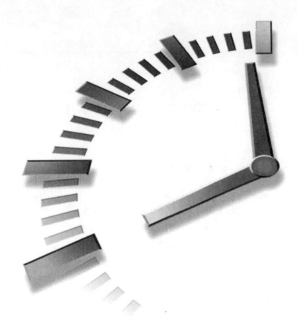

HOUR 6

Formatting Text with Word Pro

Now that you know your way around Word Pro and have typed a few paragraphs, it's time to learn some formatting tricks. This and the next hour both deal with formatting. In this hour, we'll talk about formatting individual characters; the next hour covers formatting entire paragraphs and pages.

Highlights of this hour include:

- Changing the font and font size
- Setting a different default font for new documents
- Making text bold, italic, or underlined
- Changing the text color
- Inserting special typographical symbols that aren't on your keyboard

Formatting: An Overview

Formatting refers to any special commands you issue that make typed text look different. Formatting could include making a word bold, making it appear in a different font, indenting the paragraph it is in, and changing the page margins.

Character formatting is any formatting that affects individual characters. To apply character formatting, you select the text and then issue the command. For example, to make a word bold, you select it and click the Bold button on the status bar. Even if you were to make an entire paragraph bold, it would still be considered character formatting because you could have applied the formatting to less than the entire paragraph if you had wanted to.

Paragraph formatting is formatting that applies to an entire paragraph. To apply paragraph formatting to a single paragraph, you position the insertion point anywhere in the paragraph, and then issue the command. To apply paragraph formatting to more than one paragraph, you select each of the paragraphs you want to affect before issuing the command. Paragraph formatting includes tab stops, indents, line spacing, and borders that surround certain paragraphs.

Page formatting (also called *document formatting*) is formatting that applies to an entire document, division, or section. Page formatting includes margins, headers and footers, page backgrounds/borders, and columns.

NEW TERM *Sections* and *divisions* are ways of partitioning off certain pages or areas of a document so that you can apply different page formatting. For example, if you wanted the margins different on the first page of the document, you would create a section break to separate it from the rest of the document. See Hour 7 for details.

Changing the Font and Size

Windows came with a few fonts, and SmartSuite provides many more. You may also have fonts already installed on your PC from other Windows-based applications, such as other word processing programs. Generally speaking, all fonts (at least all TrueType fonts) can work with all Windows-based programs.

NEW TERM *TrueType fonts:* Most of the fonts on your system are *TrueType* fonts. TrueType is a font format designed specifically for Windows. These fonts are fully scalable (which means you can use them in any size) and they work on any printer.

Font size is measured in points. Most TrueType fonts can be used at any size, from 6 (really small) to 72 and above (really huge). Normal text in a report or letter is usually either 10 or 12 points.

Point size: A *point* is 1/72 of an inch.

Changing Font and Size with the Status Bar

The easiest way to change the font and size of text is to use the status bar controls. Select the text you want to change and then click the Font or Font Size button on the status bar. Make your selection from the drop-down list that appears. Figure 6.1 shows a new font being chosen. The fonts on your system may be different than those shown in Figure 6.1, depending on what other applications and fonts you have installed.

FIGURE 6.1.

Change font and font size from the status bar.

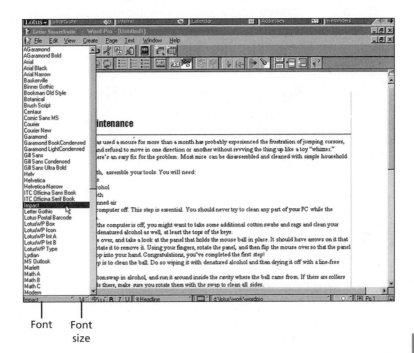

Font   Font
        size

6

Changing Font and Size with the Text Properties InfoBox

You can also change font and font size from the Text Properties InfoBox. Open it by choosing Text, Text Properties. From this InfoBox, you can select a font and size from their respective lists, as shown in Figure 6.2. Notice the little symbols next to each font on the list? The ones with TT next to them are TrueType fonts. The ones with a printer icon next to them are built into the printer.

Figure 6.2.

The Text Properties InfoBox offers font and size controls.

Changes you make in an InfoBox take effect immediately; you don't have to close the box first. You might want to leave the Text Properties InfoBox open as you work if you do a lot of formatting. To make it take up less space, double-click on its title bar to shrink it so that only the title bar and tabs appear. To enlarge it again to be usable, double-click the title bar again.

Browsing Fonts and Sizes with the Toolbar Buttons

Yet another way to change the font and size is to select the text and then use two special buttons on the toolbar:

Cycle Through Typeface Options. Every time you click this button, it changes the typeface to a different font. It starts with the first font alphabetically on your list and progresses through them with each click. This is useful for browsing if you don't know the name of the font you want or are unsure what look you are trying to achieve.

Cycle Through Font Size Options. Each time you click this button, the font size increases. The amount that it increases depends on the font. With most TrueType fonts in most sizes, it goes up one point for each click.

A shortcut for increasing the size is the F4 key. To decrease the size, press Shift+F4.

Changing the Default Font and Size

When you create a plain document in Word Pro, the default font is Times New Roman and the default size is 12 points. You can change this default so that future plain documents use some other setting.

To Do: Changing the Default Font and Point Size

1. Close all open documents. (This is important.)
2. Choose File, Open. The Open dialog box appears.
3. Select Lotus Word Pro SmartMaster (*.mwp) in the Files of type box.
4. Specify the drive and folder where the SmartMaster is located (probably c:\lotus\smasters\wordpro).

▼   5. On the list of files that appears, double-click default.mwp.

       6. Choose the new font or size from the status bar controls or the Text Properties InfoBox.

       7. Choose Text, Named Styles, Redefine. The Redefine Style dialog box opens. There is only one style—Default Text Style. See Figure 6.3.

FIGURE 6.3.

Redefine the one style contained in the default.mwp template.

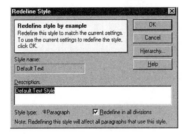

       8. Click OK to redefine the default text style to the settings you chose in step 6.

▲   9. Choose File, Close, and click Yes to save the changes.

The next time you start a new, plain document, it will default to the font and size you chose.

Changing Text Attributes and Colors

Text attributes are properties of the text, other than its font and size, that affect its appearance. Table 6.1 provides a list of the text attributes that Word Pro supports.

TABLE 6.1. TEXT ATTRIBUTES YOU CAN APPLY IN WORD PRO

Attribute	Example
Bold	**My Text**
Italic	*My Text*
Underline	<u>My Text</u>
Word Underline	<u>My</u> <u>Text</u>
Double Underline	My Text
Superscript	H^2O
Subscript	Footnote$_1$
Strikethrough	~~My Text~~
Small Caps	MY TEXT
Uppercase	MY TEXT
Lowercase	my text

6

There are two other text attributes, Hidden and Protected, that don't appear in Table 6.1. These are special attributes that work with Team Security (File, Team Security). After you mark text as hidden, you can turn off its display with File, Team Security, Show Hidden Text. After you mark text as protected, you can choose File, Team Security, Allow Editing of Protected Text to make the text uneditable.

Text color is self-explanatory. You can choose from a wide array of colors for both the text background and the letters themselves. Unless you have a color printer, however, the colors are useful only onscreen. Black-and-white printers print colored text (and backgrounds) in various muddy shades of gray.

Changing Text Attributes from the Status Bar

The controls on the status bar for changing text attributes are not comprehensive, but they are a very convenient way to apply the most commonly used attributes.

The status bar contains three buttons for text attributes—**B** (Bold), *I* (Italic), and <u>U</u> (Underline). Select the text and click on one of these buttons to apply the formatting. (There are many other attributes you can apply to text, but these are the only ones that work from the status bar.)

To change the color of the text, click the Text Color button on the status bar (it's the colorful button to the left of the B, I, and U buttons). Up pops a palette of colors. Click the color you want to change to, as shown in Figure 6.4.

FIGURE 6.4.

You can select from a rainbow of text colors to apply to the selected text.

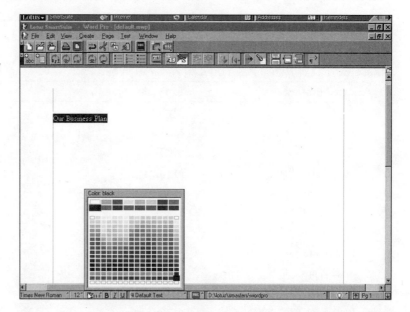

Changing Text Attributes from the Text Properties InfoBox

The Text Properties InfoBox provides access to a comprehensive array of text attributes. Just choose the one you want from the Attributes list. Refer to Figure 6.2.

To change the text color from the InfoBox, open the Text Color drop-down list and pick from the palette. (It's the same palette you saw in Figure 6.4.) You can also specify a text background color with the Background drop-down list. Usually, the background color is Transparent or none. To set it to a different color, just choose one. Notice that the check in the Transparent checkbox goes away when you select a color. To return the text to transparent background again, click the Transparent checkbox again to reenter the check mark.

Applying a colored background to the individual letters places the colored background only where there is text. If you have indented the first line of the paragraph a few spaces, for example, there will be no color behind that indented part. Character-based backgrounds are useful for making certain words or phrases stand out in a paragraph, but the effect doesn't look that great when applied to entire paragraphs.

If you want the colored background to apply to the entire area of the paragraph, including any tabbed areas like that, apply the background color to the paragraph instead of the individual letters. To do so, click the Color and Line Style tab in the Text Properties InfoBox and set the Background drop-down list there to the appropriate color.

Other Ways to Change Text Properties

You can click the **Cycle Through Attribute Options** button on the toolbar to cycle through Bold, Italic, and Underline formatting. The cycle goes like this—Bold, Italic, Bold and Italic, Underline, and then back to Normal again.

However, cycling through attributes you don't want is usually not the most efficient method. A better alternative is to use shortcut keys to apply the attributes you need:

Ctrl+B	Bold
Ctrl+I	Italic
Ctrl+U	Underline
Ctrl+W	Word Only underline
Ctrl+N	Normal (default font, size, and attributes)

6

One nice thing about the shortcut keys is that you can build one attribute on top of another. Suppose, for example, you want to make some text both bold and underlined. Select it, press Ctrl+B, and then press Ctrl+U.

Inserting Special Typographical Characters

There are many special typographical symbols that do not appear on your keyboard, but that Word Pro can produce. Examples include a copyright symbol (©), a built fraction (½), and accented letters used in some non-English languages (such as á).

One way to enter these special characters is to use an ASCII code for them. Each character has a three-digit numeric code. To enter a character, hold down the Alt key and type its code on the numeric keypad on your keyboard (with the NumLock on). For example, Alt+212 is a plus sign, and Alt+225 is ß. The only trick to this is you have to know what number to type, and most people don't know. Another disadvantage of this method is that different fonts have different symbols for each numeric code. A ß in Courier font, for example, is a ⇓ in Symbol font.

A better, easier way is to use Word Pro's Symbol feature to browse the available symbols and choose the ones you want.

To Do: Inserting Word Pro Symbols

1. Choose Text, Insert Other, Symbol. The Symbol box appears. See Figure 6.5.

2. Scroll the list of characters until you find the character you want to insert. Change the font if needed by choosing a different one from the Font drop-down list.

FIGURE 6.5.

The Symbol box helps you select and insert non-typed symbols.

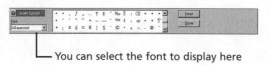

— You can select the font to display here

3. Click the character you want to insert and then click the Insert button.

4. When you are finished inserting symbols, click the Done button.

The Symbol feature in Word Pro inserts not only untypeable symbols but also typesetting characters such as long dashes (—). You can also set up these typesetting characters to work with SmartCorrect. For example, if you are using the copyright symbol frequently, you should add the symbol to your SmartCorrect list. First, insert the symbol into a document using the Text, Insert Other, Symbol command, and then copy the copyright symbol. Select Edit to SmartCorrect and choose Add Entry. In the SmartCorrect entry box, type (c). Paste the copyright symbol into the Replacement text box. Click OK twice. Now when you need to insert a copyright symbol, all you have to do is type (c) and press the spacebar.

 Notice that when you type quotation marks around a phrase, Word Pro automatically "curls" them so the beginning and ending ones are different. Choose Edit, SmartCorrect for a dialog box in which you can control this and other automatic corrections.

Summary

In this hour, you learned how to apply formatting to your typed characters. You learned how to change the font and size, apply special attributes and colors, and insert symbols that are not found on your keyboard. This basic, foundation-building knowledge will help you in upcoming chapters, as you explore more global formatting and find out how to use named styles and templates to make formatting easier and more intuitive.

Q&A

Q I chose a different font and size, but the text didn't change. What am I doing wrong?

A You probably forgot to select the text first. Simply having the insertion point positioned in a word or phrase is not enough. You must select the text to apply character formatting.

Q How can I choose a different default font for this one document I'm working on without resetting the default for all documents?

A When you create a document with the Create a Plain Document button, its default font is specified in a style called Default Text. To change the default font in the document, modify that style. See Hour 8 to learn how to edit styles.

Q I'm trying to insert a symbol but I don't see the symbol I want on the list.

A Try a different font. Open the Font drop-down list in the Symbol box. Try a font such as Symbol or Wing Dings, both of which contain some unusual and eye-catching symbols. If you are writing technical papers for a particular profession, you may want to investigate getting a font that contains nothing but special symbols relevant to your profession. (Mathematicians find this especially useful.)

6

Hour 7

Formatting Paragraphs and Documents

As you learned last hour, Word Pro offers three types of formatting—character, paragraph, and document. You nailed the first kind in Hour 6; now it's time to master the other two. By the end of this hour, you'll be setting margins and tabs, making bulleted lists, and centering lines of text like a pro.

Highlights of this hour include:

- Setting and removing tab stops
- Changing text alignment
- Indenting paragraphs
- Changing the line spacing
- Creating bulleted and numbered lists
- Setting margins and paper specifications

Introducing Paragraph Formatting

Paragraph formatting is any formatting that affects an entire paragraph when you apply it. An indent is a classic example of paragraph formatting. When you set an indentation for a paragraph, the entire paragraph is affected, not just a few words or letters.

Any of the paragraph formatting can be applied to more than one paragraph at a time. Just select all the paragraphs you want to work with before you issue the command.

Changing Text Alignment

The default text alignment for a paragraph is left, which is what you are reading now in this book. The text neatly aligns at the left in a straight vertical line, whereas the edges on the right do not all come out the same. (The right edge is referred to as "ragged.")

Word Pro offers three other alignments—Center, Right, and Full. Center, obviously, makes each line of text in the paragraph centered, while Right makes the right edge smooth and the left ragged. Full cleverly inserts extra space between letters and words as needed so that both the left and right edges are vertically aligned. Figure 7.1 shows examples of the different alignments.

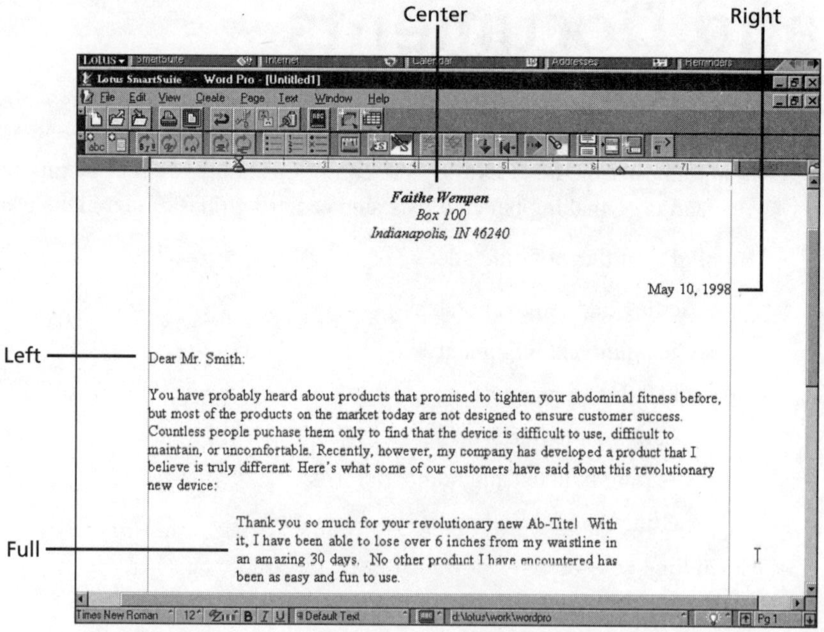

FIGURE 7.1.

Word Pro's four Alignment settings for a paragraph.

To Do: Changing Text Alignment

▲ To Do ▼

1. To change text alignment for a single paragraph, click in that paragraph. To change it for multiple paragraphs, select the paragraphs.

2. Choose Text, Alignment to open a submenu of alignments.

3. Choose the alignment you want from the submenu—Left, Center, Right, or Full Justify.

You may have noticed on the submenu in step 3 that shortcut key combinations appear next to each type of alignment. You can use these instead of using the menu to set alignment. They are:

Left	Ctrl+L	Center	Ctrl+E
Right	Ctrl+R	Full Justify	Ctrl+J

You can also set alignment from the Text Properties InfoBox. To open it, choose Text, Text Properties or press Alt+Enter and then click on the Alignment tab to display the options shown in Figure 7.2. Click on the desired alignment button to change the alignment of the selected paragraph(s).

FIGURE 7.2.

The Alignment tab in the Text Properties InfoBox contains alignment and indentation settings.

Creating Paragraph Indents

Indents control the right and left positioning of paragraphs. You can think of them as special right and left margin settings that apply to individual paragraphs rather than the entire document. In Figure 7.1, for example, the fully justified paragraph at the bottom is also indented on both the right and left sides. Indentation serves to set certain paragraphs apart, such as long quotations, and make them more noticeable.

Indenting with Shortcut Keys

There are several ways to set up an indent. The fastest way to left-indent a paragraph 1/2 inch is to press F7. (You can also choose Text, Alignment, Indent for the same result.) Each time you press F7, it moves in (that is, to the right) another 1/2 inch.

7

A reverse indent is called on *outdent*. To create an outdent, press Shift+F7 (or choose Text, Alignment, Outdent). Outdenting with Shift+F7 works only if the paragraph has been indented; it will not move the paragraph beyond the document margins.

 If F7 does not work for indenting, try this: Choose File, User Setup, Function Key Setup, and make sure that the Assign Function Keys to CycleKeys option button is selected.

Indenting with the Text Properties InfoBox

The Text Properties InfoBox's Alignment tab (refer to Figure 7.2) contains a very complete array of indentation options:

 Left indent. Indents the left side; leaves the right side alone. This is the kind of indent you get with F7.

 First-line indent. Indents the first line of the paragraph; leaves the other lines alone. Some people like to indent the first line of each paragraph to enhance readability. (An alternative to using this kind of indent is to simply press Tab once at the beginning of each paragraph.)

 Hanging indent. Indents the whole paragraph except the first line, leaving the first line "hanging" off the left edge. This is useful for bulleted and numbered lists, but you can create both of those items much more easily with Word Pro's Bullets & Numbers command, as you'll learn later in this hour.

 Full indent. Indents from both the left and the right. This is the kind you see in Figure 7.1. It's useful for setting off quotations.

To turn off all indents, click the No Indent button.

The default indentation amount for each of these indentation types is 1/2 inch. However, you can change that and some other options by clicking the Options button in the Text Properties InfoBox. This opens the Indent Options dialog box, shown in Figure 7.3. You can enter a precise amount of indent for each of the four types. This can be especially useful when you want to have more than one indent type for a paragraph—for example, if you want both a left indent and a first-line indent.

Indenting with the Ruler

You can also indent paragraphs by dragging the indentation markers on the ruler. This is my favorite method because it is so quick.

FIGURE 7.3.

*Specify your indenta-
tion options here.*

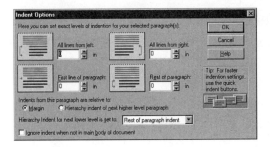

The ruler is not displayed by default and shows only in Layout view. To turn it on,
switch to Layout view if you're not already there and click the Show/Hide Ruler button
on the toolbar or choose View, Show/Hide, Ruler.

On the ruler are some triangles and a rectangle. These control the indents for whatever
paragraph the insertion point is in. You can drag these along the ruler to change the
indents.

Figure 7.4 shows the ruler controls. To adjust the left indent for the whole paragraph,
drag the rectangle. The top triangle controls the first-line indent only; the bottom triangle
controls the subsequent lines only. On the right end, things are simpler; a single triangle
controls the right indent for the entire paragraph.

Subsequent-line indent   First-line indent

FIGURE 7.4.

*Markers on the ruler
control the current
paragraphs' indenta-
tion.*

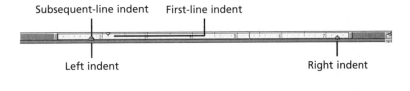

Left indent   Right indent

It is very easy to point at the wrong marker and change the indent inappro-
priately, especially on the left, where there are three tiny markers very close
together. Watch the mouse pointer as you position it over a marker. A symbol appears next to it to indicate which marker will be selected if you drag
at that moment.

7

Setting Tabs

Each time you press Tab, the insertion point moves to the next tab stop in the document.
By default, Word Pro has tab stops every 1/2 inch. These can be overridden, however, by
creating your own stops.

Types of Tab Stops

There are four types of tab, stops, based on how the text aligns with them. With the default kind, Left, the text starts at the tab stop and runs to the left. The three other kinds are

- **Centered**. The text is evenly centered at the tab stop.
- **Right**. The end of the text aligns with the tab stop and runs back toward the left.
- **Numeric**. The text aligns under the tab stop by a decimal point. This is used to line up columns of numbers under a tab stop when some numbers are longer or shorter than others.

By using tab stops, you can create some fairly sophisticated tables of data, such as the multicolumn information shown in Figure 7.5.

Tabs enable you to create multicolumn tables like the one in Figure 7.5, but it's, easier in many cases to use Word Pro's Table feature to do this kind of work. See Hour 9, "Graphics and Tables," for details.

FIGURE 7.5.

Each of these columns uses a different kind of tab stop.

Ruler symbol means this line has custom tab stops

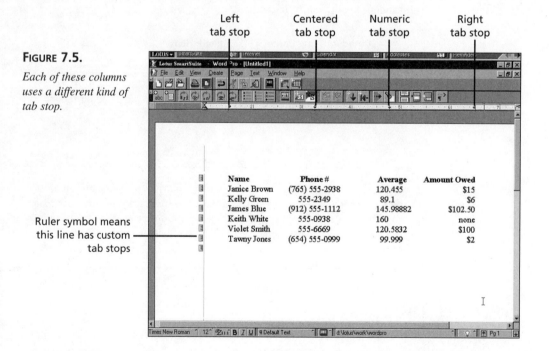

Name	Phone #	Average	Amount Owed
Janice Brown	(765) 555-2938	120.455	$15
Kelly Green	555-2349	89.1	$6
James Blue	(912) 555-1112	145.98882	$102.50
Keith White	555-0938	160	none
Violet Smith	555-6669	120.5832	$100
Tawny Jones	(654) 555-0999	99.999	$2

Setting Tab Stops with the Ruler

To set a tab stop on the ruler, click on the ruler where you want the stop to be. This places a left-aligned stop. (Remember, if the ruler is not displayed, switch to Layout view and click the Show/Hide Ruler button on the toolbar.)

If you want to place a different kind of tab stop than left-aligned, right-click on the ruler *before placing the tab stop* to display a shortcut menu. On that shortcut menu, choose the kind of tab you want to set. For example, to place a numeric tab, choose Create Numeric Tabs. After choosing the type, you can then click on the ruler to place it.

If you make a mistake and place the wrong stop type, drag the stop down off the ruler to delete it. If you place the stop at the wrong location, drag it to the left or right to reposition it.

To clear a single tab stop, drag it off the ruler. To clear all stops at once, right-click the ruler and choose Clear All Tabs.

Need more control than the ruler can provide for your tab stops? Right-click the ruler and choose Set Tabs. This opens the Set Tabs on Ruler dialog box, which you'll learn about in the following section.

Setting Tab Stops with the Text Properties InfoBox

On the Misc. tab in the Text Properties InfoBox, you'll find some commands that help you set tabs:

- **Tab Settings**. Open this drop-down list to choose from a variety of pre-set tab schemes, such as Evenly Spaced Every.
- **Inches**. Enter a number here to go along with your setting in the Tab Settings drop-down list. For example, to have evenly spaced tab stops every 1 inch, choose Evenly Spaced Every in the Tab Settings and then enter 1.0 here.
- **Set Tabs**. Clicking this button opens the Set Tabs on Ruler dialog box, shown in Figure 7.6.

The Set Tabs on Ruler dialog box provides an alternative to setting tabs as you learned in the preceding section. You might use it if you needed the stops to be set very precisely, for example, at certain numbers. You can also use it to set tab leaders.

NEW TERM   A *tab leader* is a repeated character (such as a dot) that helps your eye follow the line across the screen. See the table of contents of this book for an example.

7

Figure 7.6.

Use this dialog box to set tabs with precision control.

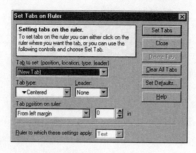

To Do: Setting Tabs

To set a tab in this dialog box, follow these steps:

1. Choose one of the tabs from the Tab to Set drop-down list, or choose New Tab if none of those preset tabs meets your needs.

2. If needed, change the stop type from the Tab Type drop-down list.

3. Choose a leader type if needed from the Leader drop-down list.

4. If needed, change the Tab Position on Ruler drop-down list to describe what the tab position is in relation to. (Most of the time the default "From left margin" is fine.)

5. Set the position in the In box. For example, to set a tab at 1 inch from the left margin, enter 1.0.

6. Click the Set Tabs button to set that tab.

7. Repeat these steps to set as many tabs as you need or click Close to close the dialog box.

> As I mentioned earlier, the default tabs are left-aligned stops evenly spaced every 1/2 inch from the left margin. If you want to a different spacing interval for these, click the Set Defaults button in the Set Tabs on Ruler dialog box. A special box appears asking how far apart you want the default tabs to be in the future.

Setting Line Spacing

You can control both the spacing between lines within a paragraph and the spacing before and after each paragraph. For example, when I am writing a book, I usually have the intra-paragraph spacing set to single, with one line of space following each paragraph, so it looks like there is a blank line between them.

To set line spacing, open the Text Properties InfoBox (Text, Text Properties or
Alt+Enter). On the Alignment tab (see Figure 7.7), you can choose an intra-paragraph
spacing from the Line Spacing drop-down list. For example, you might want double
spacing. Some spacing choices open dialog boxes where you can choose your own settings. Multiple, for example, lets you choose any number of lines for spacing, such as 3
for triple spacing.

FIGURE 7.7.

*Choose your line spac-
ing from the Alignment
tab of the Text
Properties InfoBox.*

You can precisely control the line spacing by choosing Custom. In the dialog
box that appears, you can specify spacing in picas, a unit of typographical
measurement.

To set spacing before or after a paragraph, choose it from the Above or Below drop-
down lists. You can choose a number of lines (such as 1 or 2) or an exact measurement
(with Custom).

Numbered and Bulleted Lists

As you learned previously, you can set hanging indents that work nicely when creating
bulleted and numbered lists. However, Word Pro has a separate Bullets & Numbering
feature that not only sets the hanging indents for you, but also inserts an appropriate bullet or number and, in the case of numbered lists, even does the numbering for you.

The easiest way to create a bulleted or numbered list is with the toolbar buttons. Follow
these steps:

1. Type the paragraphs that should be bulleted or numbered. Make sure each item is a
   separate paragraph.
2. Select the group of paragraphs.
3. Click the Insert Default Bullet or Insert Default Number button to convert the paragraphs to a list (see Figure 7.8).

7

Insert Default Bullet button   Insert Default Number button

FIGURE 7.8.

Numbered and bulleted lists are as easy as clicking a toolbar button.

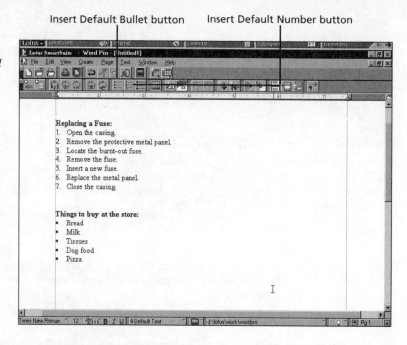

 If you accidentally apply a bullet or number to a paragraph that does not need one, select that paragraph and click the Insert Default Bullet or Insert Default Number button again to toggle it off.

A much more powerful (but somewhat more clunky) way to assign bullets and numbers is with the Text Properties InfoBox. Choose Text, Bullets & Numbers to open it up to the Bullet & Number tab shown in Figure 7.9. Select the text you want to affect and then click on a bullet or number option here to apply it to the text.

Choose from a variety of special bullet characters

FIGURE 7.9.

Choose from a wide array of bullets and number styles and options.

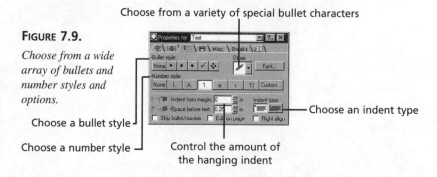

Choose a bullet style

Choose a number style

Control the amount of the hanging indent

Choose an indent type

Setting Margins, Orientation, and Paper Size

Margins are a document formatting feature. Your margins affect the entire document (or the entire division or section if you have your document divided into multiple sections or divisions.)

The default margin settings are 1 inch on all sides. To change margins, choose Page, Margins. This opens the Page Layout Properties InfoBox, which contains tabs for the various document-wide settings under your control (see Figure 7.10). Enter the new margin settings in the Top, Left, Right, and Bottom text boxes.

Click here to set separate margins for left and right

FIGURE 7.10.

Set margins for the entire document from this InfoBox.

Click here for Portrait orientation

Click here for Landscape orientation

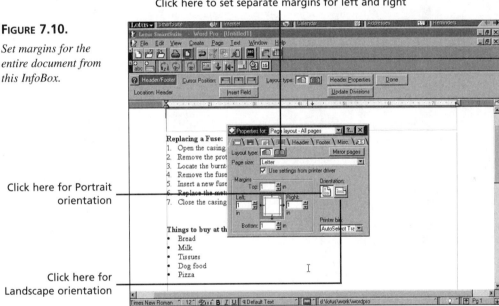

If you are creating a booklet or other two-sided document, you may want different margins for the left and right pages. Click the Left/Right button next to Layout Type to indicate that your settings are for only the right or only the left pages (see Figure 7.10). Then choose the right or the left from the Properties For drop-down list.

7

Page orientation refers to the direction that the text runs on the page. The default is Portrait, in which the text runs along the narrow edge of the paper. The pages are taller than they are wide. The alternative is landscape, in which the text runs along the wide edge. To choose an orientation, click the appropriate button in the InfoBox. See Figure 7.10.

You can also set up your document for a different paper size. The default is Letter, which is 8 1/2 × 11. Open the Paper Size drop-down list in the InfoBox to choose something different.

> You can change the margin settings by dragging on the ruler. There is a small gray bar that separates the bright yellow from the dim on each end of the ruler. These bars are your margin markers. You can drag them to the left or right to change them. To make sure you are grabbing a margin marker rather than an indent, point at the marker and notice the mouse pointer. A little picture appears on it, mirroring what it is pointing at. When it is pointing at a margin marker, the little picture looks like a bar.

Page Backgrounds and Watermarks

Word Pro has some wonderful page background controls that can make your documents really special. While you're in the Page Layout InfoBox, click the Color, Pattern & Line Style tab to display these controls. From here you can

- Place a line or shadowed box around each page and choose a line style and line width.
- Apply a Designer border, which goes beyond the traditional sense of "border" and is actually a graphic image like a piece of clip art that surrounds the page.
- Choose a background color for the page and a pattern (optional) that uses a second color.
- Choose a Shadow for the page, giving it a 3D effect.

Similarly, the Watermark tab in this InfoBox lets you add a watermark image to your page. On this tab you can choose from a variety of watermark messages, such as "Confidential," and choose the size and placement of the image.

 A *watermark* is a faint image that appears behind your text on a page. It is reminiscent of the brand name that appears very faintly on fine stationery.

Summary

In this jam-packed hour, you learned about the formatting options that apply to paragraphs and documents. You can now set tab, indents, alignment, and margins with confidence, making your documents the best they possibly can be. Even though this session is over, you might want to extend it into one more hour, practicing the skills you learned.

In the next hour, you'll find out how to automate some of your formatting in Word Pro to save yourself some time. The two principal means for this are styles, which apply formatting to individual paragraphs and characters, and templates, which start you out with preformatted text and pre-created styles.

Q&A

Q I have a one-line paragraph, and I set it to Full Justify, but it won't stretch itself out to fill the full space between the right and left margins. It looks just like it did when it was Left aligned. What am I doing wrong?

A Nothing. Word Pro does not full-justify the last line of a paragraph because it is often a partial line. Full justify works only with multiline paragraphs.

Q I'm trying to make the two triangles line up on the left edge of the ruler so that the first line indent will be the same as the other lines in the paragraph, but whenever I drag the bottom triangle, the top triangle moves too.

A You are inadvertently dragging the rectangle rather than the bottom triangle. When you drag the rectangle, it moves the two triangles together. If the triangles are apart, they will remain apart by exactly that same distance as you drag the rectangle. Make sure you are grabbing the bottom triangle.

Q I set up one line of spacing between paragraphs, but it looks like there is a lot more space between each paragraph than I specified.

A You probably specified one line in both the Above and Below settings. If the first paragraph has one line above and one line below it, and so does the next paragraph, then you get a total of two lines between them. You should set only one or the other: Below or Above.

Q I tried to change the margin settings by dragging on the ruler, but it changed the settings for only one paragraph.

A You accidentally changed the indent setting for that paragraph rather than changing the margin. It's easy to make this mistake—the markers are very small and very close together. Try again.

7

HOUR 8

Shortcuts for Formatting

Well, after the last two hours, you should be an expert on formatting, right? Formatting can make the difference between an adequate document and a really cool one. The only problem is that formatting takes time, and you won't always have time to spare.

In this hour, we'll explore some Word Pro features that can make it much easier for you to format. Highlights include:

- Creating your own SmartMaster templates
- Applying styles to text
- Creating your own styles
- Copying formatting with FastFormat

Using SmartMaster Templates

You learned about SmartMaster templates, in a general way, in the first few chapters of this book. They are preformatted "head-starts" for creating various kinds of documents. Sometimes they include sample text; other times they just use formatted placeholders.

SmartMasters can save you a great deal of time because you don't have to "reinvent the wheel" when you want to create a common business document. For example, if you want to write a letter, you can base it on one of the letter SmartMasters and not spend time figuring out where to put the date or what kind of signature block to use.

Starting a Document with a SmartMaster

This stuff is review for you—you learned about this already in Hour 4. But just in case you've forgotten:

To Do: Starting a Document with a SmartMaster

1. Choose File, New Document. The New Document dialog box appears.

2. Click the Create from Any SmartMaster tab.

3. On the Select a Type of SmartMaster list, click the type you want (see Figure 8.1).

4. On the Select a Look list, click the look you want. Check out the preview in the pane to the right.

5. When you find the look you want, click OK. For example, try letter1. The SmartMaster creates a new document.

FIGURE 8.1.

Choose the Word Pro SmartMaster that's right for the job you need done.

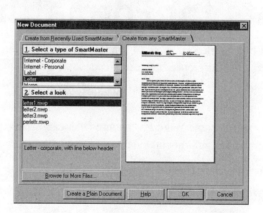

With the new document onscreen, you have some work to do. Most SmartMaster templates contain fields that you need to fill in. For example, in Figure 8.2, which was created from the Letter1 template, several lines of instruction appear. [Click here to type recipient's name] is the first such line. When you click on that line, it disappears! Go ahead and try it now. It disappears because it's merely a placeholder for the information you need to fill in. When you click away from the instruction, it returns. If you type some real text over it, the placeholder disappears permanently.

FIGURE 8.2.

In many SmartMaster templates, fields with instructions serve as placeholders. Click on it and type the requested information (for example, recipient address).

There are four fields here

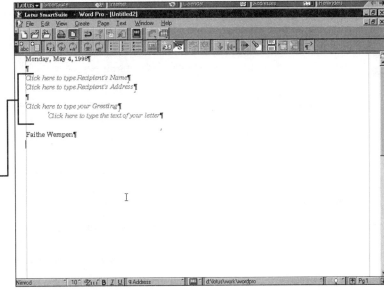

Editing a SmartMaster Template

Word Pro's SmartMasters are very nicely designed, but perhaps you would like to make a change to one of them. For example, the Letter1 template uses 10-point type for the letter; perhaps you would prefer that it used 12-point instead.

It's easy to make a change to a SmartMaster template. Just open the template as you would open any document. Select the text (or field) to change and make your change. Then save your work. Sounds easy, eh?

To try it out, follow these steps to change the Letter1 SmartMaster template to use 12-point type.

To Do: Editing a SmartMaster

▲ To Do ▼

1. Choose File, Open. The Open dialog box appears.

2. Open the Files of Type drop-down list and choose Lotus Word Pro SmartMaster (*.mwp).

3. Open the Look In drop-down list and choose the drive that contains your SmartSuite files (probably C:).

4. Double-click the Lotus folder, double-click the smasters folder, and then the word-pro folder. A list of SmartMaster templates appears.

▼ 5. Double-click on letter1. That template opens for editing.

▼   6. Choose Text, Select, Entire Document.

    7. Click the Font Size button on the status bar and click on 12 on the list of sizes that appears.

    8. Choose File, Save As. The Save As dialog box appears.

    9. (Optional) If you want to preserve the original Letter1, type a new name in the File Name text box (for example, Letter12, because of the 12-point type). Then click the Save button.

▲   10. Choose File, Close.

The next time you use Letter1, the letter it creates will have 12-point type.

Creating Your Own Templates

You can create your own templates from scratch and use them just like a SmartMaster. To create a template, set up a normal document the way you want the template to look and save it as a template with Save As, making sure you save them in the Lotus\Smaster\Word Pro folder with a file type of Lotus Word Pro SmartMaster (*.mwp). If you see a dialog box with additional options in it, click OK to move on. (You shouldn't have to change any of the options.)

Word Pro offers some specialized features that are useful when creating a template. Try these out on your own if you are interested in building more powerful templates:

- You can insert a code so that the current date always appears. This is useful when creating templates for memos and letters. Simply position the insertion point and choose Text, Insert Other, Date/Time.

- You can create text entry fields just like the ones that prompt you for data entry in the SmartMasters that come with Word Pro. To use this feature, position the insertion point and choose Create, Click Here Block. Fill in the fields in the dialog box that appears to specify what instructions will appear.

Working with Styles

Styles can save you lots of time because a style can apply several kinds of formatting in one swoop. For example, suppose you want all the headings in the document to be 14-point bold Arial. You could create a style that included all those attributes and then apply it to each line that you wanted to make into a heading.

NEW TERM   *Styles* are named formatting specifications. You format text the way you want it and then create a named style for that formatting. You can then apply the same formatting to other text.

When you work with a template, the styles associated with it appear on your Style list. The Style list is in the middle of the status bar. Click its button to open the list, as shown in Figure 8.3. Different SmartMasters have different lists of styles. Plain documents have a basic, generic set of styles appropriate for a variety of documents.

FIGURE 8.3.

Pop up the Style list from the status bar.

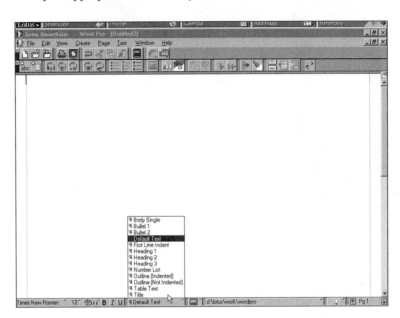

There are two kinds of styles—Paragraph and Character. You can't tell just by their names which is which. Character styles contain only character formatting, such as making text bold, while Paragraph styles contain both character and paragraph formatting, such as making a paragraph bold and centered. (This will be important later when you create new styles.)

Applying Styles

To apply a style, select the text you want to affect. Open the Style list and click the style you want to apply.

If the text had previously set paragraph formatting, the style will not override it. For example, if the paragraph was centered and then you applied a style that specifies left alignment, it would remain centered. To reset a paragraph so that all of the style's settings apply to it, select the text and choose Text, Named Styles, Reset to Style, or click the Reset to Style button on the toolbar.

Defining a New Style

Word Pro defines styles "by example." To create a style, you first format some text using all the attributes that you want the style to have. Then you issue the command to create the style.

To Do: Defining a New Style

1. Format some text the way you want it. Your formatting can include paragraph settings (such as indents and tabs) and character settings (such as fonts and colors).

2. Select the text. If you are including paragraph settings, select the entire paragraph.

3. Choose Text, Named Styles, Create, or click the Create Style button on the toolbar. The Create Style dialog box opens.

4. Type a name for the style in the Style Name box (see Figure 8.4).

FIGURE 8.4.

Create a new style from the example you created by formatting text.

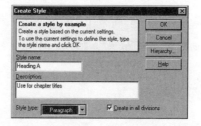

5. (Optional) Type a description for the style in the Description box. You might use the description to explain under what circumstances the style should be used.

6. If this style includes paragraph formatting, leave the Style Type drop-down list set to Paragraph. If you do not want to include the example text's paragraph formatting, change this to Character.

7. Click OK. The new style now appears on your Style list on the status bar.

The Hierarchy button in the Create Style dialog box is used to "cascade" style settings. For example, suppose you have some text that is currently formatted with the Address style, which uses 12-point type. You change some of its formatting and create a new style with it called ZIP, which also uses 12-point type. If you want the fact that ZIP uses 12-point type to be linked to Address using it, you can set this up in the Hierarchy dialog box so that if you ever change the Address style to use, say, 10-point type, the ZIP style will change also.

Changing a Style

Changing a style, like creating one, is done by example.

To Do: Modifying a Style

1. Apply the style to some text.
2. Reformat that text with the desired changes.
3. Choose Text, Named Styles, Redefine. The Redefine Style dialog box opens.
4. (Optional) Change the description if desired.
5. Click OK. The style is redefined to the current formatting.

> You cannot modify the style type for a style (Character or Paragraph). You must delete the style and re-create it to change this feature.

Managing Styles

Word Pro offers a one-stop shop for managing the list of styles in a document. You can rename and delete them, assign function keys, and even copy styles from other SmartMaster templates. Just choose Text, Named Styles, Manage to open the Manage Styles dialog box, shown in Figure 8.5.

FIGURE 8.5.

Keep your list of styles tidy with this dialog box.

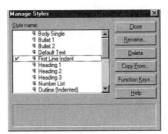

To select a style in this dialog box, click on it. A check mark appears next to it. You can select more than one style at a time; the check mark doesn't disappear next to a style until you click on it again to turn it off.

Deleting Styles

If there are styles on the Style list that you are never going to use in the current document, you can delete them. They aren't hurting anything, but you may prefer a leaner Style list that shows only the styles you actually use.

When you delete a style, you do so only from the current document. If the style came from a SmartMaster template that you used to create the document, that style is still safe-and-sound there and will reappear the next time you create a new document with that template.

To delete a style, click to place a check mark next to it and then click the Delete button. A Delete Style dialog box appears; click Yes to complete the deletion. You can delete several styles at a time by selecting them all first.

Renaming a Style

You might want to rename a style to give it a more meaningful name based on your own work. For example, if you start a new document with a SmartMaster that provides a style called Heading 1, you might want to rename the style to Chapter Title so you can remember what you are using the Heading 1 style for.

You can rename only one style at a time. If more than one style is selected, the rename button becomes unavailable.

To rename, click the style you want to rename and click the Rename button. A dialog box appears prompting for the new name and description; enter them and click OK.

Assigning Function Keys to Styles

Function keys can be helpful for diehard keyboard users who don't like to reach for the mouse whenever they need to apply a style. When you assign a function key to a style, pressing that key applies the style to the selected text.

To assign a function key from the Manage Styles dialog box, click the Function Keys button. (You don't have to select the style first.) In the Function Keys dialog box that appears, open the drop-down lists and choose styles to associate with the listed function keys. In Figure 8.6, for example, the style Default Text is being assigned to the F6 key. When finished, click OK.

FIGURE 8.6.

Word Pro enables you to assign styles to ten different function keys.

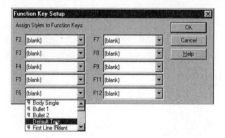

Copying Styles from Other Templates

Each of the SmartMaster templates has its own unique set of predefined styles. You may find that you like some of the styles in one template and others in a second one. Fortunately, you aren't stuck with a single set. You can pick and choose which styles you want to work with.

> To create your own template with exactly the styles you want, start a new template as you learned earlier in this hour. Base it on one of the SmartMasters that has some of the styles you want. Delete the styles you don't want and add styles from other templates as needed. Save your work as a template and use that template to create new documents in the future.

To Do: Copying Styles from Other Templates

1. In the Manage Styles dialog box, click the Copy From button. The Copy Styles From dialog box appears.

2. Click the Browse button to browse for the SmartMaster template you want.

3. Double-click the template you want. Its styles appear in the Select the styles to copy box, as shown in Figure 8.7.

FIGURE 8.7.

You can select which of the template's styles you want to incorporate in the current document.

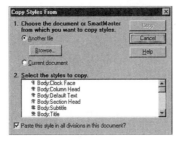

4. Click to place a check mark next to each of the styles you want to copy.

5. Click the Copy button. If one of the styles you chose already exists in the template, a dialog box asks you whether you want to overwrite the current style or choose another name.

▲   6. Click the Close button to close the Manage Styles dialog box.

Copying Formatting with FastFormat

You don't have to create a style in order to transfer formatting from one piece of text to another. Just use the FastFormat command, designed to do this very thing. Suppose, for example, you had formatted a cross-reference using a special font in bold and italic. If you wanted to format another cross-reference later in the document, you could use FastFormat to copy the formatting in a single step, rather than using the three-step process of applying the font, applying bold, and applying italics.

To Do: Copying a Format

1. Format the original text the way you want it and then select it.

2. Choose Text, FastFormat, or press Ctrl+T. Your mouse pointer changes to a vertical line with a little paintbrush next to it.

3. Drag across the text that you want to reformat. The formatting of the original text is "painted" onto it.

4. When you are finished reformatting text, press Esc to cancel FastFormat mode.

Summary

In this hour, you learned how to save some time by taking advantage of Word Pro's templates and styles. You learned how to use and modify existing styles and templates, and how to create your own. Now you're ready to set up your own templates and include your own styles in them to automate the document-creation tasks you perform most frequently.

Q&A

Q I deleted some styles, but they reappeared when I started a new document. How can I delete them permanently?

A You probably deleted the styles from the document you were working on. To delete them permanently, you need to delete them from the SmartMaster template on which the document was based.

Q I want to open a SmartMaster template for editing, but none of the names appear in my Browse box.

A Two things: First, did you change to the folder that contains your SmartMasters? It is probably c:\Lotus\Smasters\Word Pro. Next, did you change the File Type to Lotus Word Pro SmartMaster? If you don't do this, only regular Word Pro documents show up on the list.

Q I want to assign some other key combination to a style rather than using one of the function keys. Is there any way to do this?

A Unfortunately, no. However, you can create a script that applies the style, and then assign that script to a toolbar button, as an alternative to using the function keys. See Hour 10 for details.

Q I need to repeat a tab setup frequently; can I use a style for that?

A Yes. Set up the ruler with the correct tab stops, enter the text, select the text, and then follow the steps outlined above (making sure the style is a paragrraph style). Then whenever you want to change the ruler to have that particular tab setup, simply apply the style.

8

HOUR 9

Graphics and Tables

Graphics and tables are two features that some people would call "advanced," but they really aren't that difficult to use, and they can make a dramatic difference in the look of your document. Graphics can enliven any document and convey a visual image.

A table can help you align columns of data precisely, no matter how long or short the lines. In this hour, highlights include:

- Inserting a graphic image in a document
- Moving and modifying a graphic
- Using Word Pro's Drawing tools
- Creating a table
- Modifying and formatting the table

Inserting Graphics

Graphics include clip art, scanned images, charts and graphs, images you may have found on the Internet, and even pictures you have drawn yourself in a drawing or painting program. You can, for example, place your company logo as a graphic at the top of your letterhead. Graphics appear in Word Pro in frames.

 Frames are sectioned-off areas that hold special elements such as graphics, charts, and imported objects that are not a native part of Word Pro.

Adding a Graphic

To place a graphic, position the insertion point where you want the graphic to appear. Don't worry if there is already text there; it moves over to accommodate the graphic you insert.

To Do: Inserting a Graphic

1. With the insertion point positioned where you want the graphic to appear, choose File, Import Picture. The Add Picture dialog box appears.

2. By default, the folder that appears is the one that contains the clip art that Word Pro provides.

   - If you want to insert some clip art, click on the file you want. If you aren't sure which one, click on the first one and check out the sample area (see Figure 9.1.). If it isn't quite right, try another until you find the image you want.

   - If you want to insert an image that's stored somewhere else on your PC, change the folder and drive to point to its location and then select it from the list. (Remember, you learned to change folders and drives in Hour 4.)

FIGURE 9.1.

Select a graphic image to be imported into Word Pro.

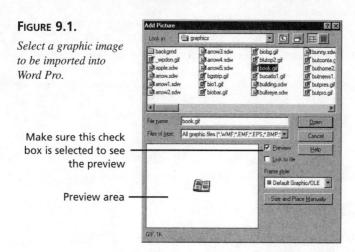

Make sure this check box is selected to see the preview

Preview area

3. Click Open to place the image into your document.

4. Move or resize it as needed, using the techniques described in the following section.

> If you want to place the graphic in an exact size and position, instead of clicking Open in step 3, click Size and Place Manually. The dialog box closes and your mouse pointer becomes a crosshair with a rectangle attached to it. By holding down the left mouse button, drag to draw a box where you want the image in your document. Note that the image may be distorted (too tall or too wide) if you don't drag the box to the same proportions as the original image. However, you can always resize it after placement, as described in the next section.

Moving and Resizing a Graphic

Graphics can be moved anywhere on the page. Any text that is already there moves over to make room.

To Do: Moving and Resizing Graphics

1. Click once on the graphic to select its frame. When the frame is selected, little black squares called *selection handles* appear around the border (see Figure 9.2).

2. Position the mouse pointer:

   - To move, position it over the edge of the frame, but *not* over a handle. The mouse pointer should appear as a hand.

   - To resize, position it over the handle that you want to drag. The mouse pointer should appear as a double-headed arrow. Choose a side handle to resize in one dimension, or a corner handle to resize in two dimensions.

3. (Optional) If you are resizing and you want to maintain the graphic's aspect ratio, hold down the Shift key.

NEW TERM The *aspect ratio* is the ratio of height to width. If you don't maintain it as you resize, the graphic can get squashed or stretched so it doesn't look right.

4. Hold down the left mouse button and drag to move or resize.

Drag a handle to
resize

Drag the border any-
where except on a
handle to move

You can also move graphics with Cut and Paste, commands that you are already familiar
with from earlier hours. Simply select the graphic and press Ctrl+X to cut it. Click where
you want it to go and press Ctrl+V.

You can control how the surrounding text wraps around the graphic by
working with the Frame Properties InfoBox. You'll see how to do that in the
following section.

Changing the Graphic Properties

There are many fine-tuning settings you can specify for a graphic. They're contained in
the InfoBox for its frame. To open it, right-click the graphic and choose Frame
Properties.

There are many commands on the shortcut menu that you see when you
right-click a graphic, but most of them simply point to different tabs in the
same InfoBox.

Let's look at four of the tabs in the InfoBox that are especially useful when working
with a graphic in a frame.

Lines and Colors

The first (leftmost) tab in the InfoBox is called Color, Pattern, & Line Style. In it, you can control the background color and pattern for the frame and whether or not it has a border around it (see Figure 9.3).

Choose a border design and width

FIGURE 9.3.

You can both place a border around your image and give it a background color.

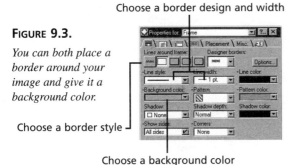

Choose a border style

Choose a background color

9

Image Size in Frame

The Watermark tab (the second from the left) is where you'll find the controls for the image itself. These controls resize the image, but leave the frame as is. So, for example, you could make the image smaller without decreasing the size of the frame (see Figure 9.4).

FIGURE 9.4.

Resize the image without resizing the frame here.

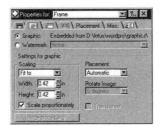

 If you make a mistake in changing the image size and want to return to the original size, choose Original Size from the Scaling drop-down list.

Frame Size

On the Size and Margin tab (see Figure 9.5), you can specify a precise size measurement for the frame, if dragging it to resize is not specific enough for your needs. You can also specify two extra settings:

- A *margin*, which controls the amount of space between the image inside the frame and the frame boundary.
- *Padding*, which controls the amount of space between the outside of the frame and any text that wraps around it.

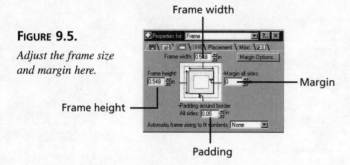

FIGURE 9.5.

Adjust the frame size and margin here.

 You can set individual margin and padding settings for each side of the frame. Click the Margin options button to open the dialog box that controls this. Choose Outside of Frame from the drop-down list to set padding or Inside of Frame to set margins.

Frame Placement

The Placement tab is one of the most important for a frame (see Figure 9.6). With it, you can control how the surrounding text wraps around the frame and which part of the document the frame is tied to.

An example makes the latter clearer. Suppose you have an article in Word Pro that contains a picture. You refer to the picture in the fifth paragraph, which is near the bottom of the page. You later add two paragraphs before it so that the paragraph that explains the picture is now bumped to the next page of the article. If you tie the picture to that paragraph, the picture will move to the next page too.

FIGURE 9.6.

Choose where the frame will be placed and how surrounding text will react to it.

Here's a sampling of what you can accomplish with the Placement tab:

- Click a button in the Wrap Options section to choose how the surrounding text will wrap around the image.

- To make the surrounding text wrap irregularly around an image, click the Irregular Wrap checkbox. The frame around the image turns to a dotted line, which you can drag to make the text wrap differently at different spots.

- Choose a placement from the Place Frame drop-down list. Choices include Same Page as Text, which keeps the frame with the text it is next to; and On All Pages, which repeats the frame at the same spot on every page.

- For more advanced placement options, click the Placement and Anchoring button to open a Placement Options dialog box. Here you can specify precise anchoring for the frame.

NEW TERM *Anchoring* refers to the way the frame is tied to a specific paragraph of text or a specific spot on a page.

9

Deleting a Graphic

To delete a graphic, just select it (by clicking on it) and then press the Delete key on the keyboard. You can also cut-and-paste a graphic to move it from one page or document to another. (Remember, to cut use Edit, Cut, or Ctrl+X; to paste use Edit, Paste, or Ctrl+V.)

Working with Tables

Tables are grids of cells that help you organize multiple columns of data. A table in Word Pro has a lot in common with a 1-2-3 spreadsheet. Both have rows and columns that intersect to form cells.

You can create an empty table and then type into its cells, or you can convert existing text into a table. After your table is created, you can format and resize it as needed.

Creating a Table

A blank table can be created in two ways. One is to choose Create, Table—a Create Table dialog box appears. Specify the number of rows and columns you want and click OK. The other way is to click the Create Table Grid button on the toolbar. When you do, a grid appears below the button. Hold down the left mouse button and drag your mouse on the grid to choose a number of rows and columns, as shown in Figure 9.7. When you are finished, stop dragging and release the mouse button. Word Pro creates a table that matches your specification.

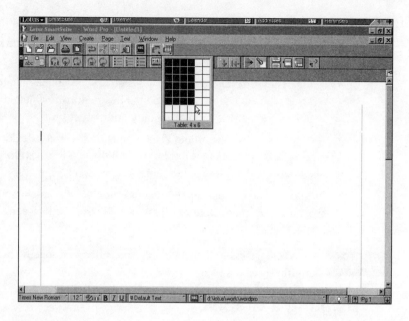

FIGURE 9.7.

An easy way to create a table is to drag on the Create Table Grid.

You can also convert text into a table. You select the text and choose Create, Table. Here's what happens next:

- The number of paragraphs in the selection determines the number of rows in the table. Each paragraph is a row.
- The number of tab stops in each paragraph determines the number of columns. If there are no tab stops, the table will have only one column. If some paragraphs have more tab stops than others, the largest number will be used.

Entering Text in a Table

To type in a table, click in the cell you want to begin with and start typing. The cell expands to contain your text, and the text wraps to multiple lines as needed.

To move to the next cell, press the Tab key. To move to the previous cell, press Shift+Tab. You can also move among the cells by using the arrow keys on your keyboard.

Calculating Columns of Numbers

Even though you have a powerful calculating tool in 1-2-3, you may still occasionally rely on a Word Pro table to perform some calculations. For example, you can list several rows of numbers and total them in the bottom row.

Even though you don't see the labels, the cells in a Word Pro table have names, just like 1-2-3 cells. The top left cell, for example, is A1 because it's at the intersection of column

A and row 1. To turn on these labels so you can work with them more easily, click the Show/Hide Table Headings SmartIcon on the toolbar.

You can also rely on a SmartIcon to total a row or column quickly. Just position your insertion point in the last cell of the row or column and then click one of these SmartIcons:

 Inserts the sum of the column

9

 Inserts the sum of the rows

To edit a formula that has been inserted into a cell or to type your own formula to be placed there, click this SmartIcon:

 Opens an Insert Formula dialog box, where you can edit or enter a formula, just like in 1-2-3.

If you don't understand formulas and cells, read ahead to the 1-2-3 chapters (Hours 11 through 15) and come back, and it will make more sense.

Adding and Removing Rows and Columns

Your best friend for adding and removing rows and columns is the Table toolbar, which appears whenever you are working with a table. Use these buttons:

 Inserts a new row directly below the selected one.

 Inserts a new column directly to the left of the selected one.

Note that for these two buttons, you don't have to have an entire row or column selected. Instead, it takes its cue from whatever cell the insertion point happens to be in at the moment.

 You can also insert a row using Ctrl++ (that's Ctrl and a single plus sign).

Another way to insert rows and columns is through the menu system. Choose Table, Insert, Row, or Insert, Column. Or, to open a dialog box where you can do either or both, choose Table, Insert, Row/Column.

To delete rows or columns, position the insertion point in any cell in the row or column and then click one of these SmartIcons on the toolbar:

Deletes the selected row.

 Deletes the selected column.

You can even delete the entire table:

 Deletes the entire table.

If you make a mistake, don't forget that the Edit, Undo command brings back your accidentally deleted table.

Changing Column Width

The easiest way to change a column's width is to drag its border. Position the mouse pointer over the right border on the column you want to resize so that the mouse pointer changes to a double-headed arrow. Drag the border to column's new width.

 You can also change the column width from the Table Cell Properties InfoBox. See "Formatting a Table" later in this chapter.

Formatting a Table

When formatting a table, you have a choice of what exactly you want to format. Do you want to format the text within a cell, the cell itself, or the entire table?

To format the text in a table, select it and format it normally. Use the status bar controls, the menus, and the Text Properties InfoBox as needed.

To format individual cells, you can turn to the Table toolbar and the Table Cell Properties InfoBox.

On the Table toolbar, use these buttons to change the formatting of an individual cell (or group of cells):

 Joins two or more adjacent selected cells into a single cell.

 Vertically aligns text in the cell to the top.

 Vertically centers text in the cell.

Vertically aligns text in the cell to the bottom.

 Selects the entire row so you can issue some formatting command that affects it.

 Selects the entire column.

 Selects the entire table.

The InfoBoxes for a table work the same as other InfoBoxes, except instead of one InfoBox, you have three. You can open the InfoBox you want by clicking on the appropriate SmartIcon:

 Opens the Text Properties InfoBox, for formatting text in the selected cell(s).

 Opens the Table Cell Properties InfoBox, for formatting the selected cell(s).

 Opens the Table Properties InfoBox, for formatting the table as a whole.

You can also open these InfoBoxes by right-clicking the cell and choosing them from the shortcut menu.

The InfoBoxes contain a dizzying array of formatting choices. I won't belabor the Text Properties InfoBox here because you've worked with it before, but I do want to point out some things in the other two.

In the Table Cell Properties InfoBox:

- On the Color, Pattern, and Line Style tab you can choose borders to surround the cell(s) on one or more sides, and you can choose a background color and pattern for the cell(s).

- On the Size and Margin tab, you can set the height and width for the cell(s). When you resize the height of a cell, its entire row changes. When you resize the width of a cell, its entire column changes.

- On the Number Format tab, you can specify formatting for any numbers that you place in the cells, just like in 1-2-3. For example, you could format numbers to appear as currency.

- On the Styles tab you can create and apply styles that format the cells.

In the Table Properties InfoBox:

- On the Color, Pattern, and Line Style tab you can place a border around the outside of the table as a whole.

- On the Size and Margin tab you can specify margins and padding for the table, just like you saw with a graphic earlier in this hour.

- On the Placement tab, you can use the Quick Alignment buttons to align the table in the document (for example, to center it or align it with the left or right margin).

- On the Misc. tab you can make the table protected so that no one can edit it accidentally.

Summary

In this hour, you learned about graphics and tables, two great ways to make a document look more polished and professional. You can now insert a graphic, move it around, resize it, and even delete it with confidence. You can also create tables of various sizes and shapes, resize their columns, add and remove rows and columns, and create formulas that calculate numbers in cells. That's quite a lot for one hour's labor!

In the next hour, we'll look at some more advanced layout features, such as running headers and multiple columns. We'll also take a peek at Word Pro's scripting language, LotusScript.

Q&A

Q I have some clip art I bought separately. Can I use it?

A Probably. Word Pro supports many graphic formats, including all of the most popular clip art formats. To see a list of the formats Word Pro supports, choose File, Import Picture and open the Files of Type drop-down list.

Q Can I place a graphic in a table?

A Sure. Click inside the cell you want to place the graphic in and issue the File, Import Picture command as usual. The graphic sizes itself to fit in the cell.

Q How do I add a caption to a picture?

A Right-click the picture and choose New Caption. In the Create Frame Caption dialog box, choose the wording and placement you want and click OK. The caption is placed as a "frame-within-a-frame."

Q **I want all my frames to have borders around them. How do I set that up as the default?**

A You need to edit the style for default graphic frames in the appropriate SmartMaster template. (You learned how to edit templates in Hour 8.) Set up a graphic frame the way you want them all to be and then open the Frame Properties and click on the Style tab. Click Redefine Style and click OK.

9

HOUR 10

Advanced Word Pro

This is the final hour we'll spend on Word Pro, so let's go out with a bang! In this hour, you'll learn how to create fancy multicolumn layouts, and how to create headers and footers that contain page numbers, document info, and more. We'll also take a look at automating your commonly performed tasks with LotusScript scripts (macros).

Highlights include:

- Laying out your text in columns
- Working with sections and divisions
- Creating headers and footers
- Recording your own scripts
- Assigning scripts to SmartIcon buttons

Creating Multiple Columns

Why do you suppose newspapers lay out their stories in several columns? The answer is readability. It's much easier for the eye to follow a narrow column of text than a wider one. You can create readability in your own documents by increasing the number of columns.

There are two kinds of columns—parallel and newspaper. Parallel column layouts are like tables, which you learned about in Hour 9. (There is a separate command for them, Create, Parallel Columns, which you might want to experiment with on your own.) The kind of columns we're talking about in this hour are *newspaper columns*, in which the text snakes from the bottom of one column to the top of the next.

Don't go overboard with column usage. Their appropriateness depends on the type of document you are creating. For a newsletter, three or four columns is perfectly acceptable, but for a business report, one column is the norm and two is the most you can get away with.

The most straightforward way to set up multiple columns is to apply the setting to the entire document. To do this, follow these steps:

1. Switch to Layout view so you can see the columns. Multiple columns do not show in Draft view.

2. Choose Page, Page Properties, opening the Page Properties InfoBox.

3. Click the Newspaper Columns tab to display the columns controls.

4. Set the Number of Newspaper Columns to 2 or more. The other controls in the box then become available (see Figure 10.1).

FIGURE 10.1.

Choose the number of columns here for your document.

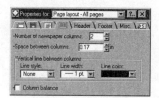

5. (Optional) Adjust the Space Between Columns setting if desired.

6. (Optional) If you want a vertical line between columns, choose a line style, width, and color.

7. (Optional) If you want the text in the columns to be split evenly between the two columns if there is not enough text to fill them both, click the Column Balance check box.

8. Close the InfoBox. Your document appears in multiple columns, as in Figure 10.2.

FIGURE 10.2.

This document uses two columns.

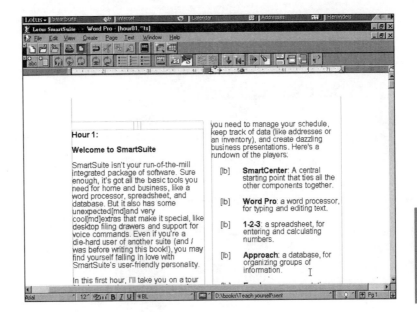

In some situations (actually in most!), you will not want the entire document to be multi-column. Instead, you might prefer a full-width heading, such as a newsletter masthead, followed by the multicolumn text. In order to have different column settings in the same document, you must create a new *section*. Then position the insertion point in the section you want to format and use the above steps to change the number of columns.

 A *section* is an area of a document that has its own page layout settings, such as margins, number of columns, running header and footer, and so on.

Working with Sections and Divisions

Word Pro really shines in the area of document management. For a large project, instead of creating many smaller documents, you can create one huge document and make it manageable by breaking it into sections and divisions.

Divisions and sections are both ways of carving up a document organizationally, but they have different purposes. A *section* is a divider placed primarily for formatting purposes, such as to have a different number of columns in part of a document. A *division* is a more major divider, placed so that you can apply a whole different SmartMaster to part of a document or insert a whole existing document.

Creating a Section

If you want to break up a document for formatting purposes, such as to have two different margin settings, a section is the way to go. The following procedure shows how.

To Do: Creating a Section

1. Switch to Layout view if needed. You cannot create a section from Draft view.

2. Choose Create, Section. The Create Section dialog box opens (see Figure 10.3).

3. (Optional) If you want to name the section, type a name in the Section Name text
    box. If you name a section, its name will appear on a tab for it if you set up Word
    Pro to display section and division tabs.

FIGURE 10.3.

*Create a new section
to apply different page
formatting within the
same document.*

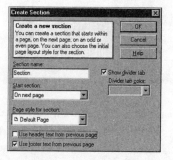

4. In the Start Section drop-down list, choose where the new section will start. The
    most common settings are On Next Page (which inserts both a section break and a
    page break) and Within Page (which creates only a section break, not a page
    break).

5. The other options in the Create Section dialog box are specialized, and you proba-
    bly will not need to use them. Click OK to go ahead and create your section break.

Now your document is divided into multiple sections, and you can set separate document
settings for each section. Click to move the insertion point into the section you want to
affect and then format normally. The formatting in the second section applies to the rest
of the document, from the break to the end. If you want only a middle part of the document formatted differently (for example, in multiple columns), you must create another
section break where you want the special formatting to stop.

Creating a Division

While sections simply separate different page formatting, divisions separate entire documents within documents. You can insert a new document in a section that has an entirely
different layout (and is based on a different SmartMaster). You can also insert preexisting

documents into a division, making your original document a sort of organizing container for multiple documents.

To Do: Creating a Division

1. Position the insertion point where you want the new division to start.

2. Choose Create, Division. The Create Division dialog box opens.

3. Do one of the following:

   - If you want to insert an existing document as a division, select the one you want from the Create a Division from an Existing Document tab, the same as you would open a document. Click OK.

   - If you want to insert a new division based on another SmartMaster, choose one from the Create a Division Using a SmartMaster tab. Click OK.

   - If you want to create a blank division, click the Create a Plain Division button.

4. Next, the Insert Division dialog box prompts you for the location of the division, as shown in Figure 10.4. Choose where the new division goes (either before or after the current one or at the insertion point).

5. If you are inserting an existing document, choose either Inserted Into Current Document or Linked to External File. The latter maintains a link with the original so the copy is updated when the original changes, while the former does not.

6. Click OK. The new division is created.

FIGURE 10.4.

Choose where the new division should appear.

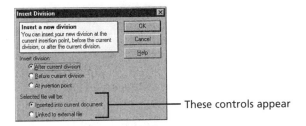

These controls appear

Working with Sections and Divisions

If you are going to work on a document that contains multiple sections and divisions, you owe it to yourself to turn on the display of divider tabs; choose View, Set View Preferences. In the View Preferences dialog box, mark the Show Divider Tabs check box and click OK. Divider tabs appear for both sections and divisions, as shown in Figure 10.5.

Sections in Division 1

Division 1   Division 2

FIGURE 10.5.

Divisions and sections appear as tabs across the top of the work area.

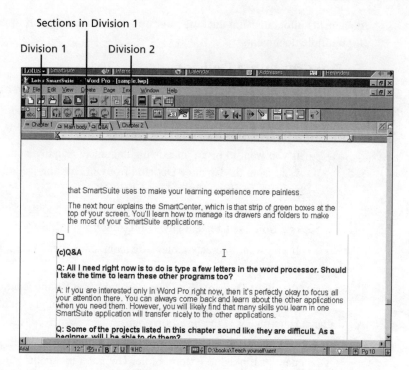

To rename a tab (as some of the ones in Figure 10.5 are), double-click on a tab and type a new name.

To jump quickly to a division or section, click on its tab. You can also right-click on a tab for a list of the actions you can take on a section or division. To delete a section, for example, choose Delete Section Mark. The text that was in that section will not be deleted, just the section designation - dfr.

Managing divisions is a complex topic that could fill an entire chapter by itself. For more information, see the Word Pro online documentation or experiment with divisions when you have some extra time. If you regularly create large, complex documents, you may find them helpful. Also, see *Using Lotus SmartSuite Millennium Edition*, published by Que.

Adding Headers and Footers

Headers and footers are repeated text that appears at the top or bottom of each page. They're commonly used in long documents (like this book!) to remind you of certain information, such as the name of the book or what page number you are on.

To work on a header or footer in Word Pro, simply display the document in Layout view and click above (for the header) or below (for the footer) the regular text. The insertion point moves into the header or footer block, and a special bar of tools appears at the top of the work area. Type whatever text you want repeated on each page. For example, in Figure 10.6, I've typed the name of the book.

FIGURE 10.6.

Type a header or footer into the header or footer block in Layout view.

Header box ────

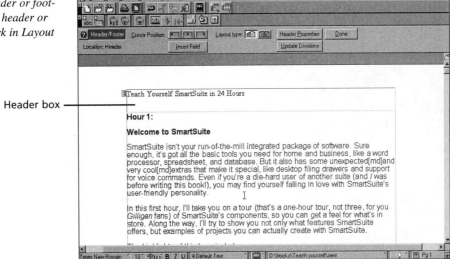

10

Aligning Text in a Header or Footer

It is customary on a header or footer to place text at any of three positions: at the left, right, or center. Word Pro offers three buttons on the Header/Footer bar to quickly move your cursor to one of those positions:

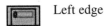 Left edge

 Center

 Right edge

You can also set and use tab stops in the header or footer block, just as you use them in the body of the document.

Adding Field Codes

Most people like to number their pages, especially when the page count exceeds two. That way, if you accidentally drop the hard copy pages, you can easily put them back in order. You can also refer to the document by page number, which makes it easier to have discussions about the document with others.

Page numbers are only one of many field codes you can place in a header or footer. These codes print different information depending on when, where, and what is printing. For example, you can insert codes that place the current date and time in the header or footer, so you will know which is the more recent printout.

To Do: Adding a Field Code

To Do

1. Click where you want the code to go.

2. Click the Insert Field button. A drop-down list appears.

3. Click on the code you want (for example, Page Number).

▲ The field code appears in the header or footer bar. It looks just like regular text, but don't let it fool you—it will print on every page exactly as needed. You can type regular text adjacent to a code to help identify it; for example, you can type "Page" before you insert a page number code.

Changing the Header/Footer Properties

The header and footer each have their own InfoBox, which you can access by clicking the Header Properties (or Footer Properties) button on the Header/Footer bar. Each has the following tabs:

- **Size and Margin**. Set the margins for the header or footer, along with the padding (the space between the header or footer and the body of the text).

- **Color, Pattern, and Line Style**. Place a border around one or more sides of the header or footer box and add a background pattern or color.

- **Watermark**. Apply a watermark to the header or footer box. (This creates a very strange look, but hey, someone might use it.)

- **Columns**. Create multiple columns in the header or footer box. (Another very strange look that doesn't have many practical applications.)

- **Misc**. Set tabs and alignment for the header or footer box.

- **Styles**. Apply styles to the text in the header or footer box, or create new styles especially for headers and footers.

Automating Tasks with Scripts

A full-service word processor would not be complete without its own scripting language, and Word Pro does not disappoint in this regard. Although few beginning users will take advantage of the full power of the LotusScript language, almost everyone can benefit from creating a few simple scripts to automate common tasks.

NEW TERM A *script* is a set of recorded program actions, also known as a *macro*. For example, if it takes five commands in Word Pro to format some text the way you want it, you could record that sequence of five commands in a script.

What might you want to write a script for? To get some ideas, just think of the multistep tasks that you perform frequently. For example, perhaps there is a standard closing paragraph that you add to the end of many different letters. You could automate the creation and formatting of that paragraph and signature block.

Script-writing does not involve any programming because Word Pro includes a script recorder. It's kind of like a cassette tape recorder. You turn it on, you perform the actions, and then you turn it off. Voilà, you've created a script. If you made any mistakes, you can easily edit them out of the final product.

10

Recording a Script

You can record any menu commands and keyboard typing in a script. The only thing you can't do in a script is select something with the mouse.

To Do: Recording a Script

1. Get ready to perform whatever actions you are going to record. That means preselecting the text to act on, positioning the insertion point, and so on.

2. Choose Edit, Script & Macros, Record Script. The Record Script dialog box appears.

3. If you want to record the script into the current document, choose Into This File and type a name for your script in the text box.

   If you want to record the script into a separate file, choose Into Another File and enter the name to create for that file.

> You can also make a script available to any file by attaching it to a SmartIcon, which you'll learn about later in this hour.

▼   4. Click OK. The dialog box goes away, and you are now recording. A red
       "Recording" message appears on the status bar as a reminder.

    5. Perform the actions you want to record. This can include typing, formatting, menu
       commands—whatever is needed. If you make a mistake, use Undo (Ctrl+Z) to cor-
       rect it and go on; you can edit the script later.

    6. Click the word "Recording" on the status bar to stop recording.

    7. If you are recording to a separate file, a message appears saying that the file does
       not yet exist. Click Yes to create it.

    8. Next, the Script Editor window opens, showing the actions you recorded (see
       Figure 10.7). Browse through the recorded commands and delete any lines that you
       know are mistakes.

FIGURE 10.7.

*Every action you per-
formed while recording
appears in the
LotusScript program-
ming language.*

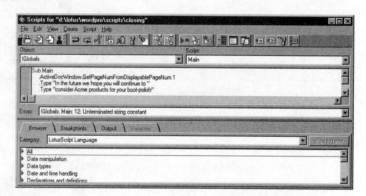

    9. If everything looks right, choose File, Save Scripts. If a message appears telling
       you that saving scripts will save the document you are working in, click OK.

▲ 10. Close the Script Editor window.

If a message appears that your script has an error, click OK. Look through the script for
lines that appear in red. If you can figure out what is wrong with the line—great! Go
ahead and correct it. If not, you might just try rerecording and saving with the same
name to replace the faulty script.

Editing a Script

In Figure 10.7, the Script Editor window, you got a taste of what editing a script is like.
You open the script in the Script Editor and add/make changes to various lines.

Obviously, unless you are a programmer, it is difficult to learn the LotusScript programming language on-the-fly and write coherent scripts. That's why I showed you how to
use the recorder in the preceding section. It's much better for beginners to record scripts
and then perform minor editing with the Script Editor.

To open a script for editing, choose Edit, Script & Macros, Show Script Editor. Open the script you want to edit if it does not already appear there. To choose from among the various scripts in the file, choose from the Scripts drop-down list. To open a different file, use File, Import Script.

> Don't spend too much time trying to edit a script that contains errors. It is often faster and easier to rerecord the script from scratch.

Running a Script

Running a script, of course, is the whole point of creating one.

To Do: Running a Script

1. Choose Edit, Script & Macros, Run. The Run Script dialog box appears (see Figure 10.8).

2. If the script is saved in the current file, choose it from the Run Script from Current File drop-down list. Or, if the script is in another file, type that filename or click Browse and locate it.

3. Click OK. The script runs.

Assigning a Script to a SmartIcon

It's not terribly convenient to run a script from the Edit menu, as you just saw. That's why many people prefer to assign their scripts to SmartIcons on the toolbar, for easier access to them.

To Do: Assigning a Script to a SmartIcon

1. Open the script in the Script Editor if you have not done so already. (Use Edit, Scripts & Macros, Show Script Editor to open the editor.)

2. Save the script as a Script Source. To do this, in the Script Editor, choose File, Export Script. Choose Script Source (*.lss) as the file type and give the script as a unique name. Save the file in the Scripts folder.

> For the script to work correctly as a SmartIcon, you it must begin with the words "Sub Main." If it begins with something else, like "Sub {name of macro}," change it to Sub Main before you export it in step 1. If you need it to retain its original functionality in the file where you originally created it, don't save your changes when exiting the Script Editor after exporting.

▼   3. Close the Script Editor window. Back in Word Pro, choose File, User Setup, SmartIcons Setup. The SmartIcons Setup dialog box opens.

4. Scroll to the bottom of the list of available icons to the ones that have no text next to them. There are a variety to choose from; pick the one that reminds you of your script. I like to use the one that looks like a cassette tape, for example, to remind me that it's a recording.

5. Click the Edit Icon button. The Edit SmartIcons box appears. See Figure 10.8.

FIGURE 10.8.

You can edit the icon picture here and (more importantly) assign a script to it.

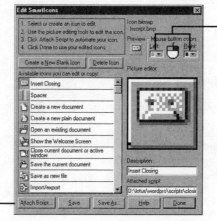

Use these buttons to change the colors for editing the icon

Click here to assign a script

6. (Optional) If you want to change the icon image, click on the image to "draw" there. Change the drawing color from the Left and Right drop-down lists.

7. Click the Attach Script button.

8. In the dialog box that appears, locate the exported script file from Step 1 and double-click it to select it.

9. (Optional) Type a description of the macro in the Description text box. This is what shows up when the SmartIcon bubble help pops up.

10. Click Done. If you see a message that the icon has been modified, click Yes to save your changes and go on.

11. Relocate the icon on the list of available icons and drag it to the toolbar at the top of the dialog box. This places the icon on your default Word Pro toolbar.

12. Click OK.

▲   13. Start a new document and click your newly created SmartIcon to test its operation.

Summary

In this hour, you topped off your Word Pro course of study by learning how to create multiple columns in your documents. You also learned about section and division breaks, headers and footers, and how to create time-saving scripts and attach them to SmartIcons for easy access.

On to the next hour. In the words of the great Monty Python, "Now for something completely different." Lotus 1-2-3. Well, actually, 1-2-3 is not *completely* different from Word Pro; you'll find that they have a lot in common, and that the skills you have gained in the past few lessons will give you a real head start.

Q&A

10

Q How do I insert a page break that starts text flowing into the next column, rather than onto the next page?

A Choose Text, Insert Other, Column Break.

Q Can I have different headers and footers for different divisions and sections?

A All sections in the document use the same header and footer, but divisions have separate ones. To have different headers or footers in parts of a document, create a division.

Q Where can I go to learn more about the LotusScript script-writing language?

A There are several excellent references right at your fingertips. In Windows, choose Start, Programs, Lotus, LotusDoc Online. Several manuals are there, including *Getting the Most Out of LotusScript* and *LotusScript Language Reference*. You can also use the online Help in the Script Editor window.

Q How do I remove a SmartIcon for a script that I've added to the toolbar?

A Choose File, User Setup, SmartIcon Setup. Make sure the SmartIcon palette that contains the script's SmartIcon is in the preview bar and then drag the icon off that bar.

PART III
1-2-3

Hour

HOUR 11

1-2-3 Basics

Now that you've become a Word Pro whiz, you're ready to tackle the second major program in the SmartSuite package: 1-2-3. Don't worry if you've never used a spreadsheet before; we'll ease into some spreadsheet basics in this hour, and you'll learn to do some basic data entry.

Highlights of this hour include:

- Understanding how 1-2-3 workbooks operate
- Moving around on a spreadsheet
- Typing and editing in cells
- Selecting ranges
- Data entry shortcuts

Getting Started with 1-2-3

Hours 3 and 4 led you through all the basics of working with a SmartSuite application, and 1-2-3 operates just the way you learned. You can start it from the Start menu or from the SmartSuite drawer in the SmartCenter.

When you start 1-2-3, the Welcome To box lets you choose between opening an existing workbook and creating a new one. If you plan to follow along with the examples and steps in this hour and the upcoming ones, click the Create a Blank Workbook button to start a new, blank sheet on which to practice.

Introduction to Workbooks

NEW TERM   A *spreadsheet* is a two-dimensional grid of rows and columns into which you enter data and formulas. A *workbook* is a 1-2-3 file that contains one or more spreadsheets.

When you start a new, blank workbook, it contains only one spreadsheet. You can tell because there is only one spreadsheet tab (A) at the top. See Figure 11.1. You can add more sheets to your workbook as needed. (You'll learn to do that later in this hour.) For now, let's just look at the basic, two-dimensional spreadsheet.

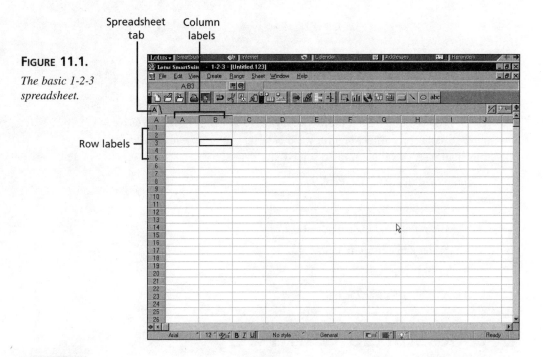

FIGURE 11.1.

The basic 1-2-3 spreadsheet.

NEW TERM   *Cells* are the individual boxes on a sheet into which you enter your text and data.

A good way to envision cells is as a stack of boxes, like a post office box system. Each cell is a separate entity, with its own sides, name, and format settings. Cells take their names from the row number and column letter in which they reside. This is called a *cell address*. For example, in Figure 11.1, the top row contains cells A1, B1, C1, and D1, from left to right. The second row contains cells A2, B2, C2, and D2.

The row and column designations are strictly determined by their position. For example, if you moved column A to the right of column D, it would no longer be column A; it would be the new column D, and all the columns to the left of it would shift up one letter (B would become A, C would become B, and so on.) The row numbering and column lettering, therefore, serves no purpose except to help you identify where you are on a spreadsheet at any given time.

Moving Around in a Spreadsheet

By "moving around" on a sheet, what we really mean is moving the *cell cursor*. The cell cursor is the dark outline that rests on the *active cell* (see Figure 11.2). For example, when you first open a new workbook, the top left cell is active (A1). It's important to know which cell is active because the characters you type and the formatting commands you issue apply to whatever cell is active.

FIGURE 11.2.

The active cell is the one with the cell cursor's black border around it at the moment.

The active cell's row and column labels appear pressed in

Cell cursor

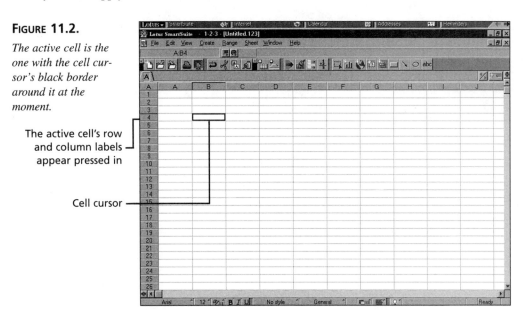

11

The simplest way to select a cell (making it active) is to click on it with the mouse. You can also move the cell cursor to a cell by pressing one of the keyboard arrow keys. This moves the cell cursor one cell in the direction of the arrow you pressed.

Table 11.1 shows some of the many ways to move the cell cursor around on a spreadsheet.

In Table 11.1, you may see some columns identified by multiple letters, such as IV. When 1-2-3 runs out of single letters, it starts with AA, then AB, and so on, until it gets to AZ. Then it starts with BA, BB, and so on. The last column in a 1-2-3 sheet is IV.

TABLE 11.1. CELL CURSOR MOVEMENT

Key	Moves...
Arrow keys	One cell in the specified direction.
Ctrl+ right or left arrow keys	One screenful in the specified direction.
Ctrl+Home	To cell A1 on the first sheet of the workbook.
Enter	Down one row, if you have it set up to do so under File, User Preferences, 1-2-3 Preferences, Classic. Otherwise it just stays on the current cell.
Home	To cell A1.
Page Up	Up one screenful.
Page Down	Down one screenful.
Shift+Enter	Up one row, if you have it set up to do so under File, User Preferences, 1-2-3 Preferences, Classic. Otherwise it just stays on the current cell.
Tab	One cell or one screenful to the right, depending on your settings under File, User Preferences, 1-2-3 Preferences, Classic.
Shift+Tab	One cell to the left.
End, then Home	To the lower-right corner of the active area (the area containing data).
End, then an arrow key	To the next cell in the specified direction that contains data and is next to a blank cell.

If your cell cursor does not move down one cell when you press Enter, your copy of 1-2-3 may be set up to use Classic Keys. To change the behavior of the Enter key, choose File, User Setup, 1-2-3 Preferences. Click the Classic Keys tab and choose "Tab moves right one cell; ENTER confirms and moves down."

If you can't see the cell onscreen that you want to make active, you can bring it into view with the scroll bars or with some of the methods in Table 11.1.

> If you use the scroll bars to locate a cell, don't forget to click on it to make it active. Simply bringing a cell into view with the scroll bars does not make it active. Many people have made the mistake of scrolling to a particular cell and immediately typing, thinking they were typing into the visible cell. Actually they were typing into the previously selected active cell.

Typing in a Cell

There are three things you can enter into a cell:

- Text
- Numbers (to be calculated)
- Formulas (to calculate numbers)

We'll look at formulas in the next hour; for now, let's focus on text and numbers.

To enter data into a cell, move the cell cursor to the cell and type. Press Enter or make another cell active when you're finished. When you press Enter, the cell cursor moves down to the next cell in that column, and the data you entered aligns itself according to these rules:

- If 1-2-3 considers what you entered to be a number, it aligns it to the right edge of the cell. Numbers can include digits, commas, decimal points, dollar signs, and percentage signs.
- If 1-2-3 considers what you entered to be text, it aligns it to the left edge of the cell. If a cell contains even one letter, or a non-math symbol (like a colon), the entire cell is considered text.

Figure 11.3 shows text and numbers aligned in cells.

> You can force 1-2-3 to consider a particular number text by entering an apostrophe in front of it ('). This is useful for numbers that are never used for calculations, such as ZIP codes. If you don't want to give up the number's calculating capability but you still want it to align differently, explore 1-2-3's Alignment formatting, discussed in Hour 13.

11

FIGURE 11.3.

Text aligns to the left; numbers align to the right.

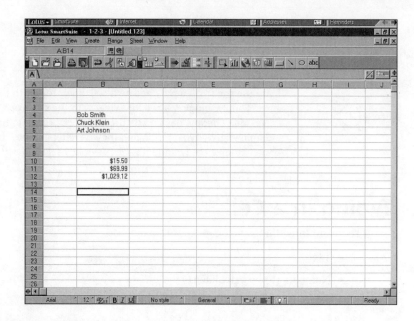

Selecting Ranges

When you move the cell cursor around, you are selecting which cell will be active. Anything that you do—typing, formatting, and so on—affects the active cell.

Sometimes, you might want to affect more than one cell at a time. For example, perhaps you want to format an entire row to show dollar signs next to the numbers. In cases like that, you select a *range* of cells. A single cell is still active, but other cells are included in a grouping with it too, so that commands you issue to affect the active cell also affect the other selected cells.

When referring to a range, it is customary to refer to it in this way: the top-left cell address, followed by two periods, and then the bottom-right cell address. For example, the range of B2, B3, C2, and C3 would be "B2..C3."

Remember that selecting is always a prelude to some other action, such as formatting, moving, or copying. When you select a range of cells, you're saying to 1-2-3, "Please apply the command I'm about to issue to this group of cells."

Selecting Rows and Columns

The most common range that most people select is an entire row or column. To do so, just click on the column letter or row number. The entire row or column is highlighted, as shown in Figure 11.4. The first visible cell in that row or column becomes the active cell, and it remains white to distinguish it from the others.

FIGURE 11.4.

Here, a single column is selected.

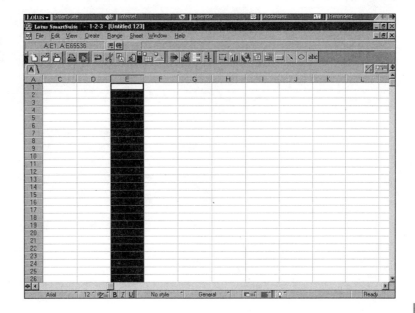

This is a little tricky. The active cell in a selected row onscreen is the leftmost visible cell—that is, visible onscreen when you select the row. For example, if you had scrolled to display so that the leftmost visible column was C and then clicked on the 5 to select row 5, the active cell would be C5.

If you were to type some characters while a row was selected, the text would be placed in the active cell, and the rest of the selected cells would be ignored. However, if you were to issue a command, such as a formatting directive, it would affect all cells in the entire row or column. (There are ways to enter data into many cells at once; see "Data Entry Shortcuts" later in this chapter.)

Selecting Ranges of Cells

Selecting a range of cells is a bit more involved than clicking on a row or column indicator. You must drag your mouse across the cells you want to select. For example, to select the range of cells B2..F14 (that is, the cells in a block with B2 in the upper-left corner and F14 in the lower right), follow these steps:

1. Position your mouse pointer over B2.

2. Hold down the left mouse button.

3. Drag the pointer to F14.

4. Release the mouse button. That range of cells is selected (highlighted). See Figure
    11.5.

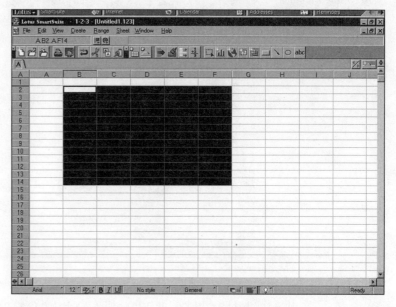

Note that in the above steps you started with B2, so it remains the active cell. If you had
started with F14 and dragged up to B2, F14 would be the active cell.

> You can also select using the keyboard. Click the first cell you want and then
> hold down the Shift key and press the arrow keys to extend the selection. To
> select a large range where some of the cells are not in view, click on the first
> cell of the range, scroll to the last one (opposite corner), and press and hold
> down the Shift key while you click on it.

Other Range Selections

Besides rows, columns, and single ranges, you may occasionally need some of these
selection techniques:

*   To select a noncontiguous range (that is, different cells or groups of cells spread
    out over the worksheet), select the first range and hold down the Ctrl key while
    you select additional cells or ranges with the mouse.

*   To select the same range on more than one sheet in your workbook, make the
    selection on one sheet, and then Shift+click on the tab of the other sheet(s), one-
    by-one, to select them.

- To select an entire spreadsheet, click the Sheet button, which is the button at the intersection of the numbers and the column letters. It contains a letter that corresponds to the sheet (for example, sheet A's button reads "A").

Editing a Cell Entry

How you edit a cell's content depends on what kind of editing you want to do. The simplest kind of editing is to replace what's already there. To do this, move the cell cursor to that cell and type the new text. It replaces what's there.

Changing the existing text without completely retyping it is easy.

To Do: Editing Contents of a Cell

1. Move the cell cursor to the cell. Its content appears in the formula bar.
2. Click in the formula bar to move the insertion point there. See Figure 11.6.
3. Use the arrow keys to move the insertion point or click where you want it. Edit normally, as you would in your word processor.
4. Press Enter to finish.

FIGURE 11.6.

Edit the cell's content in the formula bar.

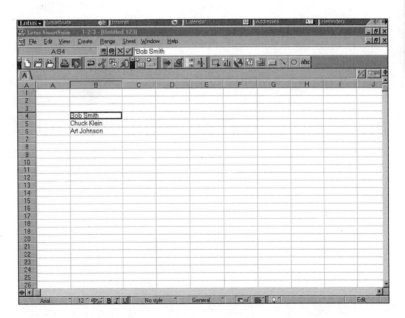

11

The formula bar gets its name from the fact that if you enter a formula in a cell, that formula appears there. The cell itself displays the result of the formula. When entering text or numbers in a cell, the formula bar and the cell itself both display the same thing. You'll learn about formulas in Hour 12.

You aren't forced to use the formula bar for editing; another way to edit cell content is to double-click on the cell. The insertion point moves directly into the cell itself, and you can edit from there, bypassing the formula bar.

Clearing a Cell

Clearing a cell involves removing one or more of the following from the cell: its content (text, numbers, or formula), its text formatting, its border formatting, its comments, and its scripts.

If you clear only the cell's content, any formatting you have applied to that cell remains and attaches itself to whatever you put in that cell later. For example, if you make the text bold and then clear the content, any new text you put there will be bold. To clear the content, select the cell and press Delete.

To clear some of the other things from the cell, choose Edit, Clear. A Clear dialog box appears, with checkboxes for each of the elements you can clear from a cell. Click checkboxes to mark the ones you want to clear from it and click OK.

Inserting and Deleting Rows and Columns

Even if you plan your worksheet carefully, you still will need to make changes. Perhaps you need to add an extra row or two at the top or get rid of a column that you ended up not using.

To insert a row or column, select the row or column before which you want the new one inserted. If you want to insert multiple rows or columns at once, select an equal number to begin with. For example, to insert three columns to the left of the current column B, select columns B, C, and D. Then choose Range, Insert Columns (or Insert Rows, as the case may be), or just press Ctrl++ (that's Ctrl plus a plus sign).

To delete rows or columns, select the ones to be removed and choose Range, Delete Columns (or Delete Rows), press Ctrl+– (that's Ctrl plus a minus sign).

Adding More Sheets to Your Workbook

As you learned at the beginning of this hour, each new workbook starts out with a single sheet, called A. You can add more sheets to meet the needs of any size project.

To Do: Adding Sheets to a Workbook

1. Right-click the existing worksheet tab and choose Create Sheet.

2. In the Create Sheet dialog box, enter the number of sheets to create. The default is 1.

3. Choose an option button to indicate whether the new sheets will come before or after the current one.

4. Click OK.

Then, to use a different sheet, click the tab for the sheet you want to bring to the top. It works just like the tabs in dialog boxes that you worked with in the Word Pro hours.

If you have several sheets in a workbook, you may find it difficult to remember which is which by letter name alone. To rename a sheet to something more meaningful (such as Sales or Expenses), double-click the tab. A text box appears where you can type a new name. Press Enter when finished. A sheet name can be up to 15 characters.

Data Entry Shortcuts

1-2-3 offers a couple of really nice time-savers for entering repetitive data. Fill-by-example looks at the data you have entered in a few cells and determines how you want the other cells to be filled. There is also a Fill dialog box you can work with where you can specify explicitly what you want in your fill area.

Fill-By-Example: Repeated Data

The easiest fill is to simply repeat the same cell entry in multiple cells.

To Do: Repeating Cell Entry

1. Type the entry in one cell.

2. Click on that cell to highlight it.

3. Position the mouse pointer at the edge of the cell so that the Fill-By-Example arrows appear on your mouse pointer. See Figure 11.7.

4. Drag to select a range in which to fill the entry. When you release the mouse button, the entire range is filled with that entry.

Figure 11.7.

The Fill-By-Example arrows indicate that the area you select by dragging will be filled.

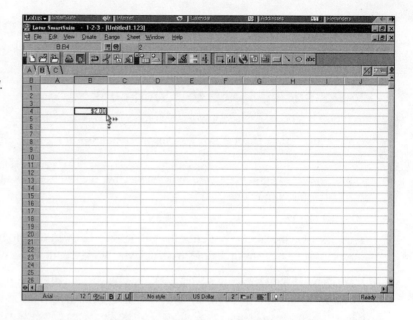

> Another way to fill a range with the same data is to copy and paste. Select the cell containing the data and press Ctrl+C to copy. Select the range to fill and press Ctrl+V to paste.

Fill-By-Example: Data Series

You can also use Fill-By-Example to fill a series, such as A, B, C or January, February, March. All you need to do is give 1-2-3 the first couple of entries, and it takes over from there.

To Do: Filling by Example

1. Type the first entry in a cell.

2. Select the cell.

3. Position the mouse pointer at the edge of the cell so you see the Fill-By-Example arrows on the mouse pointer as in Figure 11.7.

4. Drag to select the area you want filled. When you release the mouse button, the area is filled.

Using the Fill Dialog Box

If you can't get 1-2-3 to properly fill the series you want with Fill By Example, try the Fill dialog box. It enables you to specify exactly the fill you want. To open it, choose Range, Fill (see Figure 11.8) .

FIGURE 11.8.

Use the Fill dialog box to set up specific fills that do not have to be based on an example.

In the Fill Using list, choose Numbers, Dates, or Times. The controls below that list change depending on your selection. Figure 11.8 shows it for Numbers.

Next, enter your criteria for the fill in the blanks provided. For example, in Figure 11.8, it is going to start at $2.00 and enter a $1 increase in each of the cells, stopping when it gets to $32,767 or when it runs out of cells in the range, whichever comes first.

Finally, choose the range. You can either enter the range's name in the Range box, or you can click the Cell Selector button next to it to minimize the dialog box while you select the range right on the worksheet. (After you select the range, the dialog box reappears.)

Click OK when finished, and 1-2-3 fills the range as requested.

Summary

This hour provided a hands-on introduction to 1-2-3. You now know how to interpret cell addresses, and how to enter data into cells and edit it. You can select cells, clear their content, and enter repeated or series data without typing it all in manually. Now you're ready to learn how to enter powerful formulas that perform calculations on your 1-2-3 spreadsheet data. Such calculations are the heart and the primary purpose of 1-2-3.

Q&A

Q **I'm trying to issue a command, but 1-2-3 appears frozen. The mouse moves, but no menus will open. What's wrong?**

A You probably forgot to press Enter after typing some text or numbers into a cell. Until you press Enter (or move to a different cell), 1-2-3 won't do anything else.

Q When are we going to work with the SmartMasters for 1-2-3?

A I'm going to leave these for you to explore on your own. You know all about SmartMasters from your Word Pro experience, and you know how powerful and handy they can be. But most of the skills you need to learn in 1-2-3 are best learned on a plain, blank workbook, so you aren't distracted by the SmartMasters' special features.

Q How do I delete a cell completely, not just erase its contents?

A To remove a cell so that all the other cells in that row or column move over to fill its spot, use the Range, Delete command. A dialog box appears asking whether you want to shift the existing cells up or over. Make your selection and click OK.

Q How can I rearrange the sheets in my workbook?

A You can drag-and-drop a sheet by dragging its tab. You can also do it from the menus: choose Sheet, Move or Copy Sheet. In the dialog box, select the sheet you want to move. Click Before or After to indicate positioning, and then select where you want to move it. Click OK.

Q I entered some text in a cell and then in the next cell to the right, and now the first cell's content appears cut off.

A Your text is still there. To display it, you just need to widen the column. See Hour 13 for details.

Hour 12

Calculating with 1-2-3

The main purpose of 1-2-3 is to perform calculations on numbers. This is the feature that it really excels in. (No pun intended, for you Microsoft converts.) And it doesn't take a CPA to do it, either. In this hour, you'll learn how to create your own formulas, how to incorporate 1-2-3's built-in functions into your calculations, and how to control what happens when you move and copy formulas from cell to cell.

Highlights of this hour include:

- Creating a simple formula
- Understanding operators and precedence
- Adding up columns and rows of numbers
- Using 1-2-3 functions
- Moving and copying formulas
- Absolute versus relative cell references

What Is a Formula?

A formula is an expression that calculates a value. The following are formulas you may already be familiar with:

2+2

6*7

500–45

In 1-2-3, all formulas begin with a plus sign, so the above formulas would look like this in 1-2-3:

+2+2

+6*7

+500–45

> If you are using only numbers in your formulas, like 2+2, you can omit the leading plus sign and 1-2-3 will assume it. However, when you are writing formulas that include cell references, like +A1+A2, the leading plus sign is necessary. Therefore, it's a good habit to place the plus sign at the beginning no matter what.

Don't confuse the plus sign that starts a formula with the math operators in the formula itself; the plus sign at the beginning does not mean to add anything, it merely means "here comes a formula." If you are accustomed to working with Excel, you may occasionally slip and begin a formula with an equals sign, which is what Microsoft Excel uses. 1-2-3 accepts this but converts it to a plus sign when you press Enter.

These formulas are simple; they use basic math operators and regular, whole numbers. If you were to put one of these formulas into a cell, the formula bar would show the formula you entered, and the cell itself would show the result.

1-2-3 uses these basic math operators:

Operator	Meaning
+	Addition
–	Subtraction
/	Division

Operator	Meaning
*	Multiplication
^	Exponentiation

All of the preceding should seem familiar, except perhaps exponentiation. That's when you raise the value to the nth power. For example, 2^3 is 2 to the 3rd power, or 2×2×2, or 8.

Besides doing simple math, you can also refer to the contents of other cells in a formula. For example, say that you have entered 15 in cell A1 and 20 in cell A2. In cell A3, you could enter:

+A1+A2

Cell A3 would then display 35, the answer to the formula. The formula itself continues to appear in the formula bar (see Figure 12.1). If you changed the number in A1 to 40, cell A3 would change to display 60. Formulas automatically update to any changes to the cells that make up the formula.

FIGURE 12.1.

The formula in cell A3 sums A1 and A2.

Cell shows formula result

Formula bar shows formula

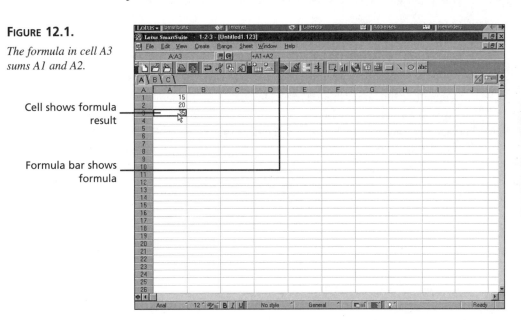

12

Order of Operations

When you use more than one math operator in a formula, 1-2-3 handles them in a particular order—exponentiation first, then multiplication and division, and finally addition and subtraction. These rules are the same that mathematicians follow, so if you have had any math classes, you are probably already familiar with this.

For example, suppose you have the following formula:

+12+5*6-2^3

Here's how 1-2-3 would work it out.

First, it would discard the leading + sign. Next, it would calculate the exponentiation—
2^3 is 8. So now we have 12+5*6-8.

Next, the multiplication: 5 times 6 is 30. So now we have 12+30-8. Because all remaining operators are of the same precedence, you can do them in any order. (Left to right is fine.) So 12+30 is 42, minus 8 is 34.

If you want the order of precedence to occur differently than the default, use parentheses to show which operations should be done first. For example, to do the addition and then the multiplication in the following formula…

+A1+6*C4

…you would write it with parentheses around the addition formula, like this:

+(A1+6)*C4

Entering a Formula

You can type formulas into cells the same way you type regular text and numbers. Just remember one important thing: type a plus sign first. Remember in Hour 11, I told you that if your entry had even one letter in it, 1-2-3 would consider it text rather than a number, and not calculate it? Well, cell references such as A1 have letters in them. The plus sign before the formula containing a cell reference is necessary to tell 1-2-3 that it's not intended to be text, even though it has a letter in it.

Another way to enter a formula in a cell is with a mixture of typing and mouse clicking. For example, if you wanted to create a formula that referred to a certain cell, you could start out typing the plus sign and then click on that cell to place its address in the formula you're building. For example, suppose you want to add the contents of cells C3 and C4 and put the result in C4. You would do the following:

1. Click C5 and type a plus sign.
2. Click C3.
3. Type another plus sign.
4. Click C4.
5. Press Enter.

If you begin entering a formula and change your mind, you can press Esc to cancel the entry any time before you press Enter.

Quick Adding with the SUM SmartIcon

One of the most common uses for a formula is to sum a row or column of numbers. For example, in Figure 12.2, I have the gross sales for several salespeople. I would like to total up the sales at the bottom of the list.

One way to total the numbers would be to enter the following formula in cell C11:

+C3+C4+C5+C6+C7+C8+C9

That works just fine, but it's rather tedious to type. A better way is to use the Sum SmartIcon. This SmartIcon inserts the Sum function, one of 1-2-3's built-in functions, which we'll talk about later in this hour. Because the Sum function is the most common one, 1-2-3 has given it its own SmartIcon on the toolbar.

FIGURE 12.2.

To sum all the sales figures for a grand total, enter a Sum function in cell C11.

Sum button

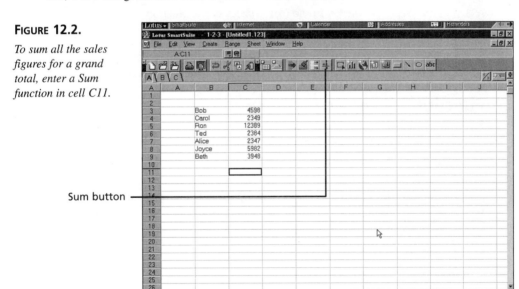

12

Here's how it works:

1. Click in the cell into which you want the result to go. For example, in Figure 12.2, I clicked in cell C11.

2. Click the Sum button on the toolbar. 1-2-3 enters the needed formula in the cell. For Figure 12.2 it would be @SUM(C3..C10).

If the range that 1-2-3 selected is incorrect, edit the formula as you would edit any other cell entry. This formula works vertically, as you just saw, and also horizontally, to sum the content of a row.

Using Functions

You just got a look at a function—@SUM. All functions have an @ (at) sign in front of their names to indicate that they are not regular text. The @SUM function is simple, but it has all the basic components of a function that you should know:

- It starts with an @ sign.
- It contains the function name in all-caps. You do not have to type the name in all-caps, but 1-2-3 makes it appear that way in the cell.
- It is followed by parentheses containing arguments.

New Term   *Arguments* provide information about how a function should be performed. 1-2-3 is rather strict about the arguments to be used. You must type all arguments correctly, in the order specified, with no extra spaces or punctuation.

One of the most common arguments is to tell which range of cells you want the function to act upon. You saw this with the @SUM function earlier. 1-2-3 guessed which cells should be acted upon, so you didn't have to make this determination yourself.

Function Examples

Here are a few examples of the many functions that 1-2-3 provides.

Average

The @AVG function averages a group of numbers. The arguments are the ranges of cells you want to average. For example, to average the numbers in cells B4..B12, you would type @AVG(B4..B12). That's just one argument, even though there are nine cells referenced in the range. You could average two or more ranges at once by typing something like @AVG(A1..A5,B2..B4).

Count

The @COUNT function counts the number of nonblank cells in the specified range. For example, suppose you have a worksheet with names listed in cells A1 through A250. You wonder how many names there are because there are many blank rows interspersed with the nonblank ones. To count the names, you could enter @COUNT(A1..A250).

Maximum

The @MAX function finds the highest value from a list. For example, suppose that you wanted to know at a glance which salesperson had the highest sales so you could award your monthly "Salesperson of the Month" plaque. You could use the @MAX function to find out. Specify the entire range of data in the argument, like this—@MAX(A1..A25). A @MIN function does the same thing for vdttm640027633 minimum value.

Entering a Function

Now that you've seen a few things that functions can do, you are probably eager to get started entering one.

Let's try an @AVG function, so you can average a column of numbers. Go ahead and enter some numbers for practice.

To Do: Entering a Function

1. (Optional) Type the label **Average** in a cell beside the one where you're planning to place the function. It's always a good idea to provide labels for each function and each number you enter.

2. Click in the cell where you want to place the function.

3. Click the Function Selector button on the formula bar. A menu of common functions appears (see Figure 12.3).

Function Selector

FIGURE 12.3.

Click the Function Selector and choose the function you want.

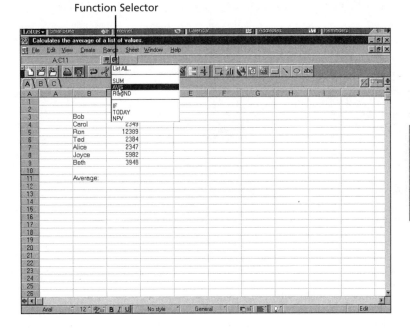

4. Because AVG is on this list, go ahead and click it. If you want some other function that does not appear, click List All and select it from the full list of functions and their descriptions.

> If there is a function you use a lot that does not appear on the menu in Figure 12.3, choose List All and click the Menu button. Click the function you want to add to the menu and then click the >> button to move it to the menu.

5. Now the function appears in the cell, with (list) in place of the arguments. Drag across the cells you want to average to place their names in the parentheses.

6. Press Enter to complete the function.

If you do not know which arguments a function takes, choose List All in step 4, and choose the function you're interested in from the list. When you select a function, a description of its purpose and arguments appears.

Moving and Copying Formulas

To move or copy a formula, you use the same procedure as you do when moving and copying text. You can drag-and-drop or cut-and-paste. It's your choice.

> The following explains the physical mechanics of moving and copying formulas and functions, but to understand exactly what gets moved or copied, you need to read the discussion of "Understanding Absolute Versus Relative References" later in this chapter.

To Do: Using Drag and Drop to Move or Copy Formulas

1. Select the cell containing the formula or function that you want to move or copy.

2. If you are copying, hold down the Ctrl key.

3. Position the mouse pointer at the top edge of the selected cell so that the mouse pointer turns into a hand. If you are copying, there is a plus sign beneath the hand.

4. Drag the cell to a new position on the sheet. An outline shows where it is going (see Figure 12.4.). When you release the mouse button, the contents are "dropped" into the new cell.

FIGURE 12.4.

Drop the outline where you want the formula or function you are moving or copying to appear.

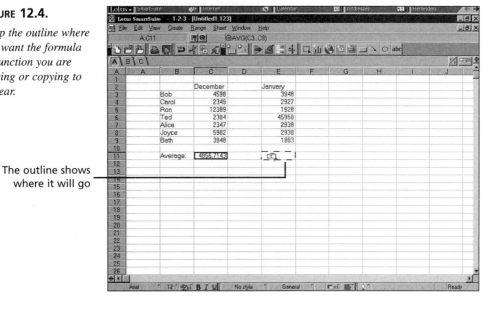

The outline shows where it will go

When you *copy* a formula or function, the copy refers to different cells than the original. For example, if you have a formula in cell C12 that reads @AVG(C3..C9), when you copy that formula to cell E12, it will change to @AVG(E3..E9). This is because of relative references, explained in the following section. In contrast, when you *move* a formula, it does not change the cells to which the formula refers. When you move a formula by dragging and dropping, the cell references do not change.

12

Remember earlier when you used Fill-By-Example to copy? You can do it with formulas too. Just drag the fill handle on the formula, and it copies it to the cells you drag across.

Another way to move and copy formulas is with the Cut, Copy, and Paste commands. Although it might seem that you would never bother with this method because drag-and-drop is so easy, don't discount it outright. I'm an experienced user, and I rarely use any method other than the Cut (Ctrl+X), Copy (Ctrl+C), and Paste (Ctrl+V) shortcut keys. Nothing else is quite as quick.

When using Copy and Paste, you can paste the copy into multiple cells. For example, to copy the formula in cell A3 to cells B3 through F3, you would do this:

1. Select cell A3 and press Ctrl+C.
2. Select cells B3 through F3 and press Ctrl+V.

Understanding Absolute Versus Relative References

Now you know the mechanics of moving and copying formulas, but do you really understand what you're doing? Probably not. 1-2-3's system of relative and absolute references can tie you in knots the first time you encounter it.

Here it is in a nutshell. When you copy a formula, say from A3 to B3, 1-2-3 is smart enough to know that you don't want an exact copy of it. If the formula in A3 were +A1+A2, chances are good that you don't want that same formula in B3. Instead, you probably want to add +B1+B2. This capability to change the formula to match the location where you copy it is called *relative referencing*. The references to the cells in the formula are *relative* to the position of the formula itself.

On the other hand, when you move a formula, say that same one (+A1+A2), 1-2-3 guesses that you probably don't want to change the formula so it doesn't change the content when you move it. +A1+A2 is still the same, no matter where you move it. This is a type of absolute referencing because the values (A1 and A2) remain constant. However, that formula is not permanently absolute. If you turned around and copied it somewhere else, the copy would be relative, like any other copy.

You can force a formula's references to be permanently absolute by placing dollar signs in front of each letter and each number that you want to stay the same when copied. For example, suppose you want the entire formula to be the same no matter where you copy it. You would insert dollar signs like this:

+$A$1+$A$2

If you want only the column letters to stay fixed but not the row numbers, omit the dollar signs from in front of the row numbers, like this:

+$A1+$A2

If you wanted only one of the cell references to remain fixed, you would use dollar signs only for that cell reference:

+$A$1+A2

The dollar signs have nothing to do with currency in a formula; they are for determining absolute references only. If you want to format the result of a formula with a currency format, you would apply that formatting to the cell in which you placed the formula.

Summary

In this chapter, you learned how to create your own calculations by entering formulas and functions. You learned how to build a formula, taking operator precedence into account, and how to select and apply a function, complete with arguments. You also learned about absolute and relative cell referencing, and how to make relative addresses absolute.

In the next hour, you'll learn how to format a 1-2-3 worksheet to make it more attractive so that your valuable calculations will be more eagerly received by your audience.

Q&A

Q I entered a formula adding up cells A1 and A2, but it doesn't calculate. The formula appears in the cell as if it were regular text.

A You probably forgot the plus sign (+) at the beginning. Edit the cell content to add that, and the formula should work just fine.

Q My formula doesn't work right, and there is a pair of little red circular arrows on the status bar. What's that?

A Those errors mean that you have a circular reference. The formula probably refers to itself, so its result can't be calculated. (For example, if you have the formula +C12+C13 in cell C12, that would be a circular reference.) To jump to the cell containing the problematic formula, click on the pair of red arrows.

Q How can I calculate a loan payment in 1-2-3?

A You can set it up yourself in a blank workbook with the @PMT function, but an easier way is to start a new workbook based on the Calculate Loan Payments SmartMaster template. It provides a grid containing all the formulas; you simply fill in the variables.

12

Q How can I find out more about the functions and what each one of them is good for?

A If you know the function name that you need help with, type it in a cell and press F1. A Help box appears providing details and examples for that function. If you aren't sure which function you are interested in, open the Help system (Help, Help Topics) and click the Contents tab. Open the Formulas and @Functions category and then open one of the categories found there (Using @Functions, Alphabetical List of @Functions, or @Functions by Category).

HOUR 13

Improving Spreadsheet Appearance

Which would you rather look at—a worksheet where everything is the same dull format, or one in which the headings and titles are bold and colorful, and the important information is shaded and boxed? The latter, of course, right? If you feel that way, then your potential readers probably do, too. Attractive formatting helps sell your reader on the idea that your worksheet is worth reading.

Highlights of this hour include:

- Changing row height and column width
- Aligning text in a cell
- Wrapping text to multiple lines
- Merging cells
- Changing the font and size of text
- Borders and shading

Controlling How Text Fits in a Cell

The first group of options we'll talk about in this hour are those that make text fit more comfortably into cells. They include column width, row height, text wrapping, and vertical and horizontal cell alignment.

Changing Column Width

One of the biggest complaints that beginners have with 1-2-3 is that their text or numbers don't fit in the cell. As you have probably seen in your 1-2-3 work, one of these things happens when a cell is too narrow to display its content:

- If you're entering text and the cell to the right is empty, the text spills over into the next cell.

- If you're entering text and the cell to the right is not empty, the text is cut off onscreen.

- If you're entering numbers, the cell displays ***** rather than the number, or it displays the number in a scientific abbreviated format like this: 2.39E+011.

There are three possible solutions: you can decrease the font size, widen the cell, or make the cell taller (increase the row height) and set that cell so that the text wraps in it. By "wraps," I mean that when the text reaches the right edge of the cell, the text starts a new line in the same cell, like in a Word Pro table. Figure 13.1 shows the problems just described and the possible solutions.

FIGURE 13.1.

When text is too long for the cell, you can widen the cell or wrap the text onto multiple lines in it.

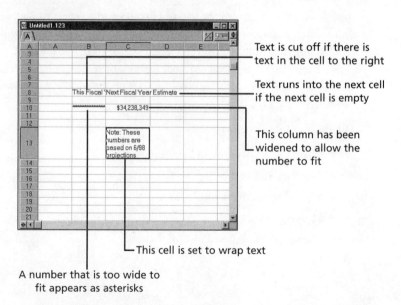

Text is cut off if there is text in the cell to the right

Text runs into the next cell if the next cell is empty

This column has been widened to allow the number to fit

This cell is set to wrap text

A number that is too wide to fit appears as asterisks

It's easy to widen a column. Just drag the right edge of the column to make it wider.

To Do: Changing Column Width

1. Position your mouse pointer at the right edge of the column label. For example, in Figure 13.2, I'm getting ready to widen column B.

2. Hold down the left mouse button and drag the column's right edge to make it as wide as you want. Release the mouse button.

Mouse pointer

FIGURE 13.2.

Position your mouse pointer to the right of the column you want to widen.

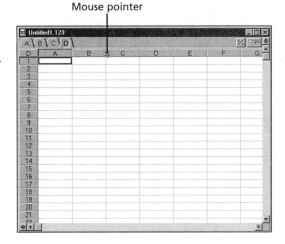

You can also widen the column so that the longest line of data in it fits precisely. To do this, right-click on the column heading and choose Fit Widest Entry from the shortcut menu that appears. Or, you can double-click the line between the column headings.

If you need to set a precise column width, choose Range, Range Properties to open the Range Properties InfoBox. Click the Basics tab, and change the number in the Width text box there, or click the Default Width option button to return the width to normal (see Figure 13.3).

13

FIGURE 13.3.

Use the Basics tab of the Range Properties InfoBox to change cell width and height precisely.

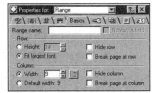

You can hide a column from the Basics Tab of the Range Properties InfoBox by clicking the Hide Column check box. To unhide it later, select a range of columns that includes it and click this same check box again.

Changing Row Height

Row height is normally determined by the largest font in that row, or the total height of multiple lines if you are wrapping text in some cells in that row. In other words, it usually adjusts itself automatically, so you do not have to worry about it.

However, if you want a special row height that does not necessarily correspond to the content of the row, you can specify it in the Range Properties InfoBox (refer to Figure 13.3). Click the Height option button and specify a height in the text box.

Text Wrapping in Cells

When I first learned to wrap text in cells, it was a great breakthrough. No more obscenely wide cells in the interest of making a lengthy bit of text fit. Text wrapping is especially helpful if you are using a spreadsheet as a mini-database to hold names and addresses because street addresses can be very long.

To Do: Wrapping Text in a Cell

▼ **To Do**

1. Select the cell(s) in which you want to wrap text.
2. Open the Range Properties InfoBox (Range, Range Properties, or click the Range Properties SmartIcon.)
3. Click the Alignment tab (see Figure 13.4).
4. Click to place a check mark in the Wrap Text in Cell check box.

FIGURE 13.4

Use the Alignment tab to control text wrapping and text alignment within a cell.

Aligning Text in a Cell

To set horizontal alignment for the cell, click one of the Horizontal Alignment buttons on the Alignment tab of the Range Properties InfoBox (refer to Figure 13.4). Your choices, just like in Word Pro, are Left, Center, Right, and Justified.

You also have a set of buttons for vertical alignment: Top, Center, or Bottom. These have an effect only if the cell height is set to be larger than the text within the cell. (This might happen, for example, if a particular row is tall because one cell in it has several wrapped lines of text. In the other cells in that row, you could set a vertical alignment.)

Notice the Orientation drop-down list on that same tab (refer to Figure 13.4). You can use it to rotate text so it runs vertically down the cell or even at a 45-degree angle, for a whimsical look. (This look could get old very quickly, so use it sparingly!)

The status bar offers a shortcut for setting alignment. Click the Alignment button on the status bar to pop up a list of alignments; then click the one you want (see Figure 13.5).

FIGURE 13.5.

Change alignment from the status bar to bypass the InfoBox completely.

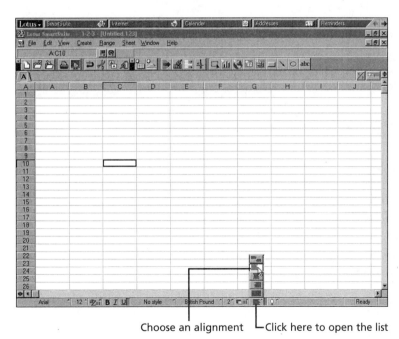

Choose an alignment └Click here to open the list

13

Setting Number Format

Number formatting can make a big difference in your spreadsheet. For example, what do you see when you look at the following number?

`12345.67`

In its plain format, you would be hard-pressed to tell what significance the number had. But if formatted in any of the following ways, its meaning becomes clear:

$12,345.67   A dollar amount

1234567.00%   A percentage

1.23E+04   A scientific notation

10/18/1933 4:04 PM   A date and time

You would never have guessed some of these from the original, but that's the whole purpose of number formatting—to take a generic-looking number and fix it up so the reader can immediately tell why it's there.

Some of the formats are self-explanatory, but others aren't so obvious. Here are a few of the ones that may need a bit of extra explanation:

- **General**. The generic format for numbers. They appear in exactly the format you enter them, including the number of decimal places you enter.

- **Fixed.** All numbers appear with a specified number of decimal places, even if they are whole numbers. This is useful for aligning columns of numbers where some have decimal places and some don't.

- **Date and Time**. Dates and times are calculated from numbers like this: The digits in front of the decimal point are the number of days since January 1, 1900. The digits after the decimal are the number of minutes since 12:00 a.m.

 Dates and times are stored as numbers because sometimes you need to use them in calculations in formulas. When you enter a date or time in a cell, 1-2-3 automatically formats that cell in Date/Time format, so you are shielded from seeing the number in its "raw" format unless you specifically format it in some other number format than date/time.

- **Scientific**. This specialized number format takes the number and moves the decimal place over so that there is only one digit before the decimal. Then it adds an E, a plus sign, and a number that indicates the number of places it moved the decimal. So, for example, 123 would become 1.23E+002. It's useful for displaying extremely long numbers in a narrow column.

- **Currency**. Besides the U.S. Dollar currency, currency formats are provided for many other countries, and each shows the appropriate currency symbol (such as the British pound symbol).

You apply number formats through the Range Properties InfoBox (Range, Range Properties) on its Number tab. Simply select the number format you want from the list and set any options for it (see Figure 13.6).

FIGURE 13.6.

Choose a number format and then set any options available for that format.

You can also apply commonly used number formats from a list on the status bar. Click to open the list and click the format to apply. A separate pop up list immediately to its right controls the number of decimal places, too (see Figure 13.7).

You can customize which number formats appear on the status bar with the Show in Frequently Used List check box in the InfoBox (refer to Figure 13.6). Just make sure it is marked for the formats that you want on your status bar list.

FIGURE 13.7.

The status bar offers the most common number formats.

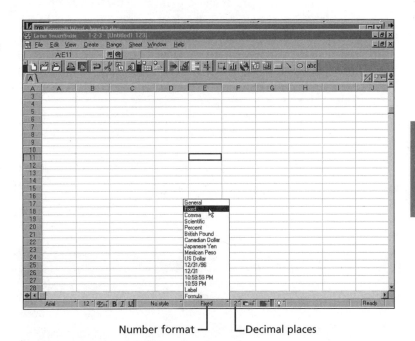

Number format ⎯ ⎸ ⎸⎯ Decimal places

13

Setting Text Properties

Text properties in 1-2-3 are the same as the text properties you learned about in Word Pro. On the status bar you have controls for Font, Size, Color, Bold, Italic, and Underline. These work the same as you learned in Hour 6. You can also use the Range Properties InfoBox (Range, Range Properties) and set text properties on its Font, Attribute, & Color tab. The only difference is that in 1-2-3, text properties apply to the entire cell, not to individual characters. You can't make part of the text in a cell bold and part not bold, for example. You are formatting the cell itself with text properties, and any text that appears in that cell takes on that formatting.

1-2-3, like Word Pro, also offers styles to expedite formatting. They work just like the styles in Word Pro. (Refer to Hour 8 as needed.) You can choose a style from the Style pop-up list on the status bar, or define a style by example with the Styles tab in the Range Properties InfoBox.

Adding Cell Borders

Each cell has four sides: right, left, top, and bottom. And onscreen, each side of each cell is marked by gray gridlines. These gridlines are utilitarian in purpose—they show you where one cell ends and another begins, but they're not particularly attractive.

Borders, in contrast, are designed to improve the look and readability of your worksheet. You can assign a border to each side of each cell individually, for perfect control over their use. For example, look at Figure 13.8. Borders have been used to separate the headings from the text beneath them and to draw attention to a note. (I've turned off the onscreen display of the gridlines so you can see the borders better.)

By default, those gray gridlines are turned on onscreen. You can turn off their display by choosing View, Set View Preferences and deselecting the Gridlines check box.

These onscreen gridlines do not print by default. You can make them print by choosing File, Preview & Page Setup and placing a check mark next to Sheet Grid Lines in the Show list.

FIGURE 13.8.

Borders can improve the appearance and readability of your worksheet.

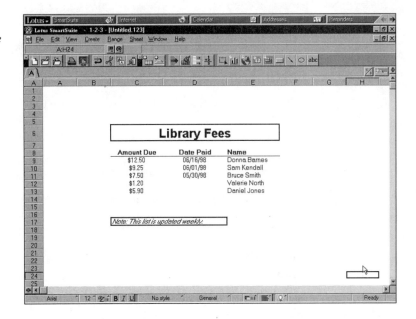

To set borders for certain cells, you use (surprise!) the Range Properties InfoBox. It has a Color, Pattern, & Line Style tab that contains all the controls you need (see Figure 13.9).

FIGURE 13.9.

Add borders to cells on this tab.

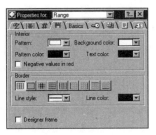

In the Border area of the InfoBox, click on the button that shows a picture of the borders you want for the selected cells:

Button	Description
	Around all sides of all cells in the selected range
	Around the outside of the selected range
	Around all sides of all cells in the range *except* those that are on the outside

13

Button	Description
	On all horizontal sides of all cells
	On all vertical sides of all cells
	On only the left side of only the cells on the outside left
	On only the right side of only the cells on the outside right
	On only the top of only the cells on the top of the range
	On only the bottom of only the cells on the bottom of the range

You can control the line style, thickness, and color of the borders with the drop-down lists in the InfoBox.

You can also use Designer borders, as you did in Word Pro. Just click the Designer Frame check box (shown in Figure 13.9) for access to the Designer Frame drop-down lists.

Adding Cell Shading

Shading can make certain cells stand out. If your lines are all one color, the eye can play tricks, and it's easy to misread a line. By making certain lines shaded, you improve their readability. (Why do you think accounting ledger paper is often striped with green shading? It's for this same reason.)

To shade certain cells with a different color or a pattern, use the controls in the Range Properties InfoBox, on the same Color, Pattern & Line Style tab shown in Figure 13.9. You can choose a pattern from the Pattern drop-down list and a color for it from the Pattern Color list. Or, you can forego a pattern and use a solid-color shading from the Background Color drop-down list.

Summary

This hour taught you how to format your worksheets for maximum visual impact. You can now not only create an accurate and newsworthy spreadsheet, but you can make it attractive enough to catch your reader's attention.

In the next hour, we'll turn our attention toward 1-2-3's charting capabilities. You'll learn how to turn boring columns of numbers into vibrant, colorful charts and graphs that tell a complex story with simple shapes and lines.

Q&A

Q Help! I've hidden a column, and now I can't get it back!

A Simple. Just select a range of columns that includes the hidden one. For example, if column B is hidden, select columns A and C. Right-click on the column headings and choose Unhide Columns from the shortcut menu.

Q I changed the row height manually for a row, and now that row won't automatically adjust to its content anymore. How do I reset a row so that it will adjust itself again?

A On the Basics tab in the Range Properties InfoBox, click the Fit Largest Font option button. This strips away any custom height you have set for the row.

Q I removed a border from a cell, but the border is still there. Why won't it go away?

A The border is probably set in an adjacent cell. For example, suppose you have a right border set for cell A1 and a left border for cell B1. Because these cells are adjacent, you see only one border between them. Then you remove the border from cell A1. But B1's border is still there, so you still see a border between them. Try removing the borders from an adjacent cell, and see if that doesn't solve your problem.

13

HOUR 14

Charting in 1-2-3

Have you ever been in a meeting where some wanna-be corporate raider pulled out a two-inch printout stack of small-print numbers? You could almost hear all the eyes in the room glazing over, right? What that guy didn't know is that the meaning of even complicated data can usually be distilled into a few well-designed charts. In this hour, you learn to create great-looking charts in 1-2-3 that convey the meaning of your data.

Highlights of this hour include:

- Creating a simple pie chart
- Creating a bar graph
- Adding titles and legends
- Formatting charts for maximum impact

Understanding Charts

A chart is kind of like a formula. It takes information from the cells you specify and "processes" it, only instead of spitting out a numerical result, a chart produces a graphical one. Figure 14.1 shows a pie chart, which is a good choice for showing percentages.

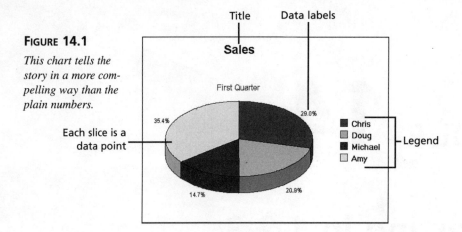

FIGURE 14.1

This chart tells the story in a more compelling way than the plain numbers.

A single number is a *data point* on the chart. All charts contain at least one *data series*, which is a group of related data points. (If you had only one data point, it wouldn't be much of a chart.) A pie chart has only one data series, which shows a pie slice for each data point's contribution to the whole. In Figure 14.1, that series is first-quarter sales.

On some charts, each data point has a *data label*, which describes the data point. (In Figure 14.1 the data label lists the percentage for each slice.) Some charts also have a legend, which is a "key" that explains what each data point stands for. For example, in Figure 14.1, the legend tells which salesperson is represented by each slice color.

NEW TERM *Data point:* An individual bit of data, such as the sales made by a particular salesman in a single month.

NEW TERM *Data series:* A related group of data points, such as the sales figures for a particular salesman for three months.

Some charts have more than one data series. In Figure 14.2, for example, another column of data has been added, and the chart shows two data series. The chart in Figure 14.2 is a *bar chart*.

FIGURE 14.2

This bar chart shows sales over time.

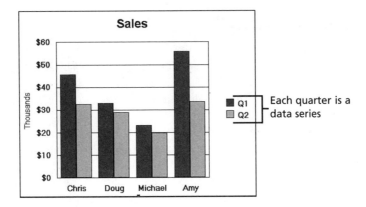

You can show the same data but present a different message by changing the way in which data points are grouped together in a data series. For example, Figure 14.2 invites you to compare each salesperson's performance individually over two quarters. In contrast, Figure 14.3 takes the same data and invites you to compare the salespeople against one another.

FIGURE 14.3

This bar chart compares salesperson performance.

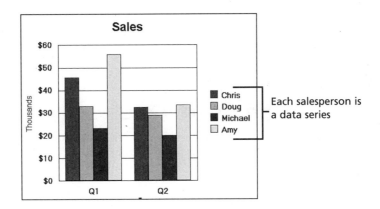

This tip will make more sense later after you have actually created a chart, but to "flip" a chart, making a different group of data into a series (as with Figures 14.2 and 14.3), right-click a chart and choose Chart Properties. On the Ranges tab, click the Options button and choose Series by Column or Series by Row.

14

Creating a Chart

To create a chart, you first enter the data into 1-2-3. That should be no problem for you, after the last hour's session. Make sure that you enter data labels too, like the names and quarter numbers in Figure 14.3. These will become labels on your chart. If you don't include them, the data may be difficult for the reader to understand.

To Do: Creating a Chart

1. Select the entire range of data to be charted, including any data labels.

2. Click the Create a Chart SmartIcon. The mouse pointer turns to a crosshair with a little chart icon on it.

3. Click on the spreadsheet where you want to create the chart. This places a chart in a default size. Or, to create a specific size chart, drag your mouse pointer to draw a box into which to place the chart.

The chart is a "live" representation of the data; if you change the content of any of the cells on which the chart is based, the chart changes automatically. The chart is part of the workbook into which it is placed; when you save the workbook, the chart is saved too. (You can't save a chart separately.)

Don't worry if your chart isn't perfect yet. You can resize easily. Also, there may be labels that are placeholders, like "Title" or "Y axis." We'll correct those later in this chapter.

Changing the Chart Type

When you create a chart, it is selected (until you click somewhere else). You can reselect it if needed by simply clicking on it again. (You must select it before you can make changes to it.)

When a chart is selected, different SmartIcons appear at the top of the screen. Many of these represent different chart types you can change to:

 Bar. Use this for one or more series, to show changes over time or between series.

 Stacked bar. This is good for simultaneously showing individual series and also how they combine to make a whole amount.

 Bar with Depth. This is a fancier version of Bar.

 3-D Bar. This places each data series in its own row. It is good for multiple data series, but can be too complex for a reader to understand at a glance.

Line. This is like a bar chart, but with dots connected by a line instead of bars. It is good for showing performance over time.

 Area. This is like a line chart, but the area beneath each line is filled in with color.

 Mixed line/bar. If you want to show two different series, one with bar and one with line, use this.

 Pie. Shows how all the data in one series combines to make a whole. Excellent for showing percentages.

 Multiple pie. Makes separate pie charts for each data series, if there is more than one.

 HLCO. High/Low/Close/Open chart, used for showing stock market (and other market) prices.

Besides choosing one of these general types, you can fine-tune the chart type. Choose Chart, Chart Type or click the Change Chart Type SmartIcon to display the Chart Type tab of the Chart Properties InfoBox (see Figure 14.4). Click the chart type you want on the list and then the button for the subtype. You can see your own chart behind the InfoBox changing to reflect your selections. Close the InfoBox when finished.

FIGURE 14.4

You can choose from several subtypes of each chart type here.

 You can create your own combination of chart types in a multiseries chart. After creating a chart, choose Chart, Series, and select the series you want to work with. Then choose a type from the Mixed Type drop-down list. This changes the type only for the chosen series; the other series in the chart remain set to the overall chart type you chose. This works with all chart types except pie, doughnut, and number grid, none of which use series.

14

Adding and Removing Labels

When you create a chart, there may be some "dummy" text on it, such as "Title" at the top or "Y axis" down the side. To replace that text with real text, simply click on it and type over it. Or, to delete the text box completely, click on it and press the Delete key. You can also move these text boxes around on the chart by dragging them, just like you did with graphics in Word Pro in Hour 9.

You can also turn on or off the display of certain labels from the Chart Properties InfoBox. Display the InfoBox (Chart, Chart Properties or click the Chart Properties SmartIcon), click the Layout tab, and then use the check boxes there to turn on or off certain elements, like the title and legend (see Figure 14.5).

FIGURE 14.5

Control the display of various optional labels here.

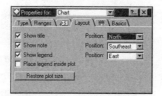

Notice the drop-down lists in Figure 14.5 with various directions? Each of these is for the check box that it shares a line with, and the directions refer to positioning on the chart. For example, the Title is set to "North," which means the top of the chart. The sides of the chart are north, south, east, and west, and the corners are northeast, northwest, southeast, and southwest.

Changing the Data Range

If you create a chart using the wrong data, the easiest thing to do is usually to delete the chart (select it and click the Cut SmartIcon) and start over. However, if you have put a significant amount of work into the chart (for example, formatting or customizing it), it may be worth your while to change the data range.

NEW TERM *Data range:* The range of cells that contains the data charted in the chart.

To Do: Changing the Data Range

1. Click the Ranges tab in the Chart Properties InfoBox, if it is open. If it is not open, choose Chart, Ranges.

2. In the Range box, type the new range to use. Or, you can click the Range Selector next to it to temporarily close the InfoBox and drag across the cells you want to select.

You can also modify the ranges for individual data series. For example, you might make one set of bars on your bar chart refer to a different group of cells, but leave the other set of bars the same as it is now.

To Do: Modifying an Individual Series

1. Choose Chart, Series. The Series Properties InfoBox opens.

> If you already have the Chart Properties InfoBox open, you can easily change to the Series Properties InfoBox with the Properties For drop-down list at the top.

2. Choose the series to work with from the drop-down list. See Figure 14.6.

FIGURE 14.6

You can set the ranges for each series individually.

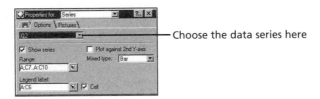

Choose the data series here

3. Change the range in the Range box or use the Range Selector to choose it.

4. If needed, change the cell containing the series label in the Legend Label box.

5. Close the InfoBox when finished.

14

Formatting a Chart

1-2-3 offers quite an array of formatting options for a chart. In addition to the Chart Properties InfoBox, an InfoBox exists for just about every chart element you can imagine—the title, the legend, each of the axes, and so on. You'll work with some of them in the upcoming sections. To change from one element's InfoBox to another, open the Properties For drop-down list at the top of an InfoBox and pick a different element.

Moving and Resizing a Chart

A chart is just like a graphic, at least for the purpose of resizing and moving. It sits on top of the worksheet. If it's sitting on top of cells that contain data you want to see, simply move the chart. To move it, drag its border (but not on a selection handle). To resize it, drag a selection handle. Refer back to Hour 9's discussion of "Moving and Resizing a Graphic" as needed.

Changing the Axes

On all charts except pies and doughnuts, you have two axes: the X axis, which runs horizontally across the bottom, and the Y axis, which runs vertically along the left side. These axes measure different things, depending on the chart, but at least one of them is usually numeric. For example, in Figure 14.7, the Y axis measures thousands of dollars. The X axis lists the names of various salespeople.

Figure 14.7 starts the Y axis at $0 and shows gridlines every $10,000. The problem with Figure 14.7 is that the salespeople's totals are so similar that it's hard to see the differences at a glance. You can change the scale used on the Y axis to accentuate the differences, as shown in Figure 14.8. The Y axis here starts at $41,000 and shows gridlines at every $1,000. It more clearly shows who is a top performer and who has room for improvement.

FIGURE 14.7

From this chart, it looks like all the salespeople are performing about equally.

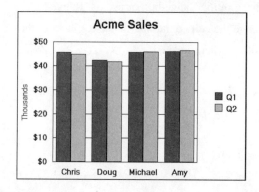

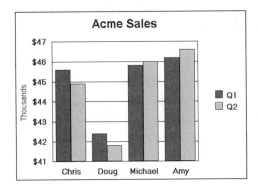

FIGURE 14.8

By changing the scale of the Y axis, differences in performance are amplified.

To Do: Changing the Y Axis Scale

1. Choose Chart, Axis & Grids, Y Axis & Grids. The Y axis InfoBox opens. See Figure 14.9.

2. Enter new measurements in the Maximum and Minimum text boxes. For example, to create Figure 14.8, I used 41,000 as the minimum and 48,000 as the maximum.

3. To set gridline frequency, change the number in the Major Ticks box.

FIGURE 14.9

Set the axis measurements manually here.

4. (Optional) Set any of the following as needed:

   • To make the bars drop from the "ceiling" of the chart, set Direction to Descending.

   • To place the Y axis on the right, set Position to Right.

   • To change the units shown on the chart, set Units to a specific unit (such as None, Hundreds, Thousands, and so on). The default is Auto.

You can also set similar properties for the X axis, although it is less commonly modified because it usually contains names or dates rather than numbers.

Formatting Labels

You can format labels just like regular text. Select the text and apply formatting from the status bar (such as font changes, size changes, and bold/italic/underline). Refer to Hour 6 for a refresher if needed.

14

Changing Data Series Properties

Each data series has its own properties, which include the color used for the series. To set series properties, choose Chart, Series and then select the desired series from the drop-down list.

The Series Properties InfoBox has three tabs. The first and most commonly used one controls the colors (see Figure 14.10). The Pattern, when set to solid, fills the bars (or pie slice or whatever) with the color chosen from the Pattern Color list. When the pattern is anything except solid, it shows a pattern made up of the Pattern Color and the Background Color.

The Line controls, also in Figure 14.10, control the lines around the series slices or bars. You can set color, style, and width.

FIGURE 14.10

You can choose the color and pattern for each data series individually.

You can use the Pictures tab to fill the slice or bar with a picture of your choosing. This can be kind of cool if the bar or slice is large, but doesn't work well for smaller pieces. Experiment with this tab on your own.

Other Chart Element Formatting

There's so much you can do with chart formatting that it would be impossible to cover it all here, but here are some starting points:

- **Legends**. Choose Chart, Legend to set the positioning of the legend in relation to the chart or to turn off the legend completely. You can also change the color of the legend and format the labels on the legend just like regular text.

- **Title**. Choose Chart, Title to control the title position, font, size, color, and background.

- **X axis**. Choose Chart, Axes & Grids, X Axis & Grid. You can make the labels larger or smaller, make them overlap (or not), add gridlines and tick marks, and change the axis scale.

- **Plot**. Choose Chart, Plot. This controls the background behind the data series. You can color it, pattern it, and even place a picture on it.

- **Note**. Choose Chart, Note. You can add up to three notes as extra chart elements (kind of like a legend or title). These can be footnotes that explain the data or any other extra text you need on the chart.
- **Table**. Choose Chart, Table. By turning on Show Data Table, you place a table under the chart that mirrors the data in the cells used to create it. This is useful if you want to use the chart by itself, without the spreadsheet. You can format this table as you would any other cells in 1-2-3.

Summary

In this hour you learned the basics of charting in 1-2-3, including how to create a chart, how to change the chart type, and how to format a chart, including changing the range, the axis, and the colors and fonts used. You may want to save some of your charts for use in a Freelance presentation, which you'll learn to create in Hour 20. Immediately ahead is another hour's worth of 1-2-3 lessons. In Hour 15, we'll tackle some of 1-2-3's more advanced and powerful features, such as specialized calculations and database management.

Q&A

Q What's the best kind of chart to use?

A It depends on what you want to show. A pie is best for showing various contributions to a whole. A bar chart is great for comparing two or more series. A line chart works well for charting progress over time. Ask yourself: What am I trying to demonstrate with this chart? Then try several chart types to arrive at the one that most clearly states your message.

Q What's the difference between a chart and a graph?

A None, really. The terms are interchangeable. Some people will tell you that a graph is a chart that has at least two axes (like X and Y), but 1-2-3 doesn't make that distinction.

Q How do I put a 1-2-3 chart into a Word document or a Freelance presentation?

A It's fairly easy, and you'll learn all about it in Hour 23, but here's a preview. To paste a static (unchanging) copy, use the Copy and Paste commands (on the Edit menu). To paste a copy that updates itself whenever the original is updated, save your work in 1-2-3 and then copy the chart (using the normal Copy command). Once you are in Word or Freelance, use the Edit, Paste Special to paste a link.

14

HOUR 15

Advanced 1-2-3

By now you know how to use 1-2-3 to create your own basic spreadsheets. In this final hour on 1-2-3, I'm going to show you some additional uses for 1-2-3 that you may not have thought of. Some involve supposedly "advanced" features of the program; others are merely innovative ideas for using the features you already know.

Highlights include:

- Managing 3D (multisheet) workbooks
- Storing database data in 1-2-3
- Creating business forms with 1-2-3
- Automating 1-2-3 with scripts

Managing MultiSheet Workbooks

I explained multisheet workbooks briefly already, but let's take a closer look. Each workbook starts with one sheet, called A. (You can rename its tab by double-clicking on it and typing a new name, but its name for calculation purposes is still A.) When referring to a cell on that sheet, its full name is A:{column}{row}. For example, the full name of the range A1..B6 is A:A1..A:B6. You don't have to use the full name unless you are making reference to a cell that is not on the same sheet, but 1-2-3 always uses the full name for a cell, so you need to understand the naming scheme.

To create additional sheets in a workbook, right-click an existing sheet and choose Create Sheet. The Create Sheet dialog box opens. Enter the number of sheets to create in the Number of Sheets text box and choose After Current Sheet or Before Current Sheet (see Figure 15.1). Click OK and your new sheets are inserted. To switch from sheet to sheet, click the tab of the sheet you want to bring to the front.

Here's a shortcut to create a new sheet: Click the New Sheet button. It's the button to the far right of the area where the worksheet tabs appear (see Figure 15.1). This creates one new sheet after the last sheet in the workbook.

New Sheet button—

FIGURE 15.1

Use the New Sheet dialog box to create a new sheet or simply click the New Sheet button.

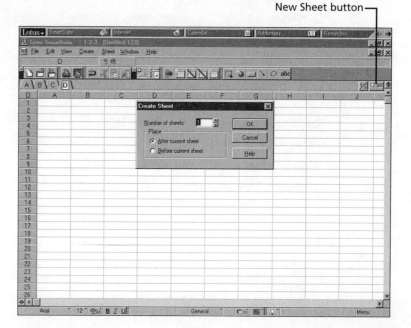

15

When referring to a range on a different sheet, just make sure that you prefix it with the sheet letter. For example, you might want to have one sheet calculate details for a project and carry over a grand total to a second sheet where you summarize. Suppose that you want to refer to the content of cell B6 on sheet A in a formula in cell C18 on sheet B. You would click on the B tab to display the B sheet and enter the following in cell C18: **+A:B6**. (Remember, the plus sign tells 1-2-3 that you want the cell's content, not the actual letters you're typing.)

Using 1-2-3 as a Database

Even though you have Approach, a great database tool that you'll learn about in upcoming hours, you may still occasionally want to store data in 1-2-3. 1-2-3 has superior calculating capabilities, so if you need to perform calculations on your data, you may find that it is faster and easier to keep in 1-2-3.

For example, if you maintain a list of club members and the amounts of money that they donate to various affiliated charities, 1-2-3 works great for calculating running totals for each member. You can do some calculations in Approach, but it takes more work to set them up there since Approach is designed for data storage rather than calculation. In 1-2-3, such formulas are simple.

When storing data in a tabular format (like 1-2-3), you create column headings near the top of the sheet for the field names. For example, if you were tracking member names and amounts due, you might have these column headings: **Name**, **Amount Due**, **As Of**. Then you would simply enter the records (that is, the information for each person) under those headings, as shown in Figure 15.2.

Sorting Data

When you have data in a listing like in Figure 15.2, you may want to sort it in different ways. For example, you might want to sort the names alphabetically, or you might want to sort according to the most money owed or the earliest As Of date.

You can sort only by the first character in a cell. If you want to be able to sort by last names, you must either put the last name first when entering names or put first and last names in separate cells.

FIGURE 15.2

To use 1-2-3 as a database, create column headings and then type your data under them.

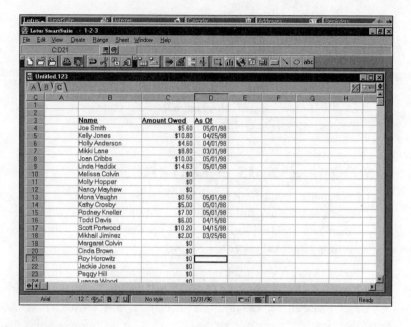

To Do: Sorting Your Data

1. Select the entire range of cells containing the data. In Figure 15.2, for example, we would start selecting in cell B4 and extend the selection to the last row in column D that contained data.

2. Choose Range, Sort. The Sort dialog box opens (see Figure 15.3).

3. If you included the row of column labels in the area you selected, make sure the Header Row check box is marked. If you did not, make sure it is unmarked.

FIGURE 15.3

You can specify which columns to sort by in this dialog box.

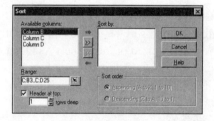

4. Click the column you want to sort by from the Available Columns list and then click the >> button to move it to the Sort By list.

5. In the Sort Order area, choose Ascending (A–Z) or Descending (Z–A).

▼   6. (Optional) If you want to add a second sort criterion (for example, if two or more
        lines have the same value for the first criterion you chose), repeat steps 4 and 5 for
        another column.

15

     7. When you are ready to perform the sort, click OK. 1-2-3 sorts the data on the
▲   worksheet.

> After you've sorted the data, you can't put it back the way it was unless it
> originally conformed to some kind of sorting. One way to get around this is
> to create a new column called Original and fill it with a series of numbers (1
> through whatever), as you learned in Hour 11. Then include that column in
> all your sorts, and if you ever need to go back to the original order, sort by
> that column.

Finding and Replacing Data

If you have a long list of data stored in 1-2-3, it may become tiresome to scroll through it
to find a certain name or value. You can use 1-2-3's Find feature to find the cell content
you want. You can also replace the found data with some other value while you're there.

The Find feature in 1-2-3 is somewhat different from the one in Word Pro. It works the
same way, but in 1-2-3, you work with a dialog box rather than a bar at the top of the
screen.

To Do: Using the Find Feature

     1. Choose Edit, Find & Replace. The Find & Replace dialog box appears.

     2. In the Find text box, type what you want to find (see Figure 15.4).

     3. (Optional) If you want to replace the found data with something, enter the replace-
        ment text or value in the Replace With text box.

     4. Open the Look In drop-down list and choose where you want to look. The default
        is Current Workbook, but you can limit the search to Current Sheet or Selected
        Range, or you can expand it to All Workbooks.

     5. In the Include area, deselect any check boxes for types of cell entries you want to
        ignore. Remember, a label is any cell entry that contains text. A value is a cell
        entry that contains numbers. A formula is a cell entry that contains either a formula
        or a function. If you don't deselect Formulas, 1-2-3 will look in the formulas them-
▼   selves (such as finding F7 in a formula that refers to cell F7).

FIGURE 15.4

Find data with the Find & Replace dialog box.

▼ 6. Click Find to find the first entry.

7. If you want to replace, click the Replace button. Otherwise click Find again to find the next instance.

8. When you come to the last entry, a dialog box appears telling you so. Click OK to clear it.

▲ 9. Click Done to close the Find & Replace dialog box.

Automating Tasks with Scripts

We spent some time in Hour 10 on the SmartSuite scripting language, and you learned how to record your own scripts. It works the same way in 1-2-3 as it did in Word Pro.

To Do: Automating Spreadsheets with Scripts

1. Choose Edit, Scripts & Macros, Record Script.

2. Enter a script name in the Script Name box.

3. Choose a location for the script from the Record Script Into drop-down list. (The default is the name of the current workbook.)

4. Click the Record button to start recording. The dialog box goes away, and two large buttons appear in the top-left corner of your worksheet: one red and one yellow.

5. Perform the actions that you want to record.

6. Click the red button to stop recording. The recorded script appears in the Script Editor window.

▲ 7. Edit the script as needed (see Hour 10) and exit the Script Editor.

To Do: Playing Back a Script

1. Choose Edit, Scripts & Macros, Run. The Run Scripts & Macros dialog box opens.

2. Choose the script you want to run and click Run. The script executes.

You can assign scripts to SmartIcons in 1-2-3, just as you did in Word Pro. See Hour 10 for details.

 Each script belongs to the sheet that was active when you created it. If you want to run a macro that is on another sheet, simply designate that sheet in the Run Scripts and Macros dialog box. Don't rerecord the macro in each sheet.

Summary

This hour topped off your work in 1-2-3 with some "power tools." You learned how to work with multisheet workbooks, creating cell references between sheets. You also looked at some of 1-2-3's analysis tools and learned how to manage database data in 1-2-3 with the Sort and Find commands. We finished up with a refresher on scripts.

In the next hour, we will start a brand-new program. You'll get an introduction to Approach, the SmartSuite database program, and learn how to create your own databases to store important business and personal information.

Q&A

Q How do I refer to other sheets in a formula?

A Precede the cell reference with the sheet name and a colon, like this: @SUM(A:A1..A4).

Q Help! I tried to sort, but my data got all mixed up.

A You may have forgotten to select the entire range of data, not just the column by which you want to sort. If you don't select the entire data range, only the selected column gets sorted, resulting in chaos. Press Ctrl+Z to undo and try again.

Q When I'm recording a script in 1-2-3, I click on the REC on the status bar to stop the recording, like in Word Pro, but nothing happens.

A The one little difference between Word Pro and 1-2-3 is that to stop recording in 1-2-3, you must click the red Stop button at the top of your worksheet rather than clicking the status bar. You can also use the yellow button to pause the recording.

15

PART IV
Approach

Hour

Hour 16

Approach Basics

Don't let the techie sound of the word "database" scare you away from trying Approach. It's actually one of the more user-friendly parts of SmartSuite! Unlike some other database programs on the market, Approach doesn't expect you to be a programmer. It works great for creating all kinds of databases, for all kinds of people.

In this "warm-up" hour, we'll go on a tour of Approach and create a new database to play with. You'll learn how to enter data and move between records and see how to switch among Approach's several views. Nothing too challenging here!

Highlights of this hour include:

- Basic database terminology
- Understanding Approach's views and modes
- Entering and editing data
- Managing your list of fields
- Starting a database from scratch

Basic Database Terminology

Strictly speaking, a *database* is any collection of information. Your local telephone book, for example, is a database, as is your Rolodex file and the card catalog at your local library.

All of the details that make up one entry are collectively called a *record*. For example, in the telephone book, each person's name and phone number is a unique record. The different kinds of information recorded for each record are called *fields*. In the telephone book, the fields include name, address, and phone number.

The data that you enter into Approach is held in a *table*, which looks a lot like a 1-2-3 worksheet. The names of the fields are column headings, and the rows are individual records. See Figure 16.1 for an example.

NEW TERM   *Database:* A collection of information.

Record: One database entry, such as information for a single client.

Field: Individual pieces of information that comprise a record; a single client's street address is a field.

Table: The container in which your Approach data is stored.

You can enter data directly into the table, or you can use a data entry *form*. Figure 16.2 shows a data entry form for the table from Figure 16.1.

As you work with your data, you may want to see a subset of it. Perhaps you want to see only certain fields or only certain records that meet the criteria you specify. (For example, you might separate children from adults in a database of people by filtering out those with birthdates less than 18 years ago.) To create a subset of your data based on one or more criteria, you use a *find*.

NEW TERM   *Find:* A find in Approach is the equivalent of a filter or query in other database programs. It weeds out the records you don't want, leaving only the ones you want to work with at the moment.

FIGURE 16.1.

The table is the basic storage tank of a database.

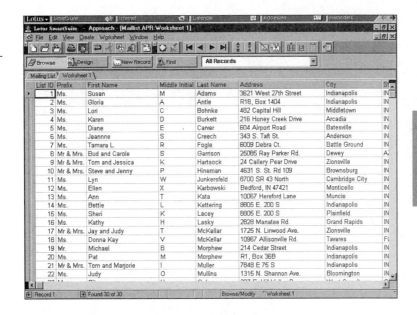

FIGURE 16.2.

Forms make data entry more convenient.

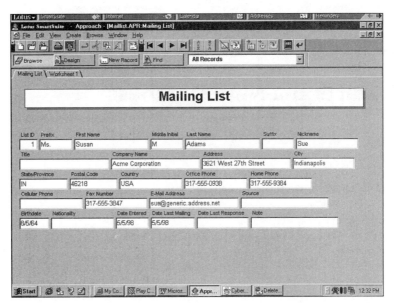

When you want to view and evaluate your data, you can do it onscreen in either Table or Form view, or you can generate a report that is optimized for printing on your printer.

Figure 16.3 shows a report in Print Preview mode, ready to be printed. Reports can incorporate filters in their design so that when you run a report, you automatically apply certain filter criteria, too.

FIGURE 16.3.

Reports filter and format your data for printing.

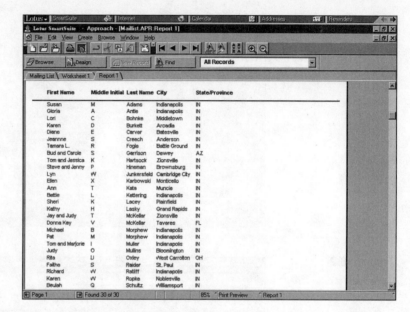

Starting a New Database

You can start a new database with a SmartMaster or from scratch, but I recommend that beginners use a SmartMaster for at least the first few databases they create. In this chapter, I'll be using an example database that I created using the Mailing List SmartMaster. Refer back to Hour 4, "Managing SmartSuite Files," if you need a refresher course in using SmartMaster templates.

Navigating the Approach Screen

Approach offers two main views of a database—Worksheet and Form. You saw these in Figures 16.1 and 16.2. The form tab's name is the same as the name of the SmartMaster you used; in Figures 16.1 and 16.2 it is Mailing List. If you have created any other views, such as reports, they appear on their own tabs, as well. In Figure 16.3, there is an extra tab called Report 1. You can switch between views by clicking the desired tab at the top of the work area.

Each of the tabbed views has several modes. The most common two have their own buttons on the Action bar—Browse and Design. Browse is the regular mode, in which you work with data. Design is the construction mode, in which you modify the view itself. Other modes include Print Preview and Find, but these are each more specialized; you'll learn about them later.

Figure 16.4 points out the onscreen landmarks to notice as you familiarize yourself with Approach.

16

Switch between Browse and
Design modes on the Action bar

FIGURE 16.4.

*Switch among
Approach's views and
modes with these
controls.*

Switch views
with the tabs

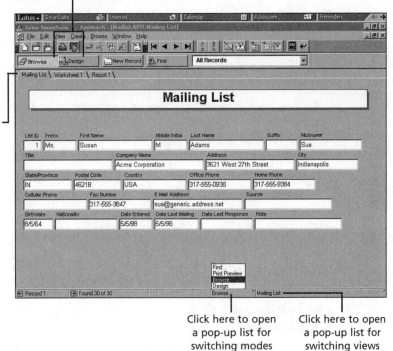

Click here to open
a pop-up list for
switching modes

Click here to open
a pop-up list for
switching views

You can have more than one database file open at once in Approach. When you do, you can tile the windows to see both at once by choosing Window, Tile Left/Right or Window, Tile Top/Bottom.

Entering and Editing Data

In this section, I'm going to assume that you used a SmartMaster template to create your database, so you already have your fields set up. If you don't, skip to "Starting with a Blank Database" at the end of this chapter because you have some extra setup you need to do before you can enter data.

> You should finalize the fields that you are using before you do your data entry. If you think you might need to make some changes to the fields, skip to "Managing the Field List" later in this hour and come back here for data entry when you're finished.

Entering a New Record

You can enter a new record from either the worksheet or the form, but the form is easier.

To Do: Creating a New Record

1. Click the New Record button. In Form view, all the fields go blank for data entry; in Worksheet view, your cursor jumps to the first blank row on the sheet.

2. Enter the data for the first field and press Tab to move to the next one.

3. Continue entering data until you reach the last field.

4. If you want to enter another new record, click the New Record button again.

Moving Between Records

After you have more than one record entered, it becomes necessary to move between them. In Worksheet view, this is not so critical because all the records appear in one big sheet. You simply use the scrollbars to bring the information you want into view and click in the correct record. In Form view, however, you can display only one record at a time.

To move among records in Form view, do any of the following (see Figure 16.5):

- Click the Next Record or Previous Record arrow buttons on the status bar.
- Press Page Down or Page Up.
- Click the Next Record or Previous Record SmartIcon.
- Click the First Record or Last Record SmartIcon.

First
Record

Previous
Record

Next
Record

Last
Record

FIGURE 16.5.

There are many ways to move among records in Form view.

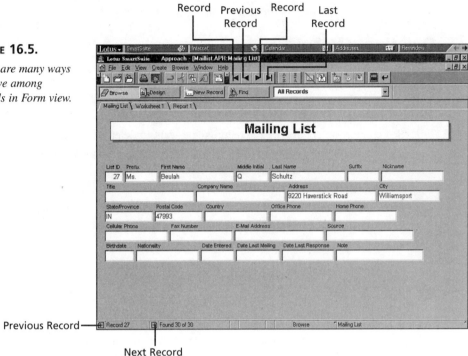

16

Previous Record

Next Record

Shortcut keys exist for moving among records too: Ctrl+Home takes you to the first record, and Ctrl+End takes you to the last one.

You can also jump to a particular record by finding it with the Find feature, which you'll learn about in Hour 17.

> All the buttons pointed out in Figure 16.5 also work in Worksheet view; they jump your cursor to the first field in the indicated record.

Editing a Record

Editing a record's data is simple. (Finding the correct record is the *real* challenge. You'll learn about that in Hour 17.) Just do one the following:

- In Worksheet view, double-click the cell containing the data to edit. This places the insertion point in the cell. Then edit normally.

- In Form view, display the record containing the field to edit. Click in the field you want to edit to move the insertion point there and then edit as needed.

Deleting a Record

You can delete records from either Worksheet or Form view. The advantage of doing it from Worksheet view is that you can select multiple records to delete in one shot.

To Do: Deleting Records in Worksheet View

▼ To Do

1. Select the rows containing the records you want to delete. To select a row, click in the area to the left of the first field. To select more than one row, hold down the Shift key while selecting the first and last ones in the group. (You cannot select non-contiguous records for deletion.)

2. Press the Delete key or right-click and choose Delete, Selected Records. A dialog box asks if it is okay to delete them.

▲   3. Click Yes. The records are gone.

As a shortcut, you can delete a record by moving the cursor to any field within it and pressing Ctrl+Delete.

> You *cannot* undo a record deletion. The usual Edit, Undo command does not work. Be very careful when choosing which records to delete.

Other Things You Can Do to Records

Besides the obvious stuff (which you just learned about), you can also:

- **Hide records**. This is sometimes useful for hiding sensitive information before printing a copy for others. To hide records, select them and press Ctrl+H or right-click and choose Records, Hide. You cannot undo a Hide command. To unhide records, open the Find drop-down list on the toolbar and reselect All Records.

- **Duplicate a record**. This comes in handy if you need to make another record that is almost like the previous one. You can save yourself some typing by duplicating the previous entry and then making changes to it. To do this, select the original record, and then right-click and choose Records, Duplicate.

- **Find records**. This is an important topic, but let's wait on it. It's covered in Hour 17.

- **Sort records**. Ditto with this one. It's pretty major, so let's wait until Hour 17, when there's more time to explore it.

Managing the Field List

The Approach SmartMaster templates provide impressive collections of predesigned fields, sometimes to the point of overkill. I guess the designers figured it was better to provide too many fields in a template and let you weed out the ones you don't want.

You'll work with your field list in the Field Definition dialog box (see Figure 16.6). To open it, choose Create, Field Definition.

16

FIGURE 16.6.

From the Field Definition dialog box, you can add, remove, or rearrange fields.

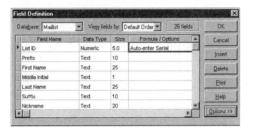

Adding New Fields

You may want to add new fields to your database so that you can track additional information. For example, suppose you find that many of your contacts have two fax numbers, not just one. You can add a second fax number field to your database to accommodate those extra numbers.

To Do: Adding a New Field

1. Choose Create, Field Definition to open the Field Definition dialog box (refer to Figure 16.6).

2. Click on the field before which you want to insert the new one.

3. Click the Insert button. A new, blank line appears on the field list.

4. Enter the name for the new field in the Field Name.

5. Click in the Data Type column. A drop-down list arrow appears. Open it and choose the data type you want (Text, Numeric, and so forth). The default type is Text. See "Understanding Field Types" later in this section for an explanation of the available types.

6. Enter the field length (in characters) in the Size field. The default is 10. If the field is to hold entries of varying lengths, such as addresses, make it plenty large. (I usually make address-containing fields 50 characters long.) If the field is to hold a precise number of characters or less, such as ZIP codes (9 digits plus one for the dash), enter the exact number.

> If you are creating a field that will hold numbers where leading zeros are significant (such as ZIP codes), make sure that you use a field type of Text, not Numeric. The Numeric type chops off leading zeros, so a ZIP code of 02345 would become 2345, which wouldn't be what you intended at all.

7. (Optional) If you want to set any options for the field, click the Options button to choose them. (See "Setting Field Options" later in this hour for more information.)

▲ 8. Click OK to close the Field Definition box.

Understanding Field Types

Each field has a data type, which determines what kind of data you can store in the field. The most common types are Text and Numeric, but you can use a variety of other types to build databases. Table 16.1 explains the types available.

TABLE 16.1. FIELD TYPES

Type	Purpose
Boolean	Stores a value of Yes, Y, or 1; or No, N, or 0. Useful for storing information that requires a simple yes or no, such as whether a contract has been signed.
Calculated	Stores the result of a formula. You create the formula when you define the field. You do not enter data into this field for each record; you let Approach calculate the field value based on the formula. For example, you could sum the values in two other fields for each record.
Date	Stores a date. Rejects entries that are not valid dates.
Memo	Stores a large quantity of text. This is useful for entering long notes about particular records. You cannot sort by this field, but you can search in it.
Numeric	Stores numbers only. Rejects any text entries. Use this field type for any numbers that you need to calculate or sort arithmetically.
PicturePlus	Stores a graphic or an object that comes from an application that supports OLE. Some common OLE objects are graphics, charts, sound files, and data ranges. You can use this field to store employee photographs, inventory pictures, and so on.
Text	Stores any characters—text, numbers, or symbols. This is the default field type.
Time	Stores a time. Rejects any entries that are not valid times.
Variable	Stores intermediate values for use in macros. Beginners will not use this field type.

Setting Default Values

When creating or editing a field, you can click the Options button to display additional controls, as shown in Figure 16.7. The ones on the Default Value tab enable you to specify a default value to be entered in each record for that field. You can override the default value whenever needed, but otherwise you can skip that field when doing data entry. This can save you a lot of time.

FIGURE 16.7.

You can set default values for specific fields.

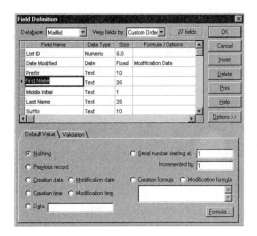

Choices include

- **Nothing**. This is the default. Reselect it to clear any other settings.

- **Previous Record**. Sets the value to the same as the preceding record in the database. For example, if the last person's ZIP code was 46240, the default for the next record you enter will be the same.

- **Creation Date** or **Modification Date**. Sets the value to the date when you either created or modified the record. (The date comes from your PC's internal clock.) This is useful in a Date Created or Date Modified field to keep track of how new the data in your database is.

- **Creation Time** or **Modification Time**. Same as above, except it's for time rather than date.

- **Data**. Sets the value to whatever data you enter in the Data text box next to this option. For example, if most of your clients are from Indiana, you could set the State field to a default value of "Indiana."

- **Serial number starting at**. Sets the field to automatically increment each record's value. This is useful for automatically numbering records in an ID number field. Use the Incremented by field to specify the increment interval (the default is 1).

16

- **Creation formula** or **Modification formula**. This sets the default calculated field. When you click on either choice, a formula builder appears. Casual users (like yourself) will probably never use this.

When you set any of these default value settings, the Formula/Options column in the list of fields shows your choice. For example, in Figure 16.7, the Date Modified field has Modification Date as its default entry.

Enabling Data Validation

When defining a field, you can specify "rules" that the entries must follow. This can help you to prevent data entry errors. For example, suppose your part numbers always begin with PT7 and a dash. If anyone enters a part number that does not begin with this, it is an error. You can set up data validation to display an error message and refuse the entry if it does not begin with PT7-.

Make your data validation selections on the Validation tab. Your choices are

- **Unique**. The value of the field must not already exist in another record (in this same field only).
- **From/To**. The value must be within a prescribed range, such as PT-7000 to PT-7999, for our earlier part number example.
- **Filled-in**. The field must not be left blank.
- **One of**. The value must match one of the values in a group that you specify. You must add the members of the group by typing each one and clicking Add.
- **Formula is True**. The value must cause a certain formula to be true. Click Formula and write the formula. For example, the formula "Number of Guests" >100 accepts only values greater than 100 in the Number of Guests field. Beginners will not use this one very often.
- **In Field**. The value must match the value in another field in the same database or in a joined database.

Deleting a Field

To delete a field from the Field Definition list, click to the left of the field you want to select. This selects the entire line in the list. Click the Delete button to delete it. If you see a warning, click OK.

Be careful not to delete a field that contains data you want to save! When you delete a field, you lose all the data in all your records for that field. You cannot undo a field deletion with the Edit, Undo command, and Approach saves your work immediately.

Reordering Fields

In the Field Definition dialog box, you can drag fields up and down on the list. Just select the field, position the mouse pointer over the field so that the pointer turns into a hand, and drag the field to a different position. You can also sort the fields by Field Name or Data Type with the View Fields By drop-down list.

However, rearranging the fields on the Field Definition list isn't the panacea that you might expect. It does not change the order of the fields on the worksheet or the form. You must change these manually in those views. Editing the layout in Worksheet and Form view is covered in Hour 19, but here's a preview:

- To reorder fields in Worksheet view, click the Design button to enter Design mode and then select and drag the column headings to the right or left to reorder the fields.
- To reorder fields in Form view, click the Design button and then the field you want to move. Position the mouse pointer over it until the pointer turns into a hand and drag the field where you want it. You may have to move other fields first to make room for it.

Changing the Field Name or Type

To rename a field, simply change its name (in the Field Name column) in the Field Definition dialog box. You can change a field's name at any time; the name is merely a label. All filters, reports, and so on that refer to the field will continue to refer to it. Renaming a field doesn't change its name in any of the views—only on the field list. You must change its name separately in each view in which it is used.

To change a field type, choose a different type from the Data Type drop-down list in the Field Definition dialog box. If you change the type for a field that has already been used to enter data, a warning box appears telling you that the field entries may be truncated or erased. That means that if you formerly stored text in a field and you change its type to Numeric, any text in any records for that field will be deleted.

16

You can also change the field size. Beware with this change, too—if you decrease the field size, any records that contain entries in that field will be truncated if they exceed the new length.

Starting with a Blank Database

The main difference between starting a database with a SmartMaster and starting with a blank is that the fields are not defined. You must create them all yourself.

When you start a blank database in Approach (File, New, Blank Database), the Field Definition dialog box appears automatically. You must create at least one field before Approach will let you proceed.

Create the fields for your database, one by one, as you learned in "Adding New Fields" earlier in this hour. The fields you create are placed on a very simple form on the Form tab. You can modify that form to make it more attractive; see Hour 19 for details.

Summary

In this hour, you learned how Approach works and how to enter data into its fields. You also learned how to modify field definitions and create your own fields. But what happens after you get all your data entered? You need to be able to manage it, of course. That means finding specific entries, sorting the list of records, and creating filters that display only the records you are interested in at a given moment. You'll learn how to do all that and more in Hour 17.

Q&A

Q Can I use data from a Microsoft Access database in Approach?

A Yes, but only the data tables. If you have any special forms, filters (queries), or reports designed in Access, they won't translate. To use Access data, choose File, Open and set the Files of Type to Microsoft Access Driver (*.MDB). A dialog box appears prompting you for the name and location of the Access file(s). Select it and click OK. Now a single folder appears in the file list: admin@ACCESS. Double-click that folder, and a list of the importable Access files appears. (The names may be funny-looking, such as D_My Documents_Filename, but you'll recognize them.) Double-click the database to import from, and a list of its tables appears. Double-click the table you want to open in Approach.

Q Why would I want to use a calculated field?

A If you need to display information on your form that depends on several different fields, a calculated field is the best way. For example, suppose you need to display the amount of money you have invested in a particular inventory item. You'll want to multiply the amount you paid per item by the number of items currently in stock. You can create a calculated field that multiplies these two other fields, and then create a report (see Hour 18) that sums all the results to provide a grand total of your inventory investment.

Q How do I put a picture or other object in a PicturePlus field?

A You can't do it directly; you have to use Windows's Cut-and-Paste. Open the image (or other object) in another application. For example, open a picture in a paint program. Select the object and copy it to the Clipboard. Then switch to your Approach database and click in the PicturePlus field for the record you are working on. Choose Edit, Paste to paste the picture into the field.

Q Why would I want to reorder the fields on the Field Definition list since they don't affect my worksheets and forms?

A Reordering on the Field Definition list puts the fields in a different order wherever a raw list of fields appears. One of these spots is the Add Field dialog box, which you use to add fields to your worksheet and form views (Worksheet, Add Field or Form, Add Field). In addition, whenever you create a new view (as you'll learn to do in Hour 19), the list of fields that you pick from appears in the order chosen from Field Definitions.

16

HOUR 17

Working with Approach Data

I have this filing cabinet in my office that is like the Bermuda Triangle—things go in, but they never come out. I stash papers in there thinking, "I'll need that someday," but my filing system isn't very good (try nonexistent!) so I can never find the scrap I need when I need it.

Approach can save you from such a plight. Once you put information into Approach, a variety of tools is available for extracting it. In this hour, you'll learn how to organize your data and how to quickly locate any individual bit of data when the moment is right.

Highlights of this hour include:

- Finding and replacing text
- Using Find by Example to filter data
- Using the Find Assistant to build filters
- Experimenting with Query by Box
- Sorting records
- Hiding certain records

What Does "Find" Mean?

In Approach, "find" means two different things. One is the same as in Word Pro and 1-2-3: You can find and replace text strings. To avoid confusion, I'll refer to this type of find as Find & Replace, even though you don't necessarily have to replace what you find.

The other, more powerful meaning of "find" in Approach is to filter out the records you don't want to see, so you're left with a subset of records tailored to your needs of the moment. Another word for it is *query*, which is the term that Microsoft Access uses for this operation. You can apply different Finds to your data at different times. For example, sometimes you might want to find only the records for people in a certain city; other times you might want to find only the records for male persons.

NEW TERM *Query:* A way of filtering out the records you want to work with. In Approach, the term query is not used except in a very specialized way; *find* is the general term that refers to querying.

Finding and Replacing Text

Approach's Find & Replace Text feature works a lot like the same feature in 1-2-3. You specify the text to find (and what to replace it with, if applicable), and it goes to work.

To Do: Finding and Replacing Text

1. Make sure you are in Browse mode. It is not available in other modes.
2. If you want to search only in certain records or fields, select them. (This is easiest to do in Worksheet view.)
2. Choose Edit, Find & Replace Text. The Find & Replace Text dialog box appears (see Figure 17.1).

FIGURE 17.1.

Enter your text to find (and text to replace if needed).

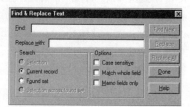

3. Enter the text string to find in the Find text box.
4. (Optional) If you are going to replace it with something, enter the replacement in the Replace With text box.

▼

5. Specify where to search. The options are different when searching in Form view than in Worksheet view:

   - In Worksheet view, your choices are Selection or Entire Worksheet.

   - In Form view, your choices are Selection, Current Record, Found Set, or Selection Across Found Set. (Not all of these options may be available; if you did not select a field in step 2, you will have only Current Record and Found Set to choose from.)

NEW TERM *Found Set:* The complete set of records that is currently displayed. If you have not done any filtering, or finding by form or with the Find Assistant, then this "found set" is the same as the complete set of records.

Selection Across Found Set: The currently selected field, in all records in the found set. For example, if you have eight records in the found set, and you have selected the NAME field, it searches only in the name field, but in all eight records.

6. Choose any of the check box options: Case sensitive, Match whole field, or Memo fields only.

7. Click Find Next to find the first instance. The dialog box changes so that only the four action buttons appear: Find Next, Replace, Replace All, and Close.

8. When a found instance appears, click Find Next to find the next one or Replace to replace it and move to the next one.

9. Repeat step 8 until you have found (or replaced) what you needed and then click Done. Or keep finding and replacing until a dialog box appears saying there are no more instances; click OK.

▲

Replace All is available, but be careful with it, as mentioned earlier in the book; you might end up making replacements that you did not intend.

Using Find to Create Data Filters

This kind of finding is different from what you just did. It finds whole groups of records that match certain criteria. You can find all the records that have Indiana in the State field. You can use multiple criteria at once; for example, find all records where the name prefix is Ms. AND ZIP Code of 46250.

17

There are two ways to create filters, or queries, in Approach. One is to find by example. This is easy as well as useful when your criteria are simple. The other, more powerful way is to use the Find Assistant. We'll look at both ways in this hour.

Finding by Example

To find using the form or worksheet, you create an example that the Find action should match. This is a simple version of what some other database programs (including Microsoft Access) call *Query by Example*, or QBE. It then displays all the records that match the example.

To Do: Finding Using the Form or Worksheet

1. Make sure you are in Browse mode.
2. Click the Find button on the Action bar or press Ctrl+F. The Action bar changes to include special command buttons, and the form or worksheet clears, so you can enter your criteria. See Figure 17.2.

FIGURE 17.2.

When finding by example, the Action bar provides extra tools.

Action bar ⎯

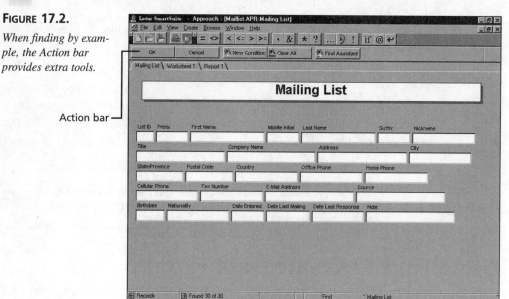

3. Enter the example conditions into any of the fields. For example, if you want to find all records with a prefix of Mr. (that is, all the male names), enter "Mr." in the Prefix field. You can also use the SmartIcons to insert operators, as shown in Table 17.1.

4. (Optional) If you want to add another set of conditions, click the New Condition button and enter it. When there are multiple sets of conditions, they are treated as an "OR" operation, and the Find operation finds all records that match either one.

> If you make a mistake, click the Clear All button. If you realize that the Find you want to do is too complicated to be expressed as a Find by Example, click the Find Assistant button and jump to the following section in this book.

5. Click OK to perform the Find. The set of displayed records changes to only the ones that match your conditions. (The search is not case-sensitive.) Notice the drop-down list in the Action bar now reports: <Current Find/Sort>. If no records are found, a dialog box appears letting you know.

6. To return to seeing all records, open the drop-down list on the Action bar and choose All Records.

17

TABLE 17.1. SMARTICON OPERATORS FOR FINDING BY EXAMPLE

This operator	Specifies
=	Equal to (Use this alone to find all blank records.)
<>	Not equal to (Use this alone to find all non-blank records.)
<	Less than
<=	Less than or equal to
>	Greater than
>=	Greater than or equal to
,	OR conditions within a field
&	AND conditions within a field
*	Wildcard for any number of characters
?	Wildcard for one character

continues

TABLE 17.1. CONTINUED

This operator	Specifies
[⋯]	Range of values (for example, A…D)
[👂]	Sounds like
[!]	Case-sensitive text find
[if]	Compound expressions
[@]	Function or field reference indicator used with another operator, such as in =@Today(). You can't use the @ (at sign) within If statements.

It's actually easier to construct finds with these operators than it might appear. Table 17.2 shows some examples.

TABLE 17.2. OPERATOR EXAMPLES FOR FIND BY EXAMPLE

To find in a field	Use this in that field
Cat or Dog	Cat, Dog
Cat and Dog	Cat&Dog
Any word beginning with "Th"	Th*
Any word ending with "on"	*on
Finds Smythe, Smyth, Smith	~Smith
"Main" but not "main"	!Main
From 46000 to 47000	46000…47000
Numbers greater than or equal to 3	>=3

Finding Using the Find Assistant

The Find Assistant is very powerful and flexible. It walks you through a series of dialog boxes to build exactly the criteria you want for your Find operation. Many people prefer to use it all the time, instead of the Find by Example, but you will surely want to use it when creating more complex finds.

To Do: Finding with Find Assistant

To Do ▼

1. Choose Browse, Find, Find Assistant (in Form view), or Worksheet, Find, Find Assistant (in Worksheet view). Or, from either view, press Ctrl+I. The Find/Sort Assistant dialog box appears.

2. On the first tab (Find Type), choose a type of find to do. For this example, we'll use Basic Find, but, for future reference, your other choices are:

   - *Find Duplicate Records.* Finds all records that *do not* have a unique value in the specified field(s).

   - *Find Distinct Records.* Finds all records that *do* have a unique value in the specified field(s).

   - *Find the Top or Lowest Values.* Finds all records that have the highest or lowest values in a specified field. (For example, it could find the top 10 or bottom 10 sales performers.) You can also find the top or bottom percent.

   - *Find Using Query by Box.* An advanced find which uses Approach's Query by Box feature to set up sophisticated criteria. You'll learn about Query by Box later in this hour.

The other three tabs in the dialog box change depending on your selection in step 2. Because the procedures are different for each type, we'll stick with the Basic Find here. You can explore the other find types on your own.

3. Click the Next button to move on to the next tab (Condition 1).

4. Choose a field and an operator, and enter the value you want for it. For example, in Figure 17.3, the field chosen is City, and the operator chosen is "Is not equal to." The value is Indianapolis. This will find only the records where City is not Indianapolis.

5. (Optional) If you want to specify alternate values, enter them in the Values column. For example, to include not only Indianapolis but also Noblesville in the found set, I would add Noblesville to the Values column in Figure 17.3.

6. (Optional) To set up additional criteria, click the Find on Another Field button and enter other criteria. This adds a Condition 2 tab to the dialog box. Return to step 4 to fill it out.

▼

17

FIGURE 17.3.

Specify a field, an operator, and a value for your Find operation.

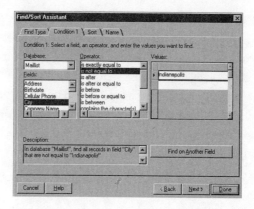

If you use the Condition 2 tab, make sure you select the appropriate option button on it: Find Fewer Records (AND) or Find More Records (OR). This determines how the new condition relates to the first one.

7. Click Next to move to the Sort tab. On this tab, you can specify the order in which the found records will appear. (This is optional; if you don't need this, skip to step 9.)

8. On the Fields list, click the field that you want to sort by, and then click the >>Add>> button. You can choose additional fields to sort by (in the event of a "tie" in the first field) by repeating with other fields. In Figure 17.4, for example, the list is being sorted by ZIP code.

FIGURE 17.4.

You can sort your found records by any field, in either ascending or descending order.

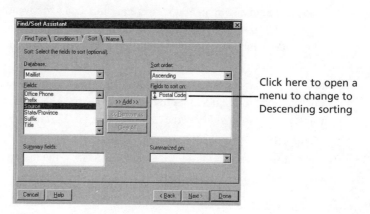

Click here to open a menu to change to Descending sorting

9. The default sort is Ascending (A to Z). To switch to Descending (Z to A), click the little arrow symbol next to the chosen field to open a shortcut menu and select Descending.

10. Click Next to go on to the Name tab.

11. (Optional) If you want to save this Find to be used again in the future, click the Named Find/Sort check box and type a name in the text box next to it.

12. Click Done. The found, sorted records appear.

13. To remove the Find and go back to seeing all records, choose All Records from the drop-down list on the Action bar.

▲

> If you name the Find, that name appears in the Action bar's drop-down list, and you can reselect it at any time.

17

Creating a Query by Box

A Query by Box is the most sophisticated kind of find that you can do in Approach. People who have lots of database experience (like programmers) love this method because it lets them write their query in a language that they are familiar with. I don't recommend it for beginners, but I want to show you that it's here, just in case you ever want to try it.

To Do: Creating a Query by Box

▼ To Do

1. Start a find with the Find Assistant, as you learned in the previous section, but choose Query by Box as the find type. Click Next to move to the Query by Box tab.

2. On the Query by Box tab, choose the field and operator from the drop-down lists and enter a value in the text box.

3. To add a second criterion, click the AND or OR button and repeat step 2. Enter as many criteria as you need. Click Next.

▲   4. Finish the Find Assistant normally.

What makes Query by Box so much more powerful? It has flexibility that the other methods don't have. You can, for example, enter a complex set of ANDs and ORs, like the one shown in Figure 17.5. This query finds all records that have the City value of Indianapolis, plus all the records that have the City value of Carmel and also a ZIP code of 46240, except those where the Street address contains "Main Street." Try doing that with a regular Find!

FIGURE 17.5.

Nested criteria like this are possible only with Query by Box.

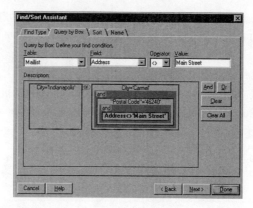

Sorting Records

You already saw how to sort records when you were finding them with the Find Assistant, so this section may be somewhat anticlimactic. But yes, you can also sort records without filtering them with Find. You might, for example, want to sort your database by last name to make it easier to browse through and look up names or by ZIP code to prepare for a bulk mailing.

To sort on a particular field, display Worksheet view and select the column on which you want to sort. Then click the Sort Ascending or Sort Descending SmartIcon, or choose Worksheet, Sort, Ascending or Worksheet, Sort, Descending. You can also use the Ascending Sort or Descending Sort SmartIcons.

To build a more complex sort with more than one field, follow these steps.

To Do: Defining a Sort

1. In Worksheet view, choose Worksheet, Sort, Define, or in Form view, choose Browse, Sort Define. The Sort dialog box appears.
2. Click the primary field to sort by and click the >>Add>> button to transfer that field name to the Fields to Sort On list. See Figure 17.6.

FIGURE 17.6.

Choose fields to sort by, just as you did with the Find Assistant earlier in this hour.

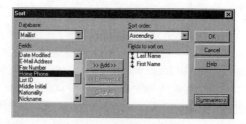

3. Choose additional fields if needed and move them over with the >>Add>> button, too. These fields are used for sorting only in the event of a tie in the primary sort field. For example, if the primary sort is Last Name, the secondary sort field comes into play only if two people have the same last name.

4. To change between Ascending and Descending, click the icon next to the chosen field(s) in the Fields to Sort On list, just as you did in the Find Assistant.

5. Click OK. The records are sorted.

As mentioned earlier, once you sort the records, there's no way to put them back the way you had them before. If the original entry order is important, create an additional field and enter sequential numbers for each field. That way, you can sort on that field to put the records back in their original order when needed.

17

Summary

In this hour, you learned how to sort and find records so you never need to scramble to find a particular record when you need it. You learned a variety of ways to find information, and how to save the Find filters you create so you can use them again. In the next hour, we'll explore Approach's charting and reporting capabilities so you can reduce your reams of complicated data to friendly, easy-to-understand reports and charts that you can present with confidence to any audience.

Q&A

Q Can I perform one Find on top of another to further narrow down the list of records?

A No. When you issue a new Find, the old one is canceled. You can, however, create a new Find that includes many conditions, including all of the conditions of the other Find you wanted to apply.

Q I'm a Microsoft Access user, and I'm confused about the terms "find," "filter," and "query." They mean different things in Access than they seem to mean in Approach.

A You're right, but don't let it give you a headache. In Access, these are three separate activities. "Find" in Access refers only to finding and replacing text. Access also has something called Filtering, which is like Approach's Find by Example. Queries in Access are sort of like the finds you perform in Approach with the Find Assistant.

Q In Form view, my Browse menu is missing so I can't access the Find command on the menu.

A You are in Design mode. Click the Browse button, and your Browse menu will reappear.

Q How can I access my named Finds that I've saved?

A If you want to edit one, choose it from the first tab of the Find Assistant. To run a named Find, choose it from the drop-down list on the Action bar or choose Create, Named Find/Sort and make your selection from a list.

HOUR 18

Creating Reports and Charts

While your database is probably a private affair that only a few people will work with, you will sometimes need to share selected information from it with a wider audience. That's where reports and charts come in. You can generate exactly the right printout to convey a message to your audience, complete with attractive formatting and graphics.

Highlights of this hour include:

- Understanding how Approach treats reports and charts
- Creating a report
- Saving and printing reports
- Customizing a report
- Creating a chart

Understanding Reports

If you have worked with other database programs, such as Microsoft Access, you may be a bit surprised at Approach's reports. In Approach, a report is simply a view. It doesn't have its own filtering and sorting capabilities; instead, it uses whatever filtering and sorting is already in place.

You can, however, specify which fields appear in a report; you can use a subset of your total field list. For example, in Figure 18.1, only certain fields are shown, not every field in the Mailing List database.

 Report: An Approach view that's designed to be printed. Reports arrange and filter your data in an attractive, easy-to-read format.

FIGURE 18.1.

A sample report in Approach.

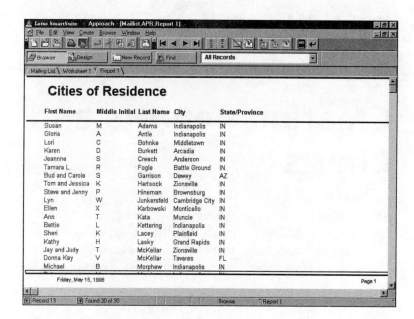

Reports, like other views, have two modes—Browse and Design. In Browse mode, you can preview the report onscreen. In Design mode, you can modify the report. (You'll learn how to modify a report later in this hour.)

Creating a Simple Report

Before you create a report, think a moment about what you want it to contain. Here are the decisions you need to make:

- What fields will it contain?
- What records will it show?
- Who is the audience for this report?

All of these answers will help you create the report correctly the first time in Approach, so you do not have to edit the report later.

You can create reports that include grouping and subtotals, but let's first look at a very basic report; we'll tackle the more specialized ones afterwards.

To Do: Creating a Report

1. Choose Create, Report. The Report Assistant opens.
2. On the Step 1 Layout tab (see Figure 18.2), enter a title for the report. (Report 1 is the default, or whatever the next available number is, but you really ought to change it to something more descriptive.)

FIGURE 18.2.

Start by naming the report and choosing its layout and style.

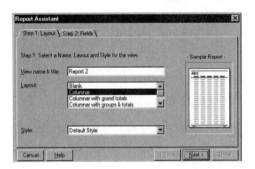

18

3. Choose a layout from the Layout list. For this example, choose Columnar, which is the layout shown in Figure 18.1. I'll explain the other layouts later.
4. Open the Style drop-down list and choose a style. The sample changes to show what each style looks like.

> You can't really get a good feel for the styles available from that little sample in the dialog box. You'll need to experiment with a few of them to find out which you like best.

▼   5. Click Next to move to the next tab, which is Step 2: Fields. See Figure 18.3.

FIGURE 18.3.

Next, choose the fields to be included in the report.

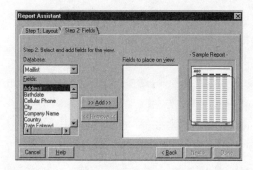

6. Click the first field you want on the report and then the Add button to move it to the Fields to Place on View list. Repeat for each field you want, in the order you want them to appear. If you get the order wrong, you must remove the fields and add them again; you can't rearrange field order.

7. Click Done. The report appears in Design mode. You can tell immediately that it's Design mode because of the grid of dots behind the report.

8. To view the report, click the Browse button on the Action bar to switch to Browse mode. (You'll learn how to modify the report in Design mode later in this hour.)

Using Other Report Layouts

When you're on Step 1 of the Report Assistant, some of the report layouts you can choose come with additional steps. Each additional step is an extra tab in the dialog box. For example, choosing Columnar with Groups & Totals causes two extra tabs to appear: Step 3: Groups and Step 4: Totals. Let's look at some of these alternate layouts and what you need to enter for them.

Columnar with Grand Totals

This report is suitable for situations where you need to perform some math operation on at least one field's data and report the result. For example, you could count the number of records, sum all the values in a particular field, or calculate the average value of a field.

When you choose this report type, a Grand Totals tab appears in the Report Assistant dialog box (see Figure 18.4). To use it, choose a field on the Fields list and click Add to move it to the Summary Fields list. Then open the Calculate the drop-down list and choose the math operation to use. Repeat with additional fields if needed.

FIGURE 18.4.

Create a grand-total summary on a columnar report.

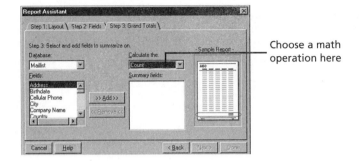

Choose a math operation here

Summary Only

This report uses the same controls on its extra tab, Step 3: Summary, which you saw in Figure 18.4. The only difference is that this report presents the summary information only, not the individual records.

Columnar with Groups and Totals

This report has all the same attributes as the Columnar with Grand Totals report, except it has an extra feature. You can group records by the values in certain fields. This is sort of like sorting, except all records with the same value for a particular field are pulled out separately in a group.

To set this up, you use the Step 3: Group tab. Choose a field to group by and click Add to move it over to the Group Fields list. If necessary, open the Group By drop-down list and choose how the grouping should occur. Default groups only when the entire value of the field is the same, but you can choose 1st Character, 1st 2 Characters, and so on, to be less specific.

If View, Show Panel Labels is checked, you can't see what you grouped by. When you use Print or Print Preview, the group field shows up. For example, suppose you group by State. You can see all the information, and it is indeed grouped by State, but the report onscreen does not show the State— it shows the word "Body." When you print, Indiana, Michigan, and so forth, print where the word Body was onscreen so you can see what governed the group. If View, Show Panel Labels is unchecked, then you can see what you grouped by onscreen, also.

18

Printing a Report

To print a report, make sure the report's view is displayed. Then choose File, Print or click the Print SmartIcon. The Print dialog box appears. Print normally, as you learned to do in Hour 3.

 The Print Preview feature (File, Print Preview) is not terribly useful for reports because it merely shows you the report in its normal Browse mode. That's because what you see on the report's tab in Approach is more or less what you get when you print.

By default, Approach prints a header and footer on each report. The header contains the report title and the column headings; the footer contains the page number and the date. You can change these when you modify the report, as explained in the following section.

Modifying a Report

In Design mode, you can make changes to your report's structure and formatting. These changes can include font choices, heading and column positioning, and more.

 You cannot modify groupings or calculations on your report once you've created it. If you need to make this kind of change, you must delete the report and re-create it with the Report Assistant.

In Design mode, each element of your report is a text box, with selection handles like the graphics and charts you worked with in Word Pro and 1-2-3. Each column is a separate text box, as are the header and the footer (see Figure 18.5). You can drag elements around on the grid, just as you would move a graphic in Word Pro (see Hour 9). To drag, position the mouse pointer over the box, but not on a selection handle, so that the pointer looks like a hand. To resize a box, drag a handle.

 In a report that contains grouping, Design mode will be very cluttered with codes for groupings. You may not be able to move columns around as freely as with a plainer report like the one in Figure 18.5.

FIGURE 18.5.

Each text block is in its own box, which can be moved or resized.

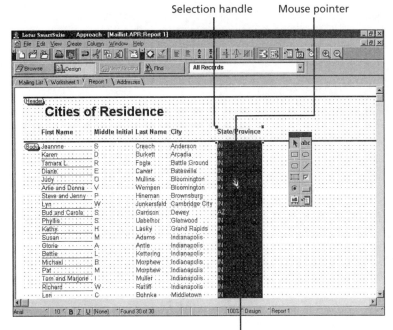

Selected box is highlighted (white on black)

18

Changing the Header and Footer

The header contains the report title. It appears on the top of every page if your report runs more than one page. To turn the header on or off, choose Report, Add Header to remove the check mark from beside that command. You can turn the footer off the same way: Report, Add Footer.

If you do not see a Report menu, it's because some individual element of the report is selected, and a menu for modifying it appears instead. To get the Report menu back, click on the report's outside border to select the report as a whole.

To modify the header, click inside its box and edit normally. You can change the text that appears there, as well as format it. (See the following section for text formatting hints.)

To modify the footer, scroll to the bottom of the report and edit in the footer's box.

You can add special codes to the header and footer, such as the current date, time, or page number. (Actually, the date and page number already appear in the footer by default, but you might want to delete them from the footer and place them in the header instead.)

To Do: Adding a Code to a Header or Footer

1. Select either the header or the footer box.

2. Choose Panel, Insert, and then the item you want to insert (Today's Date, Current Time, or Page Number). The item appears in its own, new text box.

3. Drag the new box around within the header or footer to the exact position you want.

> In Design mode for a report, there are SmartIcons on the toolbar for inserting the date and inserting the time.

To delete an element from the header or footer, click on it and press Delete.

Changing the Fonts and Formatting

You can choose from the full array of installed Windows fonts for your reports. Just select the text you want to change and use the controls on the status bar to change it, just like you do in Word Pro and 1-2-3. (Refer back to Hour 6 if you need help.)

Adding and Removing Fields

You can add or remove fields from a report without re-creating it. To remove a field, click on it to select it and press Delete.

Adding a field is somewhat more involved, but it's not too bad. Click the Add Field SmartIcon or choose Report, Add Field. The Add Field box appears, showing a list of fields. Drag a field out of that box and onto your report layout. As your cursor moves out of the Add Field Box, a thick vertical line appears, showing where the new field will be placed (see Figure 18.6). Position the line where you want the field and release the mouse button. Approach creates a column for it.

FIGURE **18.6.**

*To add a field to the
report, drag it out of
the Add Field box.*

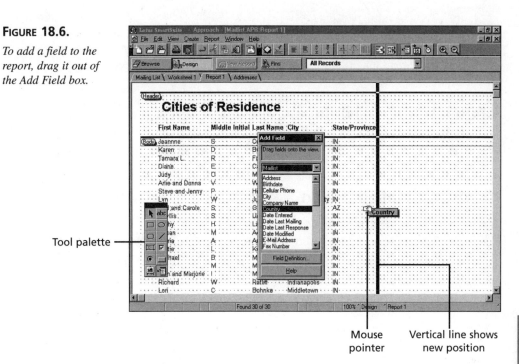

FIGURE **18.6.**

*To add a field to the
report, drag it out of
the Add Field box.*

Tool palette

Mouse
pointer

Vertical line shows
new position

18

Drawing on a Report

You may have noticed the floating tool palette in Design mode, pointed out in Figure
18.6. Some of the buttons on this palette are drawing tools that you can use to draw simple lines and shapes on the header or footer area of the report. Simply click on the shape
you want to draw and drag the mouse on the report to draw the shape.

Rectangle; hold down Shift as you draw for a square.

Oval; hold down Shift as you draw for a circle.

Rounded rectangle; hold down Shift as you draw for a rounded square.

Line; hold down Shift as you draw for a perfectly vertical or horizontal line.

Other Report Modifications

There are other things you can do to a report, but they're a little more technical and complicated than a beginner would want to get into. Some of the other buttons on the tool

palette, for example, let you place buttons on the report that you can attach scripts to, and let you add PicturePlus fields to your report. Refer to the online documentation that came with SmartSuite (Start, Programs, Lotus SmartSuite, LotusDoc Online).

Creating a Chart

As you learned in Hour 14, a chart can help make sense of a large mass of data. If you have one or more fields in your database that contain numbers, you might create a chart to help other people (or yourself!) understand the impact of the numbers.

To Do: Creating a Chart

1. Choose Create, Chart. The Chart Assistant opens.

2. Type a name for the chart in the View Name & Title text box.

3. Choose a chart type from the Layout drop-down list. (You should already be familiar with the various chart types from Hour 14.) For this example, choose Bar Chart.

4. Choose a style (2D or 3D) from the Style drop-down list. Click Next to go to the next tab.

   The next tabs you work with depend on the chart type you select. A pie chart, for example, has different information you must fill in than a bar chart. In these steps, we'll be working with the bar chart; if you are creating some other kind of chart, work on your own from here.

5. On the Step 2: X-Axis tab, choose the field that should be expressed on the X axis (horizontal) of the bar chart. For example, if you want to show the sales for various salespeople, you might choose your Salesperson field for this.

6. On the Step 3: Y-Axis tab, choose the field that should be expressed on the Y axis (vertical). You can choose more than one field here for more than one set of bars. For example, you might choose January Sales, February Sales, and March Sales. For each field you choose, make sure that the Chart the drop-down list is set to Sum.

7. Click Done. (We're ignoring that last tab in the dialog box because it's not needed for most charts.) Your chart appears, as shown in Figure 18.7.

FIGURE 18.7.

A sample bar chart created from Approach data.

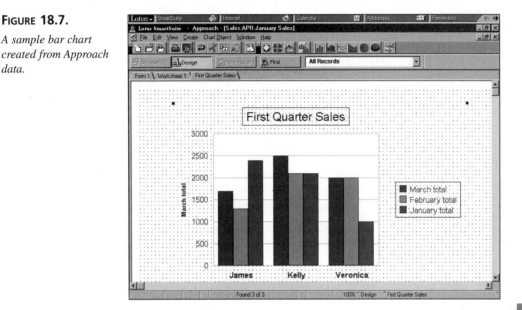

If the individual values do not appear on the X axis (for example, if the salespeople names did not appear in Figure 18.7), right-click the chart and choose Axes & Grids, X Axis & Grid. In the InfoBox that appears, click the Labels tab and make sure there is a check mark in the Show Labels Every check box.

18

Modifying a Chart

Just like in 1-2-3, there is a lot you can do to change a chart's appearance. Once you've created the chart in Approach (which is somewhat different from creating one in 1-2-3), you use most of the same procedures to modify it that you learned in the 1-2-3 charting chapter (Hour 14). Here's a sampling of what you can do:

- Right-click the chart and choose the element that you want to format from the shortcut menu. For example, to format an axis, choose Axes & Grids. An InfoBox appears showing all the options you can set for that particular element.
- Use the SmartIcons that appear above the chart to change its type, just like in 1-2-3.
- When you have clicked on the chart, a Chart Object menu is available on the menu bar. You can use it to select various parts of the chart for editing.

- Click the outside border of the chart area to change the Chart Object menu to a Chart menu. On this menu you can choose Delete Chart to delete it or Duplicate Chart to create another copy you can modify.
- You can add a data table on the chart's tab by choosing Chart Object, Table, and marking the Show Data Table check box on the Options tab of the InfoBox.

Charts are permanently in Design mode; they can't be switched to Browse. You can print right from Design mode. You can also turn off the display of the grid dots if you find them distracting; choose View, Show Grid to remove the check mark from that command.

Summary

In this hour, you learned how to create and modify reports and charts, two excellent tools for summarizing and sharing your database information. You can create any of several report and chart types now, as well as add formatting to dress up the results. In the next hour, you'll conclude your look at Approach by learning how to modify your forms and worksheets, and how to join two or more databases together.

Q&A

Q I've really screwed up my report by trying to format it. How can I get it back to the way it was?

A The easiest way is usually to delete the report and re-create it using the Report Assistant. To delete the report, choose Report, Delete Report.

Q It looks like the column labels are part of the header on the report design. Are they?

A No, the text boxes are overlapping. The text box for each column extends into the header area by an inch or so. You can resize the header or move the columns if this bothers you, but it prints just fine.

Q When I try to draw on a report with those drawing tools, it places a new field on the form instead. What am I doing wrong?

A You are probably trying to draw in the data area. You can draw only in the header and footer. When you draw in the data area, Approach assumes you are trying to insert a new field into the report, and it places the first field on the Field List, even if the Field List is not open.

Q I just can't get the hang of charting in Approach. Any suggestions?

A Personally, I like the charting capabilities in 1-2-3 a lot better than those in Approach. If I have a lot of charting to do, I copy the data from Worksheet view in Approach to the Clipboard and then paste it into a 1-2-3 worksheet. Then I create my charts from within 1-2-3.

18

HOUR 19

Advanced Approach

In this final hour on Approach, you'll learn about some "extras" that can make your work in Approach more productive. We'll start by modifying some views, which is a natural extension of the report and chart modifications you did at the end of the last hour. Then we'll move on to mail merges and joining multiple databases to round it out.

Highlights of this hour include:

- Modifying a worksheet
- Modifying a data entry form
- Creating additional views
- Printing form letters
- Joining databases

Modifying Approach Views

As you saw in the last hour, you can modify a report or chart in Design mode. You can do the same thing to worksheet and data entry forms. For example, you might want to rearrange the columns on your worksheet or add a new field that you have created.

When you create a new field in an existing database, it isn't automatically added to any of your views. You must add it manually to each view.

To modify any view (worksheets and forms included), click the Design button on the Action bar. Use the procedures in the following sections to modify the view.

Keep in mind that a view does not necessarily represent the database content. A particular view may not show every available field and may show the fields in a radically different order than they appear on the Field List. A view is just...well, a view.

Modifying Worksheets

In Worksheet view, the data appears in a table, just like on a spreadsheet. The main modifications you can perform are to add, remove, resize, and reorganize the columns.

- To add a column (that is, a field), display the Add Field dialog box (by clicking the Add Field SmartIcon or choosing Worksheet, Add Field). Drag the field name from that box onto the worksheet. A thick vertical line shows where it will go. Release the mouse button to drop it.

- To delete a column from the worksheet, right-click on it and choose Cut. This removes the column from this view, but the field it refers to remains part of the database and may appear in other views.

- To move a column, select the column and drag its heading to the right or left (your mouse pointer will look like a hand), to a new spot. You can select and drag multiple columns at once.

- To resize a column, position the mouse pointer at the right edge of the column heading and drag, just like on a 1-2-3 spreadsheet.

- To rename a column (which does not, by the way, rename the actual field in the Field List), right-click the column heading and choose Edit Column Label.

Modifying Data Entry Forms

When you work with a form in Design mode, it has a grid of dots, just like when you modified a report in Hour 18. Each element appears in its own box, and you can drag a box around (by dragging when the mouse pointer looks like a hand) or resize it (by dragging one of the selection handles). You have seen this same activity in Word Pro and 1-2-3, too, so it should be familiar by now.

Here are some activities that you should have no problem with:

- To add a field, open the Add Field dialog box (click the Add Field SmartIcon or choose Form, Add Field) and drag the field onto the form.

- To remove a field, click it to select it and press the Delete key on the keyboard.

- To move a field, drag it (when the mouse pointer is a hand) to a new position.

- To resize a field, drag one of its selection handles.

- To add graphic lines and shapes, use the drawing tools in the Tool Palette, as you learned in Hour 18.

- To edit the form title, click the title's box and then click on the title to move the insertion point into the text. Then edit normally.

And now, a few extra procedures that might not be quite so familiar.

Changing the Tab Order

By default, when you press Tab as you are entering records in Form view, the Tab key moves you from left to right and top to bottom, kind of like when you type in a word processor. You might want to change the tab order to skip certain fields that you hardly ever change or to match the order that fields appear on a hard copy sheet that you are referring to.

To Do: Modifying the Tab Order

1. Choose View, Show Tab Order. Boxes appear next to each field that show the tab order (see Figure 19.1).

2. Change the number(s) any box(es) to change the tab order for them. If you clear a box, Approach automatically assigns the last number to it, and renumbers all others.

19

> When you change a number, Approach attempts to compensate by renumbering other boxes. For example, if you change box 4 to 5, it moves the old box 5 into box 4. This may not be what you intended. Check the numbering carefully, and modify as needed.

▲   3. Choose View, Tab Order again to turn off the display of the numbers.

FIGURE 19.1.

View the tab order boxes and then change the numbers in them if needed.

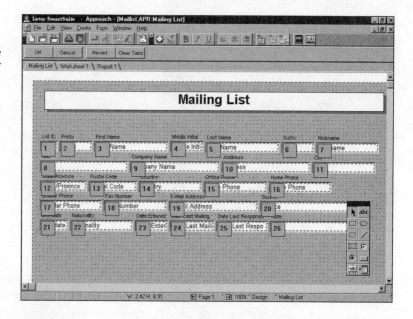

Adding Extra Labels

You might want to add extra labels to your form to help other people make more sense of it. For example, if you want them to enter the ZIP+4 postal code whenever it is available, you might add a label to that effect next to the Postal Code field.

To add an extra label, you need to create a text box. The Text Box tool (abc) is in the floating tool palette, which you first encountered in Hour 18.

To Do: Creating a Textbox

1. Click the Text Box tool on the tool palette. Your mouse cursor turns into a crosshair with "abc" next to it.

2. Drag to draw the text box where you want it. (You may want to move some fields around beforehand so there is room.)

3. When you release the mouse button, an insertion point appears in the new text box. Type your text.

4. Click outside the text box to finalize your text. If you need to edit the text later, just click inside the box again.

Adding Extra Pages

If you have more fields than will fit on the screen at once, you have two choices:

- You can scroll down and create more fields below the ones that fit onscreen. Your user will have to scroll in order to use them.

- You can create extra pages for the form. Your user will have to go to the next page during data entry to fill them in.

Generally, if you have just a few fields extra, it's better to just tack them onto the bottom, and let the user scroll. But if you have a whole series of fields that are seldom used, a second page for them might make sense. For example, suppose you primarily store business contacts in your database, but sometimes you want to enter separate information for that person's personal contacts too. You might divide the fields up into a Personal page and a Business page, each with the fields appropriate to its theme.

To add a page to your form, choose Form, Add Page. The new page appears (blank). Add any fields to it by dragging them from the Add Field dialog box (Form, Add Field). You might want to repeat certain fields from Page 1 on the second page, such as the person's name, so your user will not get confused during data entry.

To remove a page from the form, display that page and choose Form, Delete Page.

As the user is using the form, he can go to the next page with Page Down and the previous page with Page Up.

When a form has more than one page, a page number indicator appears on the status bar. You can click the indicator to open a pop-up list of pages and click on the page number you want to go to.

Creating Additional Views

By default, each database has one worksheet and one form, but you can have more of either, as your needs dictate. For example, perhaps you want two data entry forms: one for clerks to use to enter new customers' contact information and one for salespeople to use to enter information about particular products that the customers have ordered. Or perhaps you want one worksheet that contains all your fields and another that shows only the fields you use most often.

If you want to store information about both customers and products, you might consider creating separate databases and joining them, as you'll learn at the end of this hour. It is difficult to store information about radically different subjects, like customers and products, in the same database table.

You can either create a new view from scratch or you can duplicate an existing view and make changes to the copy. To duplicate a view, display that view (in Design mode) and choose Form, Duplicate Form or Worksheet, Duplicate Worksheet.

> When you duplicate a view, the copy is called Copy of [name]. You can change the name by double-clicking its tab and typing a new name.

To create a view from scratch, open the Create menu and choose the type of view you want to create (Worksheet, Form, or some other view type). When you do, an Assistant appears to walk you through choosing the fields and other options for your new view. You have worked with such assistants again and again in Approach and other SmartSuite products; just fill in the blanks provided.

To delete a view, display the view in Design mode and choose Form, Delete Form or Worksheet, Delete Worksheet.

Printing Form Letters

As you will learn in Hour 23, you can do a great mail merge with Word Pro, pulling data from Word Pro, Approach, 1-2-3, or Organizer. But you can also do a self-contained mail merge right from Approach, without opening any of those other programs.

To Do: Merging Self-contained Mail from Approach

1. Choose Create, Form Letters. The Form Letters Assistant appears.
2. Fill in the information requested on each tab. (This should be old hat for you by now.) The information it asks for includes:

   Layout. Choose the letter style (Block, Modified Block, Letterhead, or Personal). If you use Letterhead or Personal, some of the steps below do not appear. For example, if you are using Letterhead, it assumes you have your own stationery and does not prompt for a From address.

   From. If prompted for this, type your return address or choose None.

   To. Choose the fields from your database, one by one, and move them to the grid by clicking Add. This is normally a no-brainer: First Name, Last Name, Address, City, State, and Postal Code. See Figure 19.2.

FIGURE **19.2.**

Choose the fields for the address.

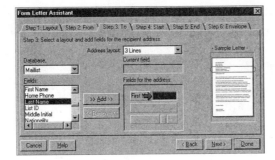

Start. Choose the salutation you want to use and which fields to include in it (for example, Dear {First Name} or Dear {Prefix} {Last Name}.

End. Enter your closing, or choose None.

Envelope. Set up specifications for printing matching envelopes or choose Do not create envelopes.

3. Click Done. Approach creates the letter, in its own view, and it appears in Design mode (see Figure 19.3.).

FIGURE **19.3.**

All the field codes are correctly entered; now it's up to you to create the letter body.

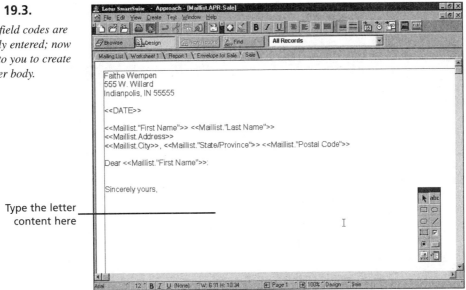

Type the letter content here

19

▼   4. Type the letter content.

5. When you are finished, click Browse. The letter displays with a real record in it. The letter is just like any other tabbed view now; you can move among records like you do in Form view.

6. (Optional) If you do not want to print letters for every record in your database, apply a Find to narrow down only the ones you want, as you learned in Hour 17.

7. Choose File, Print. The Print dialog box appears.

8. Choose All Records to print all displayed records or Current Record to print only the displayed record. (Or you can do a Find to filter the group of records, as you learned earlier.)

9. Click Print. The letter(s) print.

10. If you chose to create envelopes, a separate view was created for envelopes. Click
▲   its tab and change to Browse mode if needed. Print the envelopes by repeating
     steps 7 through 9.

> You can also print mailing labels and envelopes from the Create menu in Approach.

Joining Databases

If you are accustomed to multitable databases like those in Microsoft Access, you may wonder how to create databases with more than one set of fields. The answer is that you create two separate databases and join them together. When two or more databases are joined, you can use fields from either or both in your views. For example, you might create one database that contains a list of types of antiques, such as toys, dinnerware, books, and so on. You could join this database with one that tracks your own personal collection and categorize each of your holdings using one of those types.

Why Join Databases?

Database experts will tell you that you should use multiple tables (and therefore, in Approach, multiple databases) to organize all but the simplest of data. But how can you make such decisions in an informed way? To do that, you'll need to learn a little bit about database normalization.

When a database (or a group of databases) suffers from poor organization, information is duplicated in one or more fields, creating a greater potential for entry error. There are rules that govern how you should store tables of information; these are the rules of *Data Normalization*.

Data Normalization: To make data storage as efficient and compact as possible to eliminate the possibility for confusion and error.

There are five normalization rules, but the latter ones are fairly complicated and used mostly by database professionals. In this section, I'll explain the first two normalization rules, which are all a beginner really needs to understand in order to avoid major mistakes.

Rule #1: Avoid Repeated Information

Let's say that you want to keep contact information on your customers along with a record of each transaction they make. If you kept it all in one big database, you would have to repeat the customer's full name, address, and phone number each time you entered a new transaction. It would also be a nightmare if the customer's address changed; you would have to record the change in every transaction (see Figure 19.4.).

FIGURE 19.4.

This single database contains repeated information in the first three columns, making it hard to update.

Customers/Orders Database

Customer Name	Customer Address	Customer Phone	Order Date	Order Total
ABC Plumbing	201. W. 44th St.	(317) 555-2394	2/5/98	$155.90
ABC Plumbing	201. W. 44th St.	(317) 555-2394	5/14/98	$90.24
ABC Plumbing	201. W. 44th St.	(317) 555-2394	7/9/98	$224.50
Jack's Emporium	1155 Conner Ave.	(317) 555-4501	6/6/98	$1,592.99
Jack's Emporium	1155 Conner Ave.	(317) 555-4501	7/26/98	$990.41
Millie's Pizza	108 Ponting St.	(317) 555-2349	8/29/98	$39.95

A better way is to assign each customer an ID number. Include that ID number in a separate database that contains names and addresses; then include the same ID number as a link in a separate database that contains the transactions (see Figure 19.5.).

19

FIGURE 19.5.

These two databases share a common field, Customer ID, by which they can be joined.

Customers Database

Customer ID	Customer Name	Customer Address	Customer Phone
1	ABC Plumbing	201. W. 44th St.	(317) 555-2394
2	Jack's Emporium	1155 Conner Ave.	(317) 555-4501
3	Millie's Pizza	108 Ponting St.	(317) 555-2349

Orders Database

Customer ID	Order Date	Order Total
1	2/5/98	$155.90
2	6/6/98	$1,592.99
3	8/29/98	$39.95
1	7/9/98	$224.50
1	5/14/98	$90.24
2	7/26/98	$990.41

Rule #2: Avoid Redundant Data

Let's say you want to keep track of which employees have attended certain training classes. There are lots of employees and lots of classes. One way would be to keep it all in a single Personnel database, as in Figure 19.6.

FIGURE 19.6.

A single database can be used to hold this information, but it's not the most efficient way.

Employees/Classes/Training Database

Employee Name	Employee Address	Employee Phone	Training Date	Class Taken	Credit Hours	Passed?
Phil Sharp	211 W. 16th St.	(317) 555-4321	5/5/98	Leadership Skills	3	Yes
Becky Rowan	40 Westfield Ct.	((317) 555-3905	5/5/98	Customer Service	2	Yes
Nick Gianti	559 Ponting St.	(317) 555-7893	6/15/98	Public Speaking	9	Yes
Martha Donato	720 E. Warren	(317) 555-2930	6/15/98	Public Speaking	9	No
Cynthia Hedges	108 Carroll St.	(317) 555-5960	6/15/98	Customer Service	2	Yes
Andrea Mayfair	3904 110th St.	(317) 555-0938	5/5/98	Leadership Skills	3	Yes

But what if an employee takes more than one class? You would have to add a duplicate line in the table to list it, and then you have the problem described in the previous section—multiple records with virtually identical field entries. What if the only employee who has taken a certain class leaves the company? When you delete that employee's record, you delete the information about the class's credit hours, too.

A better way would be to create separate databases for Employees, Classes, and Training, as in Figure 19.7.

FIGURE 19.7.

A three-database breakout is the best way to handle the information in Figure 19.6.

Employee Database

Employee ID	Employee Name	Employee Address	Employee Phone
1	Phil Sharp	211 W. 16th St.	(317) 555-4321
2	Becky Rowan	40 Westfield Ct.	(317) 555-3905
3	Nick Gianti	559 Ponting St.	(317) 555-7893
4	Martha Donato	720 E. Warren	(317) 555-2930
5	Cynthia Hedges	108 Carroll St.	(317) 555-5960
6	Andrea Mayfair	3904 110th St.	(317) 555-0938

Training Database

Employee ID	Date	Class	Passed?
1	5/5/98	C1	Yes
2	5/5/98	C2	Yes
3	6/15/98	C3	Yes
4	6/15/98	C3	No
5	6/15/98	C2	Yes
6	5/5/98	C1	Yes

Class Database

Class ID	Class	Credits
C1	Leadership Skills	3
C2	Customer Service	2
C3	Public Speaking	9

Preparing Databases to be Joined

To prepare to join two databases, you must decide which database will be the "master." In a multidatabase setup, one database is the main one, and the others support it. For example, in Figure 19.7, the Training database is the main one. The Class and Employee databases exist only for the Training database to pull data from. Create the databases and save your work.

You must also make sure that you have joinable fields in the databases. These are fields in the different databases that contain the same information. For example, in Figure 19.7, the Employee and Training databases both have an Employee ID field, which provides the means to join them. Similarly, the Class database's Class ID field joins with the Class field in the Training database. (The fields need not have the same name in both databases in order to be joined.)

If you do not have joinable fields, create them now. It could be as simple as adding an ID number field. For example, look back at Figures 19.4 and 19.5. Notice that a Customer ID field was added in Figure 19.5 to the Customers database, for the express purpose of having something to link with in the Orders database.

Joining the Databases

After you have done the preparatory work, you are ready to join the databases. Follow these steps.

To Do: Joining Databases

1. Make sure all the needed databases have been created with the necessary fields and that you have saved your work.

2. Display the database that you have chosen as the master one.

3. Choose Create, Join. The Join window opens.

4. Click the Open button. In the Open dialog box, double-click the database that you want to join with the master one. Repeat this to open as many different databases as you need to join together. Each database's fields appear in their own list, as shown in Figure 19.8.

19

FIGURE 19.8.

Each database is a separate windowed list in the Join window.

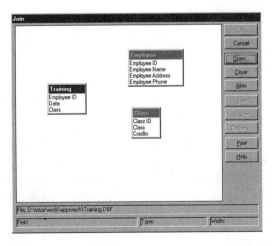

▼   5. Drag a field from one list onto the field on another list that you want to join it to. A line appears connecting them.

     6. Click the Options button to open the Options window.

     7. Select or deselect the checkboxes to set the options you want. You can choose whether to insert or delete records in the databases based on the existing content. (More on this following these steps.)

     8. Repeat steps 4 through 7 for other databases if there are others you need to join to the master one.

▲   9. Click Close to close the Join box. Now you are ready to use your joined databases in views in your master database.

A bit of explanation is in order regarding the Options you were prompted to set in step 7. They control how the two databases relate to one another. There are two sets of two check boxes, one set for each of the databases:

- **Insert**. If no records match the {database1} record, typing into a blank {database2} field inserts a new record. This is on by default.

- **Delete**. Deleting a record from {database1} deletes matching records from {database2}. This is off by default.

- **Insert**. If no records match the {database2} record, typing into a blank {database1} field inserts a new record. This is on by default.

- **Delete**. Deleting a record from {database2} deletes matching records from {database1}. This is off by default.

Some examples will make these options clearer. Suppose you created and linked the databases shown in Figure 19.7. If a new employee were hired, you would enter his information in the Employee database, assigning him an Employee ID. Then later, when he took a class, you would enter it in the Training database. But if he took a class before you got around to entering him in the Employee database, then what? If the Insert check box is on, any new entries you make in the Training database (for example, adding a new Employee ID) will also create new entries in the linked Employee database. If you turn this off, you'll see an error message if you try to enter a class in the Training database for an employee who has no number in the Employee Database.

What about the Delete check box? Suppose an employee quit who had taken a class, and you deleted his employee record from the Employee database. If the Delete check box were marked for the join between Employee and Training databases, all records of the employee's training would be deleted from the Training database automatically.

Working with Joined Databases

The handiest thing you can do with joined databases is to create views that use fields from more than one database. You can use these views for data entry, so you can enter data into several databases at once. For example, you could create a form that lets you add and change employee information and track their training at the same time.

To create a view that contains multiple databases, just look for the Database drop-down list in the Assistant. For example, in the Form Assistant in Figure 19.9, notice that you can choose which database you want from the Database drop-down list, enabling you to pick and choose the fields from all the databases that are joined to the current one.

FIGURE 19.9.

When databases are joined, you have multiple databases to choose from in the Database drop-down list when creating a new view.

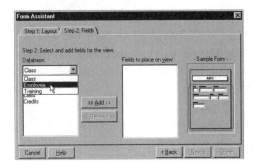

Summary

In this final Approach hour, you learned how to create new views and how to edit your forms and worksheets. You also learned how to perform a mail merge on your Approach data and how to join multiple databases to create more powerful forms and other views.

In the next hour, we'll switch gears and take a look at Freelance, SmartSuite's presentation slide creation program.

19

Q&A

Q Why don't all my fields appear on the worksheet?

A If you added fields after you created the database, the new fields must be manually added to each view. Remember, the worksheet is just a view; it's not a comprehensive picture of your list of fields. To see the complete field list, click the Add Field SmartIcon.

Q Why would I want to create more than one worksheet?

A One of the best uses for multiple worksheets is for "field filters." When you perform a Find operation, as you learned in Hour 17, you filter out unwanted records, but there is no corresponding way to filter out unwanted fields. Creating a worksheet that contains only the fields you want to see at the moment can solve this problem.

Q Can I choose different fonts and formatting for the mail merge letter I create in Approach?

A Yes. All the familiar formatting tools are available on the status bar, just like in Word Pro. Refer back to Hours 6 and 7 if you need help.

Q When I try to enter new records using a form I've created with multiple databases, I get an error message. What am I doing wrong?

A When creating multidatabase forms, make sure that whenever you include a joined field, you include the version of it from the main database. For example, in the databases shown back in Figure 19.7, suppose I was creating a data entry field that used fields from both databases. I would include the Employee ID field from the Training database, not the Employee ID field from the Employee database.

PART V
Other SmartSuite Tools

Hour

Hour 20

Creating a Freelance Presentation

Forget those awful plastic overhead slides with their bulky cardboard frames. With Freelance you can create and present your presentation right from your PC. We'll spend the next two hours looking at Freelance Graphics, SmartSuite's presentation software, and you'll learn how to create, spice up, and present your own show.

Highlights of this hour include:

- Creating a new presentation
- Creating pages
- Changing views
- Building page content
- Adding, removing, and rearranging pages

Starting a New Presentation

Like all the other SmartSuite programs, Freelance Graphics starts out with a Welcome to box, and from it you can open an existing presentation or create a new one. (You want to do the latter, of course.)

When starting a new presentation, you can start a blank one (not recommended for beginners), or you can choose a content topic and a look. The content topic determines the content of the sample text and the number and arrangement of pages. The look determines the color and font scheme. Pick one of each, depending on your needs, and click OK (see Figure 20.1). (You can change the look easily if you change your mind later.) For the examples in this chapter, I'm going to pick Business Plan as the content topic and 1998 as the look.

FIGURE 20.1.

Choose a content topic and choose a look.

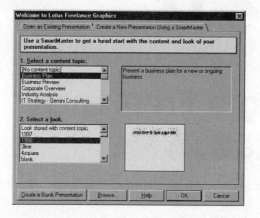

One of the choices for Look is Look stored with content topic. Each of the content topics has a default look, chosen especially to work well with that topic. If you aren't sure what look to choose, choose this default one.

If you see a message when opening your new presentation about LotusScript routines, click Yes to allow the scripts to run.

Creating Your First Page

If you started with a content topic (rather than a blank presentation or No Content Topic), the first thing you see is the New Page dialog box (see Figure 20.2). It enables you to select sample text for the first page to be created.

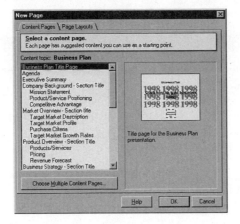

FIGURE 20.2.

Choose the sample content to use for the page.

NEW TERM Freelance calls its slides *pages*.

The first page you probably want is a title page, which is already preselected. (Later you'll want to add other, different pages.) The title page is already selected, so click OK.

Understanding the Freelance Screen

Now that you have a presentation started and have created your first page, take a moment to familiarize yourself with the Freelance controls. (Don't worry; it'll just take a moment. You'll be back to work on your presentation before you know it.)

As shown in Figure 20.3, the Freelance screen is pretty typical of a SmartSuite application. You've got the standard SmartIcons, status bar, and so on. The Guide Me button in the top-right corner works sort of like the Ask the Expert feature in Word Pro. You click on it and choose a Help topic. There is an extra set of buttons along the left side of the work area from which you can perform some common activities, such as adding a new page. We'll look at each of these buttons as we go along.

As in Approach, there are tabs for each of the available views. Current Page shows a full view of a single page. Page Sorter shows thumbnail sketches of each page. Outliner shows the text of each page. Each view has its own uses, as you will see. You can go ahead and click on each tab to check out each view now if you want.

20

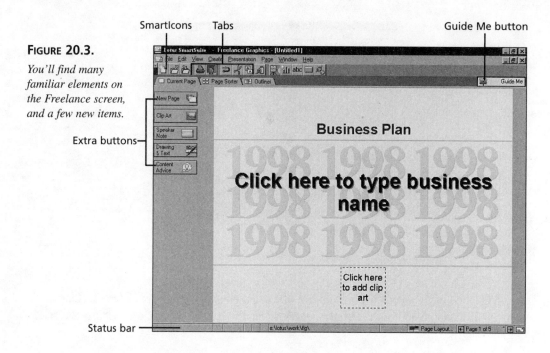

FIGURE 20.3.

You'll find many familiar elements on the Freelance screen, and a few new items.

Creating Additional Pages

To create other pages, click the New Page button. This reopens the New Page dialog box.

In the New Page dialog box, there are two tabs. You saw the first one in Figure 20.2, from which you can select sample content. When you choose sample content, it comes with a predefined layout. You can change that layout later, but not now.

The other way to define a new page is to choose a page layout, devoid of sample content. That's what Page Layouts tab is for (see Figure 20.4). You can, for example, choose a bulleted list and create your own page title and bullet content. This is useful if you need a page that does not correspond to any of the content samples.

When you have chosen the content or layout you want, click OK to create the new page.

If you are not using sample content from a template, the New Page dialog box has only the Layout tab.

FIGURE 20.4.

Choose a layout for the new page.

Think carefully as you insert each page into the presentation. You will need to decide what you want to show with each one and in what format you want to show it. If you need to change a page's layout, choose Page, Switch Page Layout to open a dialog box to do so.

For example, suppose you want to create a short presentation about your business plan. You have started your presentation using the Business Plan content topic and inserted your title page. You might use a combination of content and layout choices to build your presentation structure, as shown in Table 20.1.

TABLE 20.1. A SAMPLE BUSINESS PLAN PRESENTATION

#	Content Used	Layout Used	Explanation
1	Executive Summary	—	Summary of what you will be presenting
2	—	Bulleted list	What products you sell
3	Target Market Profile	—	Who you are trying to sell your products to
4	—	1 Chart	Past sales successes
5	—	Bulleted list	Where your products are sold
		Table	Where you advertise
6	Competitor Evaluation	—	Your competitors' strengths and weaknesses
7	Total Funding Required	—	Money you need to get started
8	—	Bulleted list	Request for action
9	—	Bulleted list	Summary

20

Moving from Page to Page

Now that you have more than one page in your presentation, you will need to be able to move from page to page. The easiest way is to press Page Up and Page Down. You can also click the Page indicator on the status bar to open a pop-up list of the pages and select the one you want. Or you can click the blue arrows to the left and right of the Page indicator to change pages.

One of my favorite ways to find an individual page is to switch to Page Sorter view (by clicking its tab). You can then easily locate the page you want and double-click it to display it in Current Page view.

Changing a Page Layout

Suppose you want to use the sample content for a page, but you want it to have a different layout. No problem; just change the layout for the page.

To Do: Changing a Page's Layout

1. Display the page in Current Page view.
2. Choose Page, Switch Page Layout. A dialog box appears that looks just like the Page Layouts tab of the New Page dialog box did.
3. Choose a different layout.
4. Click OK.

> When you change the layout of a page, the data on it does not always translate well. For example, if you have a two-column bulleted list and you change it to a bulleted list with a chart, the right-hand bulleted items get overwritten. To avoid such problems, you should carefully think through your layout choices and make changes only when absolutely needed, or be prepared to reenter your data on that page.

Building Page Content

After you have chosen the pages for the basic structure of the presentation, you are ready to fill in your own information in the placeholders provided on the pages. (Actually you can fill in the content of each page as you insert it, but I prefer to get the big picture nailed down first by developing the structure, as in Table 20.1, before I work on the content.)

Replacing Sample Text and Text Placeholders

If you created the page based on sample content, you already have a title. Change it if you like by clicking in the title's box and editing the text. Then click the sample body text on the page and type your own text to replace it.

If you created the page based on a layout, both the title and the body text are placeholders only. Click on each one in turn and type your own. Such placeholder text does not print and does not show up in Print Preview. It is merely there as a reminder to you.

When you click on some placeholder text, a text box appears, as in Figure 20.5. While you are typing in that box, you can use its controls, as well as the normal text formatting controls on the status bar, to format the text.

Consistency from page to page is very important in formatting in a presentation. If you started the presentation with a SmartMaster template Look, the text for each title, bullet, and so on is already preformatted for a consistent look. If you want to change the formatting across all slides, change it through the Master, as described in Hour 21, rather than using the individual slide's formatting controls shown in Figure 20.5.

Use these buttons to change the indent level   These buttons make the text larger or smaller   Click OK or click outside the text box to end text entry   Insertion point

FIGURE 20.5.

Type your text in the box and format it as needed. When you are finished, click OK or click outside the text box.

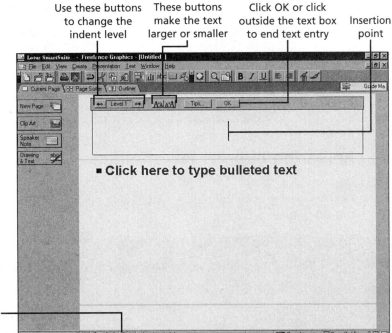

Formatting controls on status bar

20

Replacing Table Placeholders

If one of your pages is a table layout, you can easily create the table by clicking the placeholder box. The Table Gallery dialog box appears, prompting you to select a table format. Click on the button that best shows the kind of table you want. Change the number of rows or columns if needed. (The default is four of each.) See Figure 20.6. Then click OK.

Once the table is in place, you can type in its cells just as you did in a Word Pro table and in a 1-2-3 worksheet. You can also resize columns by dragging the divider lines between cells, just as you did in Word Pro and 1-2-3.

FIGURE 20.6.

Tell Freelance what kind of table you want and how large it should be.

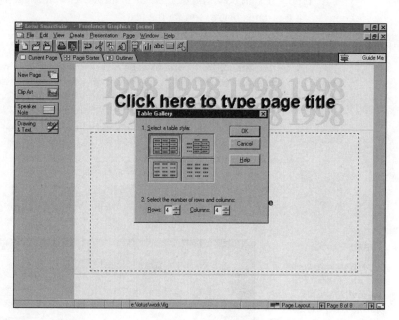

Replacing Clip Art Placeholders

When a clip art placeholder appears on a page (such as "Click here to add clip art"), you can click on it to open the Add Clip Art or Diagram to Page dialog box. From here you can select the art you want.

To Do: Adding Clip Art to a Page

1. Click the clip art placeholder. The Add Clip Art or Diagram to the Page dialog box appears.

2. Open the Categories drop-down list and choose the art category you want to browse.

▼ To Do

3. Page through the clip art using the right and left arrow buttons.

▲   4. When you find the art you want to use, click on it and then OK.

FIGURE 20.7.

Choose the clip art you want to use from SmartSuite's large collection.

Replacing Chart Placeholders

When you click on a chart placeholder, the Create Chart dialog box opens, where you can choose a chart type and look. You should already be familiar with the chart types from your work in 1-2-3 and Approach. When you make your selection and click OK, the Edit Data dialog box opens. This is where you enter the data to be used in the chart.

Notice that the first row is labeled Legend and the first column is Labels. Use them for their marked purposes, not for data. Fill in your data in the lettered columns and numbered rows starting with A1 (see Figure 20.8).

FIGURE 20.8.

Enter your data to be charted, just like in a spreadsheet.

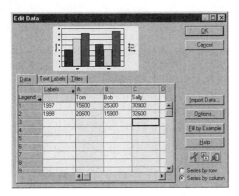

20

You can also:

- Click Import Data to import the data from another program (perhaps a 1-2-3 workbook).

- Click Options for a single check box that turns on/off the display of the preview chart at the top of the dialog box.
- Click Fill By Example to fill a row or column based on the example you set in the first few cells. This is like the Fill Series work you did in 1-2-3.
- Use the Cut, Copy, and Paste SmartIcons in the dialog box to employ cut-and-paste as needed while entering the data.
- To change the orientation of the sheet, so that Labels is the first row and Legend is the first column, click the Series by Row option button.

When you are finished entering the data, click OK to place the completed chart in the placeholder box.

Adding Your Own Graphics

You can also use your own art, such as your company's logo, but it's considered a picture, not clip art. To add it to a page, choose Create, Add Picture. The Add Picture dialog box appears. Choose the file type from the Files of Type drop-down list and navigate to the folder containing the image. Then double-click it. It appears on your page. You can drag it around to reposition it as needed or resize it. (Moving and resizing objects in Freelance is the same as in all the other SmartSuite applications you've learned about so far.)

Adding Additional Freelance Objects

Besides replacing placeholders, you can insert new objects onto a page. For example, suppose you started out with a Bulleted List page, and you decided that it needed a chart. You could switch the layout to Bullets & Chart, but you could also just stick with the Bulleted List layout and add a chart to it with the Create, Chart command. The same dialog boxes appear when adding extra objects that appear when you click on placeholders.

Removing Objects from a Page

To remove an object, click it and press Delete. If it was originally a placeholder, the placeholder reappears. You can't delete a placeholder, but they don't print or display during the presentation. If it was an additional object you added, it disappears completely.

Managing Your List of Pages

Page Sorter view is the best way to manage pages because you can see lots of pages at once. Click on the Page Sorter tab to switch to that view. See Figure 20.9. From there, you can:

- **Delete a page**. Select it and press Delete or click the Delete Page SmartIcon.

- **Move a page**. Drag a page to a new position to rearrange them.

- **Add a page**. Click the New Page SmartIcon.

- **Duplicate a page**. Click the Duplicate Page SmartIcon. (You won't want two identical pages, of course; you'll then modify one of them.)

FIGURE 20.9.

You can move and delete pages easily from Page Sorter view.

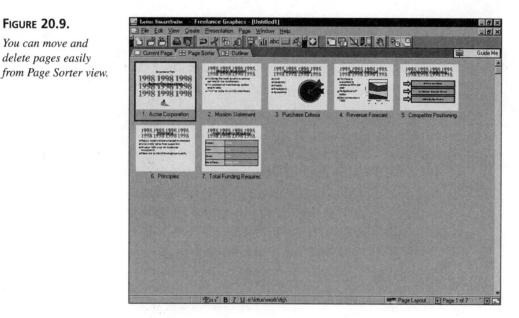

What Else Can You Do?

You already know how to do a lot of the common tasks in Freelance, by virtue of learning them in other SmartSuite programs. Don't forget that you can:

- Print by clicking the Print SmartIcon or choosing File, Print. In the Print dialog box you can choose whether to print the selected page(s) or all pages.

- Preview a print job with File, Print Preview or the Print Preview SmartIcon.

- Save your work by clicking the Save SmartIcon or choosing File, Save.

- Start a new presentation by clicking the New Presentation SmartIcon or choosing File, New Presentation.

- Open an existing presentation by clicking the Open SmartIcon or choosing File, Open.

- Change the zoom with the View, Zoom command.

20

- Move and copy objects with the Cut, Copy, and Paste SmartIcons and menu commands.
- Check your spelling by choosing Edit, Check Spelling or pressing Ctrl+F2.

Summary

In this hour, you learned how to start a simple presentation in Freelance. You learned how to get a head start with the SmartMaster templates, and how to replace placeholder blocks with your own material. In the next hour, we'll finish the job by adding cool multimedia effects and transitions to the presentation and learning how to present it onscreen.

Q&A

Q Isn't there any way to delete a placeholder block from a page? I know it won't print, but it's annoying and it's in my way.

A You can change to a different layout for the page, and if the new layout doesn't include the placeholder for that element, it won't appear. You can also drag placeholder blocks anywhere on the slide, so you can move them out of your way.

Q We didn't talk about Outliner view in this hour. What's that good for?

A Outliner view is great for entering and editing text in a presentation that is primarily text-based. You can't edit charts, tables, and graphics in this view, however, so it's limited in that way. If you want to jot down your thoughts to build slides from, Outliner view is a great place to do that.

Q In the New Page dialog box, can I choose both sample content and a layout, so that the sample text appears but in the layout I choose?

A No, you can use only one tab or the other in this dialog box. When you make a selection on one tab, your selection on the other tab is voided. You must create the page first, using the sample content you need, and then change its layout with the Page, Switch Page Layout command.

Q Can I import information from other programs for my slides?

A Sure. An easy way is to cut and paste to move or copy the material onto the slide. You can also use the Create, Object command to place a saved object from almost any other Windows-based program on your system.

HOUR 21

Polishing and Presenting with Freelance

Last hour, you created a Freelance Graphics presentation that contains the information you need to convey to your audience, but it could probably use some polishing to be the best it can be. In this hour, you'll learn how to make consistent changes to pages, insert whiz-bang multimedia elements, and present the show.

Highlights of this hour include:

- Applying master changes to formatting
- Working with multimedia elements
- Setting up transitions
- Preparing your notes
- Printing handouts
- Rehearsing the presentation
- Running the show

Applying Master Changes to Formatting

As I mentioned in the last hour, it's important to maintain consistency in your show. If the heading is in Arial font on one page, it should be in Arial on the next page. If the logo appears in the right corner on one page, it should be there on the next. You get the idea.

Changing the Font Globally

All presentations use a default font. You can format bits of individual text in other fonts, as you learned in Hour 20, but when you don't explicitly choose a font for some text, it appears in the default.

When you change the default font for a presentation, all text that has not been specifically set to another font changes. Changing the default does not override any individual font changes you have made.

To Do: Changing the Default Font

1. Choose Presentation, Change Typeface Globally. The Change Typeface Globally dialog box opens (see Figure 21.1).

2. Choose a different font from the list. The Sample area shows the chosen font.

3. Mark any checkboxes to indicate other elements for which you want the font to apply: data charts, tables, and/or organization charts.

FIGURE 21.1.

Choose a different default font for the presentation.

4. Click OK. A warning message appears.

5. Click OK again, and the font is changed on all pages.

Adding Repeated Elements on Every Page

If you have a company logo, it might be nice to place it on every page for a consistent, professional feel. It doesn't have to be a logo necessarily; you can repeat any text or graphic on all pages. Perhaps you want your company motto to appear at the bottom of every page.

It is better to place the element once, with the following steps, than to try to insert and position it on every single page. You will never be able to get them exactly the same with the latter method, and a change means changing many pages individually.

To Do: Placing Repeated Elements on Each Page

▼ To Do

1. Choose Presentation, Add a Logo to Every Page. A special setup page appears, as in Figure 21.2.

2. The dotted outline represents the area where the page content goes. If needed, resize that box to make room for the element(s) you want to add. (Resize it like any other object: Click it to select it and drag its selection handles.)

FIGURE 21.2.

Add clip art, a logo, or repeated text to this "master" page that should be repeated on all pages.

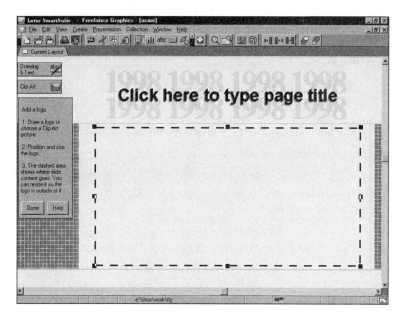

3. Do any of the following:

   Choose Create, Add Picture and place a picture on the page, as you learned in Hour 20.

   Click the Clip Art button and place a piece of clip art on the page.

   Click the Drawing & Text button and use the controls that appear to draw on the page.

▼

21

▼   Click the Drawing & Text button, and then click the abc button and place a text box containing text you want repeated on each page.

    4. Click Done when you are finished to return to viewing pages normally. Your
▲   repeated element appears on each page.

After adding a repeated element, you may need to adjust the positioning of some items on some individual pages so nothing overlaps. If many pages seem to need adjustment, you may want to go back to steps 1 and 2 and resize the content area.

Adding Sound

Sound can really perk up a tired-looking presentation. You can add sounds to any slide—perhaps a recording of your CEO welcoming everyone to the seminar.

There are two ways to add sounds to a slide. You can either assign them to individual elements on the slide or to the slide itself. If you want to assign a sound to the slide itself so the sound plays when the page appears, skip to "Creating Transitions Between Slides," later in this chapter.

To assign a sound to an element on the slide (such as a text or graphic) so that the sound plays when you click on that element, use the following steps.

To Do: Attaching a Sound to a Page Element

1. Click the element to select it.

2. Open the context menu (the actual name varies) and choose Screen Show Effects. The Properties InfoBox opens for that element, with the Screen Show tab on top. See Figure 21.3.

3. To play when the object is clicked, open the Action When Object Is Clicked drop-down list and choose Play Sound. The Play Sound dialog box appears.

FIGURE 21.3.

Choose Play Sound from the Action When Object is Clicked drop-down list.

New Term *Context menu*: Notice that when you click on different elements on a page, the menu between Presentation and Window changes. When you click on text, it's Text; when you click on some clip art, it's Group (because the art is a group of shapes), and so on. This menu is called the context menu because it changes depending on the context.

4. Locate and select the sound you want to play and click Open.

5. If you want the sound to play more than once or play continuously, click the Options button and make those setting changes. Click OK.

6. Close the Properties InfoBox.

7. To test the sound, choose Presentation, Run Screen Show, From Current Page. Click on the element to see if the sound plays.

▲ 8. To exit from the screen show, press Esc, then choose Quit Screen Show.

Building Slides Element-by-Element

By default, all elements on the slide appear at the same time. For example, if you have text, three bullet points, and a piece of clip art on your slide, they all appear at once.

You can add interest to your presentation by building the elements individually, so the audience focuses intensely on each one in turn. To do this, set up the individual elements to build, as in the following steps.

To Do: Setting Page Elements to Build

1. Click on an element to select it.

2. Open the context menu (the actual name varies) and choose Screen Show Effects. The Properties InfoBox opens for that element, with the Screen Show tab on top. See Figure 21.3.

3. Click the Display Page First, then Display {Object} button. The word "object" is replaced with Text or Object depending on what the selected element is.

4. If you want the element to appear after a certain number of seconds, enter that number in the After box. Otherwise, choose On Click, so the element will appear when you click the mouse.

5. (For text bullets only) Choose the way you want the bullets to appear from the Display Bullets drop-down list (All at Once or One at a Time). Check or uncheck the Dim Previous Bullets check box as desired if you're using One at a Time. This makes all bullets except the current one dim, to make the current one stand out.
▼ See Figure 21.4.

▼ To Do

21

FIGURE 21.4.

Bullets have a few special properties you can set, like the way the text from the bullets builds.

▼ 6. If you want a transition to happen or a sound to play when the object appears, select those from the Transition or Sound drop-down lists. (You'll learn more about transitions in the next section.)

7. Close the Properties InfoBox when you're done or leave it open and click on a different element to set its building properties.

8. When you are finished with all elements on the page, choose Presentation, Sequence Objects on Page. The Screen Show Sequence Overview appears (see Figure 21.5).

FIGURE 21.5.

Set the order in which the elements appear on the slide.

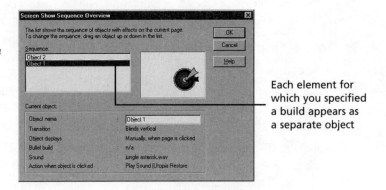

Each element for which you specified a build appears as a separate object

▼ 9. Drag the objects up or down on the list to reorder them if needed.

You can rename the objects from the generic names (Object 1, Object 2) by typing new names in the Object Name box. This can help if you have a lot of objects and a complex order in which they need to be sequenced.

▼ 10. Click OK.

11. Test your work by choosing Presentation, Run Screen Show, From Current Page. Then click or wait the number of seconds you indicated to see if the element appears.

▲ 12. To exit from the screen show, press Esc, then choose Quit Screen Show.

Creating Transitions Between Slides

The default transition between slides is Appear, which means one slide disappears and another appears in its place. Boring! Freelance offers a lot of more interesting transitions, whereby the new slide replaces the previous one by flying in, dropping in, sunbursting out from the center, or any number of other effects.

You can set transitions for the presentation as a whole (that is, so that all transitions use the same effect) or for individual slides. While the latter is more fun, it can be distracting from the presentation message, so most people choose to set one transition effect for the entire presentation.

Setting a Default Transition Effect for the Presentation

When you set an effect for the whole show, you are setting a default. You can override that default for any individual slides, as explained in the next section.

To set a default transition for the show, choose Presentation, Set Up Screen Show. The Set Up Screen Show dialog box appears, listing the various transition effects available (see Figure 21.6). Choose the effect you want and then click OK.

FIGURE 21.6.

Select a transition effect as the default for the show.

21

In this same dialog box, you can also choose how the pages will advance in your show. The default is On click or keypress, which means you will need to click or press a key each time you want the next slide. An alternative is After __ Seconds. If you choose this and fill in a number, the pages will advance all by themselves.

Setting Transition Effects for Individual Slides

You can override the default effect for any individual slide—for example, to create a dramatic effect for an important page. To do so, choose Page, Screen Show Effects, and choose a transition from the Page Properties InfoBox. The controls nearly identical to the ones for the entire show (refer to Figure 21.6).

Preparing Speaker Notes

Speaker notes are notes to yourself that you might want to refer to during a live speech. If you are preparing the presentation slides as background visuals for a live speech you are giving, check these out.

To type notes for a slide, choose Page, Create Speaker Note. A box that resembles an index card appears. Type your notes into it (see Figure 21.7). You can paste text from the Clipboard onto the card (from another program such as Word Pro, for example), format the text using the Text menu's commands, or go to the card for the next or previous page by clicking the arrow buttons. When you are done typing notes, click OK.

FIGURE 21.7.

Type your notes for each slide on these index cards.

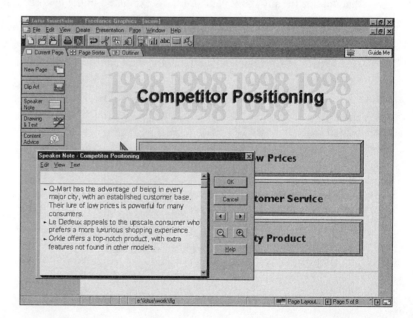

To print your notes, choose File, Print, and in the Print dialog box, click Speaker Notes. Click a layout (2, 4, or 6 notes per page) and click the Print button to print them. You can either leave them as whole sheets or cut up the printouts to make individual index cards.

Preparing Handouts

You might want to give your audience handouts—that is, printouts of your slides. It can help the audience focus on your message better because they won't have to take as many notes. On the other hand, you might not want to use handouts. Some people feel that the audience that has handouts tends to read ahead and ignore the person speaking. It's up to you; there's no real right or wrong.

To print handouts where each slide is a full page, you use the Full Page option in the Print dialog box (File, Print). If you want smaller versions of each slide, so that two, four, or six of them fit on one sheet, use the Handouts option, and then click one of the layouts presented (see Figure 21.8).

FIGURE 21.8.

Choose Handouts in the Print section of the dialog box, and then the desired layout.

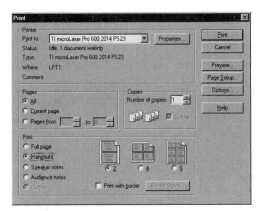

Rehearsing the Presentation

Freelance offers a really cool rehearsal feature that lets you practice giving the presentation. It times how long you spend on each slide and lets you add speaker notes as you go (since you'll probably think of some notes as you practice). These timings can help you gauge how long your speech will take, so you can know in advance whether you need to tighten things up or stretch them out.

21

Choose Presentation, Rehearse, Start to begin rehearsal. The first slide appears, along with a bar on the bottom that shows the time and provides some other controls, as shown in Figure 21.9.

FIGURE 21.9.

Practice your presentation with the timer to see how long it is running.

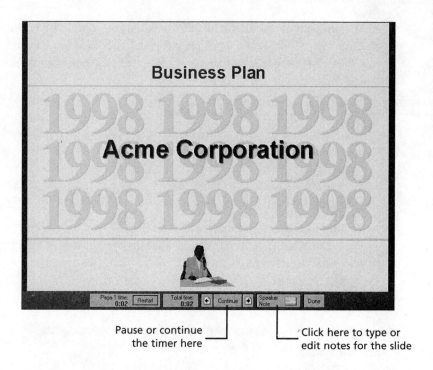

Pause or continue
the timer here

Click here to type or
edit notes for the slide

Go ahead and recite your presentation, letting the timer keep track of the time. Click the right arrow button to move to the next slide. If you need to pause the timer so you can collect your thoughts or jot down some notes, click Pause. Then you can click the Speaker Notes button to open the Speaker Notes window or do whatever else you need to take care of. When you're ready to go again, click Continue.

Click Done to exit from rehearsal mode, and a Rehearse Summary page appears, telling you how much time you spent on each slide. You can redisplay this Rehearse Summary page any time you want by choosing Presentation, Rehearse, Summary.

If you didn't make it through all the slides, don't worry; you can always come back later. If you return to rehearsal mode after leaving it, a dialog box appears inquiring whether you want to keep or clear the timings from the last rehearsal.

Running the Show

When it comes time for the big show, will you know what to do? To be safe, you should practice the show with the actual presentation controls in Freelance, after you are done practicing with the Rehearse feature.

To run the show, choose Presentation, Run Screen Show, From Beginning, or click the Run Screen Show SmartIcon. The first slide appears, filling the entire screen. Click the mouse or press a key to move to the next slide. To abort the show, press Esc and choose Quit Screen Show.

On a plain screen like this, you wouldn't expect that there would be much to do, but there are actually many controls available. Just right-click and select them from the shortcut menu that appears. The following sections detail a few of the more important commands there.

Moving From Slide to Slide

As you know, you can advance the slide by clicking or pressing any key. You can also right-click and choose Next from the shortcut menu. To go back to the previous slide, you can right-click and choose Previous.

To jump to a slide that isn't the next or previous one, right-click and choose Go To, or press Esc. Double-click the slide you want to go to in the dialog box that appears.

You can also display a control panel onscreen that contains slide navigation buttons. Right-click, choose Control Panel, and then choose the command for the position you want it to appear (for example, Lower Right).

Displaying Your Speaker Notes

To display your notes for a slide, right-click and choose Speaker Notes. Of course, you won't want to leave these onscreen for long because they obscure the slide, but it can be handy to check them briefly, in case you have misplaced your hard copy. (That's easy to do when you're nervous.)

You can also use the Speaker Notes feature to take notes during a meeting. If someone asks a question and you promise to get back to them with an answer, you might record that fact on the Speaker Note card for the slide to remind yourself.

Drawing on a Slide

When using an overhead projector, some speakers draw on the transparencies with markers to emphasize certain points. You can do this onscreen in Freelance, too.

First, you need to enable drawing. Right-click and choose Allow Drawing. The default pen is medium-width black. If you want to change the color or thickness, right-click again and choose Pen Color and the color, or Pen Width and then the width. Then—just draw. Hold down the mouse button and drag on the slide to draw on it. Release the mouse button to stop drawing.

21

Don't use the Drawing feature to make any notes that you want to keep. Drawings aren't saved; when you advance to the next slide, they're erased.

Summary

In this chapter, you learned how to improve your Freelance presentation with transitions and other special effects. You also had a chance to rehearse it, and you learned about the controls you'll use when you present it. There's certainly a lot more to Freelance than we had time to look at in these last two hours, but you can explore it with confidence on your own, armed with the basic knowledge you've gained so far.

Q&A

Q I noticed that the Create menu has an Add Movie command. What's that for?

A Freelance comes with a number of predesigned "movies," which are actually just animation sequences. For example, there is one of an arrow hitting a target that you could use to punctuate the fact that you are "on-target" with your customer focus. You can place one of them on your slide and set its timing and controls the same as you would for a sound clip. These don't appear in Current Page view; you have to actually run or rehearse the show to see them.

The Add Movie command also lets you add videos in all the popular computer video formats, such as MOV and AVI. Simply choose the type from the Files of Type drop-down list when selecting a movie.

Q Is there a way I can change the font or formatting of a certain element on each slide, like the title, without changing the overall default font for the entire presentation?

A Yes. You can use named styles in Freelance, just like in Word Pro. Format a single instance of that text the way you want it (for example, change the font of the title on one slide). Then right-click it and choose Named Styles, Redefine. In the dialog box that appears, click OK. You've just redefined all text with that style, across all pages.

Q Can I create my own page layouts to assign to individual slides?

A Yes. Just choose Presentation, Edit Page Layouts. From here you can edit any of the existing layouts (with the Edit button) or create a new layout (with the Create button).

Q I'm going to be printing my presentation in black-and-white. How can I preview what that will look like?

A Just press Alt+F9 or choose View, Show in Color to toggle the color on and off.

21

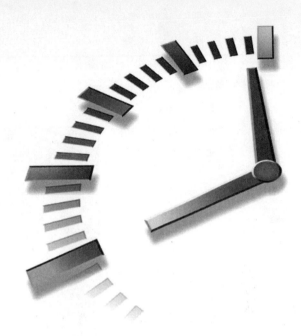

Hour 22

Working with Organizer

Organizer is a simple but powerful program that's based on a metaphor you are probably already familiar with—a day planner. Within the "binder" of an Organizer file, you'll find tabs for addresses, calendars, events, and more.

Highlights of this hour include:

- Storing contact information in Organizer
- Locating a contact
- Entering appointments
- Working with alarms
- Planning multiday events
- Working with EasyClip

A Quick Tour of Organizer

When you open Organizer, you see a "book" onscreen, with some tabs, buttons, and SmartIcons arranged around the edges (see Figure 22.1).

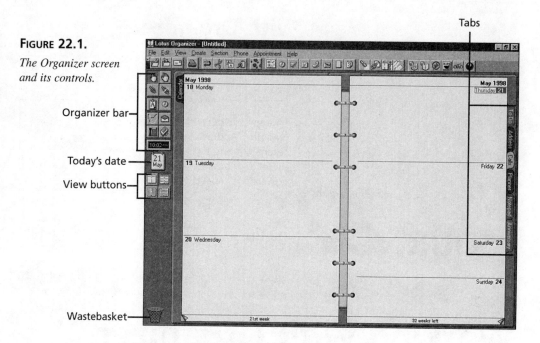

FIGURE 22.1.

The Organizer screen and its controls.

Tabs

Organizer bar—

Today's date—

View buttons—

Wastebasket—

The elements you'll work with include:

- **The Organizer bar**. This bar contains extra icons that help you manage your Organizer file. For some of them, you can drag an object to them to perform a task, such as dragging a contact to the Print icon to print it. You'll learn more about these as we go.

- **Today's date**. This serves two purposes. It appears for reference, and you can also click on it to jump to today's date in your calendar.

- **View buttons**. Each tabbed section can be displayed in several views, just like in Word Pro and Approach. Choose the view you want with these buttons.

- **Tabs**. Each feature of Organizer has its own tabbed section. Click on the tab you want.

- **Wastebasket**. To delete something from any of the sections (such as an appointment or contact), drag it to the wastebasket.

In addition to these unique elements, Organizer employs many of the standard SmartSuite controls you've come to expect, such as a SmartIcon bar, menus, and a Help system accessible through the Help menu.

Managing Contacts with Organizer

Contacts are people that you need to keep in touch with, such as customers, friends, relatives, vendors, and so on. You store their information in the Address section.

> You can add tabs to your file to have multiple instances of the same feature. For example, you can add another Address tab to store personal and business addresses in two different sections. If you think you might want to do this, do it now, before you get your business and personal addresses intermingled. See "Customizing Sections" near the end of this hour.

Entering Contact Information

To create a new contact, click the Address tab to jump to the Address section in Organizer and double-click to open the Create Address dialog box. Or, from any section, click the Create an Address Record SmartIcon. Then simply fill in the blanks in the box for Name, Address, Phone, and so on (see Figure 22.2). When you're finished, click OK. Repeat for each person you want to add.

> It doesn't matter which letter tab (A, B, C, and so forth) you click on before you add a new contact. The new contact always appear on the lettered tab that matches the entry in the Last Name field.

Home tab

FIGURE 22.2.

Fill in the blanks to create an address record for each contact.

Business tab

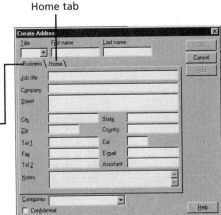

You can also import contact names from other programs, to save some time. For example, if you have addresses in Approach, you can import the DBF file.

To Do: Importing Addresses from Approach

1. Choose File, Import or press Ctrl+I. The Import dialog box opens.

2. Open the Files of Type list and choose dBASE (*.DBF).

3. Open the Into Section list and choose Address if it is not already chosen.

4. Click the Up One Level button once to see the folders for each of your applications. Double-click the Approach folder to switch to it (see Figure 22.3).

FIGURE 22.3.

Choose the Approach file you want to import.

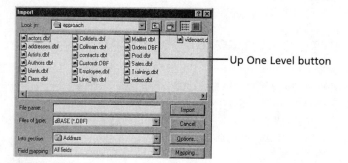

———Up One Level button

5. Click the file you want to import.

6. Click the Mapping button. The Import Mapping dialog box opens.

7. Click the Clear All button to clear Organizer's mapping choices. (They are probably not right.)

8. Click on a field on the left list, and then on the corresponding field on the right (see Figure 22.4).

FIGURE 22.4.

Select the field on the Fields in Import File, and match it with the appropriate field in the Approach file.

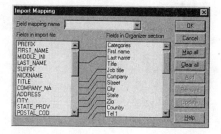

9. Repeat step 7 until all fields have been mapped to the correct Organizer field. Click OK.

▼

▲   10. Back in the Import dialog box, click Import. Your addresses are imported.

You can also import from text-only files, as you did in Approach, or from FoxPro files. Most database and personal organizer programs can export in one of these formats.

Editing Contacts

When you enter a new contact, it appears on the appropriate lettered tab. If you have more contacts than will fit on the single page for a letter, they appear on the next page. You can move from page to page by clicking the bottom corner of the page.

> The four View buttons, which were pointed out in Figure 22.1, provide four different levels of detail for your contacts. Try them out.

To edit a contact card, double-click on it. The address reopens in the Edit Address dialog box. Make your changes and click OK.

Managing Your Schedule with Organizer

Organizer displays a daily, weekly, monthly, or yearly calendar for you, on which you can schedule your appointments and meetings. It can then remind you of an appointment with an alarm. You can also set it up to schedule recurring appointments automatically, such as a weekly staff meeting.

> If you use SmartSuite with Lotus Notes and you specified this when you installed SmartSuite, a group scheduling module was also installed with Organizer. This feature isn't covered in this book, but you can get information about it through the Help system or through Lotus DocOnline.

Scheduling an Appointment

There are many methods of scheduling appointments in Organizer; I'll show you a few of the easiest ones here. First of all, you need to turn to the page in your calendar for the date on which the appointment should occur. You can:

- Click the Calendar tab to display a yearly calendar and then double-click the correct date.

- Click on the Calendar icon below the Organizer bar to display today's date, and navigate to the correct date from there by turning pages.

 You can turn pages in Organizer by clicking the bottom corners of the pages or by pressing Page Up or Page Down.

Click in the area for the day you want and a timeline appears, showing the hours in the day and the appointments already scheduled, if any. From here, double-click the line for the starting time you want to open the Create Appointment dialog box. Fill in the appointment information in the fields provided (see Figure 22.5).

Change the date
or time if needed

FIGURE 22.5.

*Enter the details of
your appointment here.*

This description will
appear on the calendar

Category use is
optional

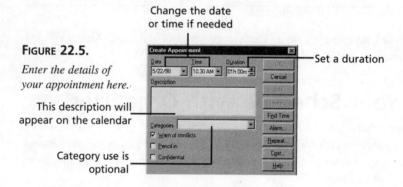

Set a duration

The only essential fields to fill in are Date and Time (which should already be correct), Duration, and Description. The rest of the options are just that—optional.

- **Categories**. One of the more advanced features in Organizer is the ability to assign categories to various events and then create reports based on them. Most casual users don't bother with this.
- **Warn of conflicts**. If you leave this marked, Organizer alerts you if you already have something scheduled for the specified time period.
- **Pencil in**. This makes the appointment tentative if you're not sure it will happen.
- **Confidential**. This prevents the appointment details from being seen by others who may have access to your calendar in a network environment.

22

- **Find Time**. This helps you find a free block of time for an appointment if you can't locate one on your busy schedule.
- **Alarm**. This sets an alarm, so you'll be reminded of the appointment in time to get there. (More on this in the following section.)
- **Repeat**. This enables you to set the appointment up to recur regularly on your calendar. (This is explained in more detail later in this chapter.)
- **Cost**. This allows you to assign a cost or customer code to an appointment for billing purposes.

When you are finished, click Add to leave the dialog box open for creating more appointments or click OK to close the dialog box.

Just like with addresses, you can double-click an existing appointment at any time to edit it.

Setting and Responding to Alarms

By default, when you create an appointment, Organizer sets an alarm to go off five minutes before the appointment. You can modify this by clicking the Alarm button in the New Appointment dialog box. From there, you can change the alarm sound, adjust when it will go off, and change other details about it. To disable the alarm for an appointment, click Cancel Alarm.

When the alarm goes off, a dialog box appears telling you of the appointment. You can click OK to acknowledge it and turn it off, Snooze to ignore it for the moment but be reminded again in five minutes, or Turn To to open the full appointment in the calendar.

Scheduling a Recurring Appointment

You can schedule a recurring appointment, such as a staff meeting that happens every week or a series of meetings that occur every day for two weeks. You enter it once, and Organizer places the instances of it on each day.

To set this up, click the Repeat button while creating or editing the appointment. The Repeat dialog box opens. Choose the interval and duration, as shown in Figure 22.6, and then click OK.

FIGURE 22.6.

Set up an appointment to repeat on your calendar.

Specify a duration to repeat throughout

Set the day or date

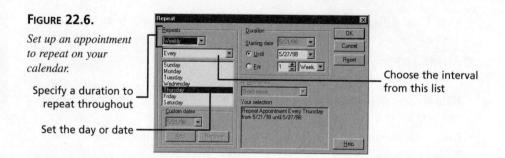

Choose the interval from this list

Keeping a To Do List

The To Do section helps you manage the things you need to do that do not involve specific-time events like meetings, appointments, or phone calls to specific people. Examples might include picking up your dry cleaning, buying copier paper, and finishing writing a proposal.

Click the To Do tab, and you find four tabbed subsections: Overdue, Future, Current, and Completed. Organizer categorizes your tasks in one of these categories based on the start date and due date you specify and whether the task is marked completed or not. Figure 22.7 shows two items on the Future tab and one on the Current.

FIGURE 22.7.

Your action items fall on one of four tabs depending on their specs.

View by priority

View by date/time

View by category

Click here to mark the task completed

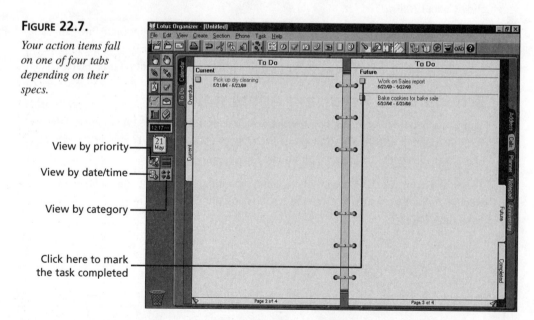

22

You don't have to organize your tasks by status, however; just click one of the View buttons below the Organizer bar to change to tabbed arrangement by date/time, by priority, or by category.

But all this is getting ahead of the game a bit; you still need to know how to create a to-do item. Simply double-click any blank spot on your To Do list and a Create Task dialog box appears. Fill in the task information (there's nothing tricky about it) and click OK.

To mark a task completed, click the check box next to it or right-click it and choose Completed from the shortcut menu.

Finding Information

Finding in Organizer is much like finding in any other SmartSuite program you have used. Choose Edit, Find, and use the dialog box that appears to specify what you are looking for. You can find a contact by entering any scrap of information you know that appears in any field.

To Do: Finding Information

1. Choose Edit, Find. The Find dialog box opens (see Figure 22.8).

2. Type what you want to find in the Find text box.

3. (Optional) Mark the Case sensitive or Whole word check boxes if needed.

FIGURE 22.8.

You can find information in any section based on any field.

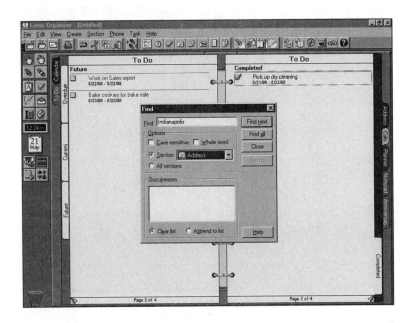

▼   4. Choose the section to look in from the Section drop-down list. If you are in the Address book when you choose Edit, Find, then Address is automatically in the Section box. If you are in the To Do list when you choose Edit, Find, then To Do is automatically in the Section box.

     5. To find the first occurrence, click Find Next. The first occurrence appears on the Occurrences list. Or, to find them all at once, click Find All, and all occurrences appear on the Occurrences list.

     6. Double-click the occurrence you are interested in to jump to it in Organizer.

▲   7. Click the Close button to close the dialog box.

Linking Information

You might sometimes have entries in one section of Organizer that relate to entries in another. A phone call that uses a phone number and name from the Address section is a good example; an appointment with someone from your Address section is another. If you link these related entries, you can easily browse them from either section. For example, in Figure 22.9, a Link icon appears on the address card for Beulah Schultz. If you click on it, you see a pop-up window that shows a linked phone call. You could click on that phone call to jump to its details.

FIGURE 22.9.

When you link entries, the linked items become accessible from other sections.

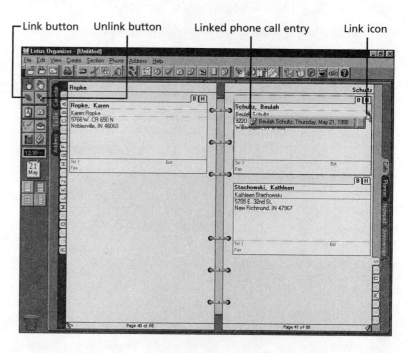

To link two entries in different sections, follow these steps.

To Do: Linking Organizer Entries

▼ To Do

1. Click the Link button on the Organizer bar. The mouse pointer turns into a chain.

2. Click the first entry you want to link.

3. Switch to the other section and click the other entry to link. A Link icon appears on each entry, showing that they are linked.

To unlink, you do almost the same thing, but with the Unlink button in step 1. Click the Unlink button and then click on one of the entries you want to unlink. A pop-up appears showing its links, as in Figure 22.10. Click the entry you want to unlink, and the link between them vanishes.

Customizing Sections

You may find it handy to have multiple copies of certain sections. For example, as I mentioned earlier, you might want two Address sections—one for business and one for personal, or one for customers and another for vendors. You might also want separate To Do sections for various projects.

To create a new section, follow these steps.

To Do: Creating a Section

▼ To Do

1. Choose Section, Customize. The Customize dialog box opens.

2. Click Add. The Add New Section dialog box appears.

3. Choose the type of section you want to add from the Section Type drop-down list.

4. Type a name for the section in the Section Name box.

> You will rename existing sections in step 7 if needed. So, for example, if you are creating an additional address book for personal use, call it Personal in step 4, and in step 7 you can rename the existing one, which is currently called Address, to be called Business.

5. Click OK. The new section is added to the list of sections in the Customize dialog box.

6. (Optional) To rename a section, click on it and click Rename. Type a name in the New Name box and click OK.

▼

7. Repeat steps 2 through 6 if needed to add more sections.

▲ 8. Click OK to close the Customize dialog box. You can now use your new section(s) normally.

To delete a section, as you might expect, you choose it from the list in the Customize dialog box and click the Remove Section button. Removing a section deletes all entries in it, so be careful not to do this in error.

Using EasyClip

When you install Organizer, it also installs a program called EasyClip, which starts when you start Windows. It enables you to quickly access your Organizer file even when Organizer is not running. It appears as an icon in your system tray (the area down by the clock on your Windows taskbar).

To access EasyClip, click on the icon in the system tray to open a menu. From it, you can create an appointment, task, address, or notepad page, or launch the full-blown Organizer.

Summary

In this jam-packed hour, you learned how to use Organizer to…well, to *organize*. You learned how to enter (or import) addresses, how to schedule appointments and calls, and how to enter to-do tasks for yourself. You even found out how to create new sections and link items together.

In the next hour, we'll start talking about how to use SmartSuite applications together by linking and copying data between them. You'll learn how to mail merge, and how to share charts, tables, and other elements.

Q&A

Q How can I make my to-do tasks show up on my calendar?

A While viewing the calendar, choose Section, Show Through. In the Show Through dialog box, make sure that To Do is selected. (By default all sections are selected.) Then click OK. Now your to-do items will appear on each day's page or area.

22

Q Can I create a link to a Word Pro or 1-2-3 file instead of to another item in Organizer?

A Yes. Open the dialog box for the call, to-do item, or other element. (Double-click it, as if you were going to edit it.) Choose Create, File Link. Enter the name for the link and the path to the file (Browse for it if needed with the Browse button). Click OK. Now you have a link to the file, and when you click on the link, the application opens and the file displays.

Q How do I filter out contacts, tasks, or other items I don't want to see?

A You can create a filter, which works a lot like a Find in Approach. Choose Create, Filter, and click the Add button. Then choose the criteria you want for your filter and click OK. Then select your new filter from the list and click Apply. To remove the filter, choose View, Clear Filter.

PART VI
Integrating SmartSuite

Hour

Hour 23

Using SmartSuite Components Together

Individually, all the tools in your home toolbox are useful. You can pound nails with your hammer, tighten screws with your screwdriver, and so on. But to do any really ambitious construction or repair project, you are probably going to need to use more than one tool. It's the same with computing with SmartSuite. You can turn out some pretty nice small items with the individual components, but larger, more ambitious projects call for multiple programs.

In this hour, I'll show you how to work with data from the various SmartSuite components to create integrated works of art (or at least spiffy business documents).

Highlights of this hour include:

- Integrating static data from one program into another
- Understanding OLE
- Creating dynamic links between files
- Creating and performing a mail merge

Copying Data Between Programs

There are many reasons to include data from one program in another. You might have some data in 1-2-3, for example, that would illustrate a point you are trying to make in a Freelance presentation or a Word Pro report. Or you might want to pull some information from Approach into 1-2-3 so you can perform some what-if calculations on it.

The simplest way to include data from another program is to use the Clipboard to copy or move it there. You are doubtless already familiar with the Cut, Copy, and Paste commands from earlier hours. Here's a brief synopsis:

1. Open the application and document containing the material to be moved or copied.

2. Select the data and choose Edit, Copy or Edit, Cut.

3. Open the application and document where you want to place the material.

4. Move the insertion point to the spot where you want it.

5. Choose Edit, Paste.

This same procedure works in all SmartSuite applications.

Importing Files into Other Programs

If you want to open an entire file in a program other than the one that created it, you must either open or import it, depending on the program. Here's how to get started in each program:

- **Word Pro**. You can open files in a variety of other word processing formats with File, Open, or you can choose File, Import/Export to work through the Import or Export assistant.

- **1-2-3**. You open files from other spreadsheet programs or from text files with File, Open. There is no specific Import command. The best way to place non-tabular data into 1-2-3 is with the Clipboard.

- **Approach**. Choose File, Import Data. This lets you open files in several database and spreadsheet formats.

- **Freelance Graphics (Text)**. To import text from a word processing or plain text file, switch to Outliner view, then use File, Open and select a text file type. The best way to place non-text objects is with the Clipboard.

- **Organizer**. Choose File, Import, and import the data file you want, making sure to map the fields, as you learned in Hour 22.

Understanding OLE

So far you have learned about *static* sharing. The data is shared, but the data loses all contact with its original source. For example, if you copy some 1-2-3 data into Word Pro and then change the original file that the 1-2-3 data came from, the copy in Word Pro does not change, resulting in out-of-sync copies. The solution to this is found in OLE.

 Object Linking and Embedding (OLE): OLE is a way of dynamically linking information so that the copied data retains its connection to its original source.

23

Linking and embedding are two different things, although you can do both at once if you like.

When you link data to its source, the data is updated every time the source is updated. If you make a change to a 1-2-3 spreadsheet with linked data in a Word Pro file, the next time you open that Word Pro file, Word Pro checks to see if an updated version of the 1-2-3 data is available. If it is, it re-copies the data so that its version matches it.

When you embed, the data is associated with the application that created it, so you can double-click the data at any time to open it in its native application. For example, you might embed a graphic that you needed to change frequently. Any time it needed to change, you could double-click it, make the change, and save your work, without having to open its native application separately.

There are two ways to do OLE in an application. The method you'll choose depends on what you want to link or embed. If you want to link or embed an entire file, you'll use one method; if you want to link or embed only a snippet of data from a file, you'll use another.

Linking or Embedding Selected Data from a File

To link or embed selected data, you start out using Edit, Copy as usual, but instead of Edit, Paste, you use a different command: Edit, Paste Special. This opens a dialog box where you can specify your pasting preferences (see Figure 23.1).

The Paste Special dialog box gives you a choice of many formats in which to paste your data. You can paste it in its native format, as plain text, or as several different kinds of graphics. Don't be boggled by all the choices, though; it's really pretty simple.

FIGURE 23.1.

*Paste Special offers a
variety of pasting
options and formats.*

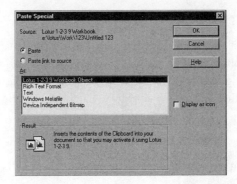

If you want to embed only, choose the Paste option button and select the native file type
from the As list. For example, in Figure 23.1, you would choose Lotus 1-2-3 Workbook
Object.

To both link and embed, choose the Paste Link Option button, and choose the native
application from the As list.

If you plan on linking, you should save the source file first so it has a name.
There needs to be a name in order to create the link. If you are merely
embedding, it doesn't matter since the name of the source file is not
retained.

To link only, choose the Paste Link option button and choose any of the types *except* the
native application from the As list (for example, Rich Text Format).

Embedding and Linking an Entire File

You can link and embed an entire existing file in a SmartSuite document. For example,
suppose you wanted to include the latest financial data from a 1-2-3 workbook as an
appendix in a Word Pro report. The 1-2-3 workbook already exists, so you could insert it
as an object in your report.

 The term *object* means different things in different contexts, but for linking and
embedding purposes, it means a named file, or some data from a named file.

To Do: Inserting an Existing Object

1. Choose Create, Object. The Create Object dialog box opens.

2. Click the Object from a File option button. A File text box appears (see Figure 23.2).

> If the Object command is unavailable on the Create menu in the application you are working with, try a different view. In some programs, such as Freelance, you can insert objects only in certain views.

23

FIGURE 23.2.

When you choose Object from a File, a File text box prompts you for a filename.

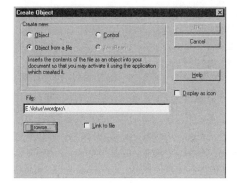

3. Enter the filename in the File text box or click the Browse button and locate it.

4. If you want to link (as well as embed), click the Link to File check box. Otherwise it will merely be embedded.

▲ 5. Click OK. The file is embedded (and linked too if you specified that).

When you embed an existing file, you have the option of linking it. However, when you create a new embedded object, that new object does not exist in a file independently, so it cannot be linked to—only embedded, as you see in the following steps.

Creating a New Embedded Object

Suppose you want to create an impromptu 1-2-3 worksheet in your Word Pro document as you are writing. In this case, the worksheet you want doesn't yet exist, so you would insert (and embed) a new one as a new object in your report.

To Do: Embedding a New Object

1. Choose Create, Object. The Create Object dialog box opens.

2. Click the Object option button if it is not already selected.

3. Choose the type of file you want to embed from the Object type list (see Figure 23.3).

FIGURE 23.3.

You can choose any object type from among the Windows-based programs installed on your system.

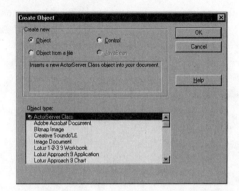

4. Click OK. The controls for the chosen application appear within the host application's window. For example, Figure 23.4 shows the controls for 1-2-3 within the Word Pro window.

FIGURE 23.4.

You have access to most of the application's features without leaving the host application.

Word Pro title bar   1-2-3 SmartIcons and menus

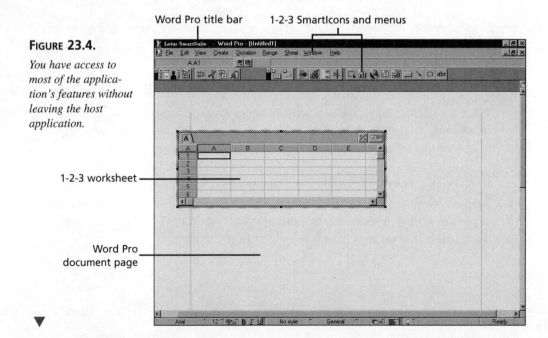

1-2-3 worksheet

Word Pro document page

5. Enter the data you want to create and apply any formatting or other program features needed.

▲   6. Click outside the object area to return the controls to those of the host application.

Performing a Mail Merge

One of the most common tasks that involves more than one SmartSuite component is a mail merge. A mail merge usually involves taking names and addresses from one source and merging them with a letter or other document to create personalized copies for multiple recipients. You have probably gotten dozens of these in the mail: *Mr. Smith, You May Already Be a Winner!*

There are three steps to performing a mail merge:

- Prepare the list of Names and Addresses. You may have already done this in Organizer or Approach. If not, you can create a table in Word Pro or type them into a worksheet in 1-2-3.
- Prepare the form letter. This is best done in Word Pro.
- Perform the merge.

In the following sections, we'll look at each of these steps.

Preparing a List of Names for Mail Merge

If you followed along with the Approach and Organizer sections, you may have already entered the content of your address book into one (or both) of those programs. If so— great. You're ready to roll. If not, go ahead and do so now. Organizer is a great place to keep addresses, as is a database in Approach created using one of the address SmartMaster templates.

If you have not yet created the list of addresses, you can do it either in a Word Pro table or in 1-2-3. With either of these programs, you need to make sure that the field names appear as column headings. In other words, the first row needs to contain labels like FIRST, LAST, ADDRESS, CITY, STATE, and ZIP (see Figure 23.5).

FIGURE 23.5.

If you enter the names in 1-2-3 or Word Pro make sure you label the columns with field names.

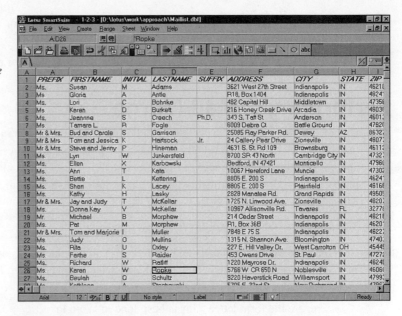

Creating a Mail Merge Document in Word Pro

Next you need to type the letter that will be sent. (Actually it doesn't have to be a letter; you can merge any kind of document using this same procedure.)

Creating a Mail Merge Document

1. Choose Text, Merge, Letter. The Mail Merge Assistant opens (see Figure 23.6).

2. Click the Use Existing button under Select Data File to open a Browse window and then locate and double-click on the file you created in the preceding section.

3. If you are using data from another program, an extra dialog box may appear asking what portion of the data you want to use. For example, when using 1-2-3 data, you're asked to choose between the entire file, a single sheet, and a selected range. Make your selection and click OK.

▲ To Do

FIGURE 23.6.

Complete the three steps of the Mail Merge Assistant to build a mail merge.

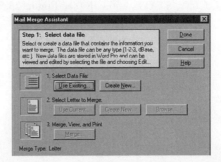

4. Next, the Merge Data File dialog box opens, asking where the field names are located. Click the Field names in the first record of the data file button and click OK. (Now you see why I insisted that you put them there in the previous section.)

5. Now you're back in the Mail Merge Assistant box. You can either click Use Current to use the current document for the letter, or Create New (and then choose a SmartMaster) to start a new one under Select Letter to Merge. Do one or the other.

   The dialog box goes away, and you're left to write your letter. A Merge bar appears across the top of the screen.

6. Write your letter. Wherever you need to insert a merge code, click the field name from the list on the Merge bar and then click the Insert Field button. A completed letter appears in Figure 23.7.

FIGURE 23.7.

Write your letter, using a combination of regular typed text and inserted merge codes.

Merge bar   Choose fields to insert

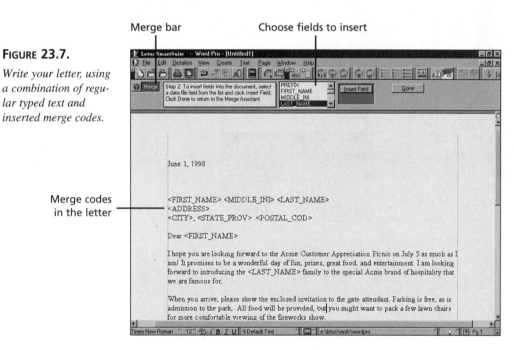

Merge codes in the letter

7. Click the Done button on the Merge bar. The Mail Merge Assistant reappears.

To complete the merge now, go on to the next section. Or, if you need to take a break, click Done to close the Mail Merge Assistant dialog box and come back to it later by choosing Text, Merge, Letter again.

Performing the Merge

When you merge, the data in the data file is combined with the letter to create personalized copies for each recipient. You can merge to a new document and review it before printing, or you can merge directly to the printer.

> The first time you do a mail merge, you should merge to a new document so that you can check your work. If you merge directly to the printer and there is an error, you will have wasted many sheets of paper.

To Do: Making a Merge

1. In the Mail Merge Assistant box, click the Merge button.

2. If the dialog box asking for a range reappears (as in step 3 of the previous procedure), make your selection and click OK.

3. If the dialog box asking for the location of the field names reappears (as in step 4 of the previous procedure), click OK again.

   Now the Merge, View & Print dialog box appears (see Figure 23.8).

FIGURE 23.8.

You're in the home stretch now; this box lets you choose what to merge and what to do with the results.

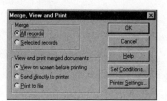

4. In the Merge section, choose All Records to merge the entire data file's data or Selected Records to merge only records you chose earlier.

5. In the View and Print Merged Documents section, choose View on Screen Before Printing.

6. Click OK. The first letter of the set appears onscreen.

7. If the first letter looks wrong, click Done to close the letters and correct the problem.

   If the first letter looks okay, do one of the following:

   - If you want to print the letters one at a time, picking which ones to print and which to skip, click the Print and View Next button or Skip and View Next button for each one. At any point during this, you can print all the remaining letters (excluding the ones you skipped) by clicking Print Rest.

   - If you want to print all the letters at once, click Print All.

8. When you are finished, click Done.

9. If you will need to perform the same merge again in the future, save your letter as you would any Word Pro document. If not, close it without saving changes.

▲

Summary

In this hour, you learned how to share data between SmartSuite applications, both with simple copying and with dynamic OLE. You also learned how to perform a mail merge using names and addresses stored in any SmartSuite application. You're almost done with your 24-hour crash course! In the hour coming up, you'll learn how to create your own Web pages for Internet use.

23

Q&A

Q Are there any drawbacks to using OLE instead of regular copying?

A The big drawback is that OLE links make your data file large and cumbersome. Every time you open, save, or print a file containing OLE links, you have to wait for the links to be updated. If you have an older computer (386 or 486) and have many OLE links in a file, it can bog down the computer so badly that it locks up, and you have to restart it. If you are embedding only (not linking), the problem is not as severe.

Q When I try to open a dBASE file from Approach in 1-2-3 and then save it as a 1-2-3 file with Save As, it doesn't work. It appears to be saving, but the saved file it creates doesn't contain my data.

A When converting between SmartSuite programs, there are sometimes a few glitches. The best way to convert data from one program to another is by copying it from its native program and pasting it into an empty file in the new program. By doing this, you ensure that you are getting only the data, not any macros, formulas, or other gook that can cause unexpected results.

Q Can I use OLE and mail merge together so that the names to be merged are always updated?

A Mail merge is dynamic by its very nature. Each time you remerge, it pulls the latest names and addresses from the data file. Just make sure you save the merge file (the letter with the codes in it). The next time you open it, choose Text, Merge, Letter again, and click the Merge button.

HOUR **24**

Going Online with SmartSuite

More and more, the Internet is becoming part of people's daily lives. All of the SmartSuite components have some sort of Internet capability; together, the SmartSuite package can help you with everything from inserting the occasional hyperlink to building a multi-page Web site. In this chapter, I'll show you what each of the applications has to offer Internet-wise, and you'll learn how to create your own Web site with SmartSuite.

Highlights of this hour include:

- Inserting hyperlinks in documents
- Creating a Web site with Word Pro
- Saving other SmartSuite data in Web format
- Organizing and publishing your pages with FastSite

What Can SmartSuite Do on the Internet?

There are three main Internet capabilities in SmartSuite:

- You can insert links to existing Internet content in regular documents, worksheets, databases, and so on.
- You can create your own Web pages by saving your work in a special format.
- You can organize Web pages and publish them to the Internet with Lotus FastSite.

I'll explain how to do each of these things, but first you should take a few moments to discover how the Internet works. This knowledge will help you greatly, especially if you want to create your own Web pages.

Some Basic Internet Terminology

The *Internet* is a vast interconnected network of computers all over the world. Most of the connected computers make information available to the public, and many of them provide Internet access to individuals and businesses as well.

> This book only covers the bare basics of the Internet. For a more complete tutorial, see *Sams Teach Yourself the Internet in 24 Hours*.

Most ordinary people don't have computers that are directly a part of this big network (the Internet) because it's expensive to maintain the connection 24 hours a day, even when you aren't using it. So instead, they get an account with a service provider, who has a big, powerful computer, called a *server*, that's hard-wired into the Internet full-time. They pay their monthly fees, and the service provider gives them an ID and password that let them connect to the server with their modems. The server provides them with an on-ramp to the Internet for as long as they stay connected by modem.

There are many different kinds of files available on the Internet, and several ways of accessing them. You can look up text-only information through a series of menus on a Gopher system, and you can download all types of files to your own computer with FTP. However, the most popular Internet feature is the World Wide Web, or Web for short.

While you are connected to the Internet, you can use a Web browser program that runs on your PC to request various Web pages from all over the world and display them on your computer screen. The most popular Web browsers are Netscape Communicator (which you can download for free from http://www.netscape.com) and Microsoft Internet Explorer (which you can get, also for free, at http://www.microsoft.com/ie4).

These Web pages are nothing more than simple text files with some HTML (Hypertext Markup Language) codes that tell the Web browser how to format the text and from what locations to pull in the pictures. The HTML code, of course, is hidden from view since your browser reads it. Here is an example of some HTML coding:

```
<p>Elvis <i>lives!</i></p>
```

When your Web browser receives the HTML text, it reads it as shown in Table 24.1. The final result shown by your Web browser looks something like this:

Elvis *lives!*

TABLE 24.1 INTERPRETING A LINE OF HTML CODE

Code	Meaning
<p>	Begin a new paragraph.
Elvis	Print the word "Elvis."
<i>	Make the text that follows italic.
lives!	Print the word "lives!" in italic.
</i>	Stop making text italic now.
</P>	End the paragraph.

Don't worry; you won't have to learn HTML coding with all its brackets and obscure abbreviations. You can apply special styles in Word Pro that will handle the conversion of HTML codes automatically when you save your work. If you do want to learn HTML, don't worry, it's fairly easy to learn. See *Using HTML 4.0*, published by Que.

To request a Web page from a computer that it resides on, you have to know its complete address; it's just like mailing a letter. This name and address is called a Uniform Resource Locator, or URL. (It's pronounced You Are Ell, not Earl, though many people pronounce it incorrectly that way.) A page's URL consists of http:// plus the address of the computer, a slash (/), and the name of the page itself. For example, here is a (fictitious) URL:

```
http://acmecorp.com/~wempen/index.html
```

Some HTML documents end in .htm rather than .html. Sometimes you may see a Web page address that does not have a document name, but only a site address, like this:

```
http://acmecorp.com/~wempen
```

24

When there is no filename, as above, most browsers look for a file with the name index.htm or index.html. In other words, if I call my welcome page "index.htm," I don't have to include the file name in the address I give to people when I invite them to look at my page.

One way to keep both public and restricted-access Web pages at the same address is to link all the public ones through the index.htm page, but not the restricted ones. Then you give your restricted pages unusual names that nobody would guess. Give their names out only to the people you want to be able to access them.

You can jump from page to page with hyperlinks, which are hot links to other URLs. They're called "hot" because you can click on one to make your Web browser open that URL. Hyperlinks can point to other Web pages at your own address, or to pages at any site anywhere in the world. For example, suppose you are promoting a music CD. You might want to have three pages:

- A welcome page that introduces the CD.
- A page that provides downloadable sample clips.
- An order form.

Each of your pages can contain hyperlinks to the other two pages, so your readers can jump freely among them. In addition, you might have other hyperlinks to other, related Web sites besides your own.

Adding Hyperlinks in SmartSuite Documents

When you insert a hyperlink into a document, you create a pointer to a particular URL. Anyone reading your document on a computer screen can click on that hyperlink to open the specified Web page in their system's Web browser. (Obviously, a hyperlink doesn't work on a hard copy printout, but the address of the link can appear on the printout, so anyone reading a printout can manually type that address into their own computer's Web browser.)

A hyperlink can point to other things besides Web pages, although Web pages are by far the most common. For example, you can point to a file to be downloaded, or an email address to send a message to.

Hyperlinks in Word Pro

To insert a hyperlink in Word Pro, choose Create, Hyperlink. The Create Hyperlink dialog box appears.

 If you want an existing bit of text or a graphic that you want to be the link, select it first, before you choose Create, Hyperlink.

24

The default action is to go to a Web page. If you want a different action, such as to send mail to an email address, choose the action from the Action drop-down list. Then enter the address in the Link To text box.

The Linked Text box's use is optional. If you put some text here, this text will be the underlined words to click on to jump to the URL. If you put nothing there, the link that appears in the document will be the same as the text in the Link To box. For example, suppose you want to visit the page http://members.iquest.net/~fwempen/imagodei. You would put that text in the Link To box. To give it a shorter name in your document, you might enter Imago Dei in the Linked Text box. See Figure 24.1.

FIGURE **24.1**

Insert a hyperlink in Word Pro by choosing a link type and typing an address.

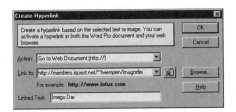

 You can cut and paste the hyperlink from some other source. For example, if you visit a page with your browser and want to link to that page, you could select its URL in the browser and press Ctrl+C to copy it. Then, in the Create Hyperlink box, you could use the Paste button or Ctrl+V to paste the link into the Link To text box.

Hyperlinks in 1-2-3

You can insert a hyperlink in a 1-2-3 cell the same way you do in Word Pro: with the Create, Hyperlink command. The Create Hyperlink dialog box is almost exactly the same in 1-2-3 as it was in Word Pro (refer to Figure 24.1), and it works the same way.

Hyperlinks in Freelance Graphics

In Freelance, you must type the text or graphic first, and then select it and choose Create, Hyperlink. Other than that, the procedure is the same as with Word Pro and 1-2-3.

> In Freelance, you might want to explore some of the other options on the Action drop-down list. For example, you can use a hyperlink to jump to a different page in the presentation, or even to open another application. You can do this in Word Pro and 1-2-3 also, but it's especially useful in Freelance presentations that you are going to distribute via email to other people.

Hyperlinks in Approach

Unlike in other SmartSuite applications, you cannot put a "live" hyperlink in an Approach database field. You can store hyperlinks in any text field, but they will not be clickable; that is, you won't be able to open their pages by clicking on them. You will have to copy the text and then paste it into your Web browser's window.

Don't let this limitation make you think that Approach has limited usefulness on the Internet, however; Approach contains many features designed to help you publish entire Approach databases on a Web site. You'll learn more about those features later in this hour.

Hyperlinks in Organizer

As you learned in Hour 22, Organizer lets you link one item to another. You can link a meeting to a contact, for example. You can use this same capability to link a URL to any other item. To do so, select the item and then choose Create, Internet Link. In the Internet Link dialog box, enter a description in the Description text box and the address itself in the URL text box. Then click OK.

Creating Web Pages

There are many great programs on the market that are specifically designed to build Web sites (that is, collections of Web pages). And I won't tell you that using SmartSuite is better, because it's not necessarily so. However:

- SmartSuite is available right now, already installed on your PC.
- By using SmartSuite to create Web pages, you avoid having to learn another new program.
- SmartSuite (especially Word Pro) can do an adequate job creating pages, if your needs are simple.
- Your data may already be in a SmartSuite program's format, eliminating the need for a conversion program.

24

> I don't want to discourage you from using SmartSuite for your Web site creation, but neither do I want you to think that you can easily create flashy, complex pages with it. If you need a professional-quality business Web site, consider a program like Microsoft Front Page 98, or learn HTML.

With those caveats out of the way, let's take a look at the various SmartSuite components' Web page creation capabilities. Generally speaking, if you want to create a new Web page, or a series of pages, Word Pro is your best bet. Word Pro has by far the best Web page creation capabilities of the suite. On the other hand, if you need to publish data from one of the other SmartSuite applications on the Internet, you should work from that program.

Setting Up Your Internet Save Location

If you are going to save your work directly to an Internet server, you must do a bit of setup beforehand. You can do this from within whatever SmartSuite application you are creating your Web content from.

NEW TERM Your *Internet server* is the big computer belonging to the company or service provider that gives you Internet access. Usually each user (including you) has his or her own special directory for saving files; you need to find out what yours is named before you do this setup.

From within any SmartSuite application (Word Pro, 1-2-3, Approach, or Freelance), choose File, Internet, Setup. This opens the Internet Setup dialog box. Fill in these fields on the FTP Hosts tab:

- Enter the address of the server you will be saving to in the Host Address text box. Do not include the path to your directory. For example, the address to save to might be ftp://ftp.yoursite.com.

- Enter the directory on that server where your files should be saved in the Initial Directory box. For example, you might enter members/ur/4342/user/~jsmith, if that's what you were told your path should be.

- If you need to log into the server with a username and password (which you probably do), clear the Anonymous FTP check box and enter a user ID and password.

If you need to set up to use proxy server, do so on the Proxies tab. You might need this, for example, if you are connecting from a company that has a firewall set up to prevent intruders. Your system administrator can provide more details if you need to use a proxy server. When you are finished with both tabs, click OK to close the dialog box.

NEW TERM A *firewall* is a program that makes a company's server less prone to hacker attacks by placing an electronic "barrier" to incoming communications. If your company uses one of these, they probably also have set up a proxy server that allows you to bypass it to access the Internet. Your system administrator can explain this more fully and tell you what proxy server settings you need, if any.

If you don't have the information handy to set up your Internet save location, you can save the Web pages you create to your hard disk, and then transfer them to the server later.

Creating Web Content with Word Pro

Creating Web pages with Word Pro could be the subject of several whole chapters. There is a lot you can do! In this section, I'll show you where to find the most important commands and features, and then let you explore on your own.

Step 1: Create the Page

To start a Web page, use one of the Internet SmartMasters. In the New Document dialog box (File, New), on the Create from Any SmartMaster tab, choose either Internet - Corporate or Internet - Personal, and choose a look to go with it. For the examples in this chapter, I'll use Personal with the Home1 look.

Step 2: Customize the Text

First things first: Customize the page as you would any SmartMaster template. Just click on a placeholder block, and type your own text (see Figure 24.2). You'll want to replace the page title and add an explanation of the Web site's purpose and content.

FIGURE 24.2

Replace the placeholder text on the page created by the template.

Click on the placeholder blocks and type your own text.

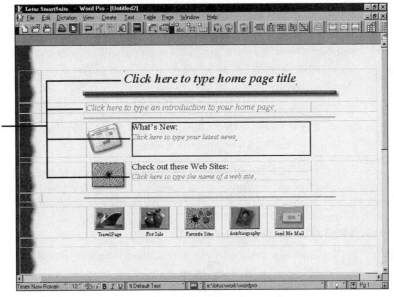

24

Step 3: Delete Elements You Don't Need

You probably won't need all the placeholder elements on the sample page. For example, you might want to get rid of the Travel button if you're not going to include travel information. To delete an element, click on it and press Delete.

The buttons along the bottom of the page are in a table. You can clear a table cell by pressing Delete, but the cell still remains. You can place your own content in that cell, or you can delete the cell itself. To do so, click inside the cell and then right-click on the cell and choose Delete Row/Column. Click the Column option button, and click OK.

Step 4: Customize the Graphics

The graphics that appear on the page are fairly general, and work well in many cases. However, you may want to replace some or all of them with your own graphics.

To replace a graphic, delete the graphic within the frame inside the cell (select it and then choose GIF, Delete), and then insert a different picture with File, Import Picture.

> If you are using your own graphics on the page, make sure they are the correct size to fit nicely in the table. You may want to resize them in a paint program like Windows' Paintbrush, or create them in exactly the right size to begin with.

Step 5: Adding Hyperlinks

Next, you'll want to make each of the graphic buttons into hyperlinks. (Don't worry that you haven't created the pages yet that they'll link to; you can do this momentarily.) Click on a graphic to select it, and then use the Create, Hyperlink command to link it to a URL.

When you choose Create, Hyperlink when a graphic is selected, the dialog box has a new text box in it: Graphic Description. Fill in a description here that will appear if the viewer's browser can't show graphics for some reason.

To create links between your pages, enter the filename in the URL box. Delete the http://, and simply type the name of the page. If you haven't created the pages yet that you'll link to, decide on their names and create the links now anyway.

Step 6: Saving Your Work

As the final step, save your work. You can do this in any of three ways.

The most straightforward method is to use File, Save. You'll want to save in HTML format, rather than normal Word Pro format, so change the Save As Type drop-down list setting to HTML (*.HTM). If a warning message appears that some of the formatting may not be available, click Yes. (This isn't a problem, since you started with an Internet SmartMaster.)

If you are creating the initial page for your Web site, the page that you will want visitors to see first, name it index.htm. Otherwise, name it some meaningful name that will help you remember its content.

A more powerful way is to choose File, Internet, HTML Export Assistant. This opens an Assistant, a series of dialog boxes in which you can make choices about the way you want your work saved for Internet use. Here's a rundown of the options you can set:

These options are found on the Content tab:

- Export. Choose Entire Document or Current Division, if there is more than one division in your document and you only want to export that division.
- Content Options. Mark any of the checkboxes here that are applicable to your situation:
- Save Divisions as Separate Files. This creates separate Web pages for each division.
- Save Sections as Separate Files. Same as above, except for sections rather than divisions.
- Include Header from Document. Places the document header at the top of each page. This is useful for placing navigation hyperlinks on every page.

- Include Footer from Document. Save as above, except it's the footer, and it's at the bottom.
- Font Face Support. Includes any special fonts you have used in the document. Otherwise the text will be displayed in the default font for the browser that each individual reader is using.

These options are found on the Layout tab:

- Navigation Arrows. If you are creating multiple pages (out of multiple divisions or sections), you can choose navigation arrows for moving among them.
- Include Link to URL. Mark this check box and enter a URL that you want to appear on every page if needed. This is useful for pointing the reader back to the home page.

Use the Save Locally button on the Preview & Save tab of the Assistant to save the files to a temporary location on your hard disk. You can then transfer them to your Internet server later. Or, choose the Save to Internet button to copy the files directly to your Internet server.

24

If you are not sure what Internet server address you should use, talk to your system administrator at your company or call your service provider if you are an individual or home user.

The final way of saving your work is with the File, Internet, Save to Internet command. This lets you save your work on the Internet server without converting it to HTML format. You save it in its native Word Pro format instead. In this way, you can share it with other Internet users of Word Pro. This is useful when you have a document that relies on some of Word Pro's features that get lost when converting to HTML format, but is of limited usefulness when you are specifically creating Web pages.

Step 7: Creating Additional Pages

Now you need to create the other pages of your site, if you are going to have a multi-page site. Repeat steps 1 through 5, again using one of the Internet SmartMasters. (Generally, it's best if you use the same SmartMaster for each page, for a consistent look.)

Creating Web Content with 1-2-3

You will probably not create your index page (that is, your "home" page) in 1-2-3. That's because 1-2-3 is not as easy or powerful for creating Web pages as Word Pro. Instead, you might open a few pages that contain 1-2-3 data and save them in HTML format, and then link to them from your index page that you create in Word Pro.

You can choose to save your 1-2-3 content in either a regular HTML table or in a special format called jDoc. jDoc format is especially good because it retains all your formatting and provides onscreen buttons to move from screenful to screenful of data. It does not display correctly in browsers that do not support Java, however, so people with older Web browsers may not be able to read it.

To Do: Saving 1-2-3 Data as a Web Page

1. (Optional) If you want only certain data from a worksheet, select it.
2. Choose File, Internet, Convert to Web Pages. The Convert to Web Pages dialog box opens (see Figure 24.3).
3. Enter a name in the File Name for Web Page text box.
4. In the What to Convert section, choose Entire Workbook, Current Sheet, or Selected Range.

FIGURE 24.3

Use this dialog box to specify how you want your 1-2-3 data saved.

5. In the Format area, choose HTML Table (available only if you chose Selected Range in step 4) or jDoc. I recommend using jDoc unless you think that your potential audience might not be using Java-capable browsers.
6. Click Next.
7. Fill in the options presented on the next screen. The options vary depending on your choice in step 5.

   If you chose jDoc, your only option is Add a Link for Downloading the 1-2-3 file. This places a link on the Web page that enables the reader to download the 1-2-3 document in its native format.

▼   If you chose HTML Table, you can choose several extra items for the page, includ-
     ing a header, description, author name, and so on. Click a check mark to indicate
     you want to include the element, and then type the text for it in the accompanying
     text box (see Figure 24.4).

FIGURE 24.4

*If you are saving 1-2-3
data as an HTML
table, there are some
additional page ele-
ments you can choose
to add.*

24

8. Click Next again to view the next set of options.

9. (Optional) To check out how the saved document will look in a browser, click the
    Preview in Browser button. When you are finished, close the browser window and
    return to 1-2-3 to finish filling out this dialog box.

10. In the Location section, choose Local or Network Drive or Internet Server.

11. Make sure the correct path to the save location appears in the Directory text box.
    Use Browse to locate it if needed.

▲   12. Click Save. Your file is saved.

Creating Web Content with Freelance

In Freelance, you use the same command as in the other programs: File, Internet, Convert
to Web pages. Then you follow along with the Convert to Web Pages assistant that
appears. Each of the options along the way is explained very well onscreen, so I won't
belabor the procedure with you here. Give it a try on your own.

Creating Web Content with Approach

In Approach, you can save Web content in several ways. The most straightforward
method, and the one that most people will use, is File, Internet, Convert View to Web
Pages command. It works like the similar commands in the other SmartSuite applications
that you have already seen, and results in a Web page that shows the content of the
currently selected view.

You can also save your entire Approach database in .APT format, a read-only Approach format that other Approach users can read. This has the advantage of preserving all the data and all the views, not just one particular view.

To Do: Saving Approach Files to an Internet Server

1. Choose File, Internet, Save to Internet.
2. Under Save, choose either Current View only or All of the Views.
3. Select what data you want to save: All Databases, Found Set, Current Record, or Blank Databases. If you selected All of the Views in step 2, your only choices are All Databases and Blank Databases.
4. Click Save.
5. Select a host server from the "FTP Servers" box.

> If you don't have any servers configured (remember, we went through this in "Setting Up Your Internet Location" earlier in this hour), click Hosts and enter the connection information. Click Save, and then Done.

6. Click Connect.
7. Specify a location on the server for the file.
8. Enter a filename with an .APT file extension in the File Name box.
9. Select Lotus Approach (.APT) in the Save as Type box.
10. Click Save.

Building a Web Site with FastSite

FastSite is a Web page organizer. You can import the pages you create with your SmartSuite applications, and link them together to create a coherent, consistent-looking site.

You will definitely want to explore FastSite on your own, as there is not enough space in this chapter to do it justice. Here are some pointers for using it.

To Do: Using FastSite

1. First, create a new site. The first time you run FastSite, the New Site dialog box appears automatically. If you don't see it, choose File, New Site.
2. While creating the new site, you're prompted to add files. Add the files you've created with your other SmartSuite applications by clicking the Add Files button and locating them. (You can add more files later with File, Add File.)

▼ 3. After you've created your new site, each page appears in a tree structure on the left side of the screen. Click on the page you want to see, and use the tabs at the top to switch between the Choose Tasks and Preview Web Pages windows.

4. If a page does not appear on the Preview Web Pages tab, a message appears there instead explaining that the file must be converted to Web format. Click the Convert button to perform this conversion. It can convert not only Web pages you've created in other SmartSuite applications, but also regular documents (non-Web format) from the applications as well.

5. When you are finished building your site, choose File, Convert to Web Pages, and convert all the pages to a format that Web browsers will understand.

▲ 6. To publish your site to the Internet, choose File, Post Web Pages to Server.

 For more in-depth coverage of FastSite, see *Using SmartSuite Millennium Edition*, published by Que.

24

Summary

In this hour, you learned how to integrate your SmartSuite documents with the Internet. We started out talking about the simple addition of hyperlinks to normal documents, and ended up working on creating Web pages and publishing them to a server. Of course, creating a Web site is time-consuming, and I don't expect for you to have finished yours in an hour! But now you have the knowledge and tools at your disposal to get started.

This is the 24th hour, so we're done with the official part of the book. Stay tuned, however, for a bonus hour on IBM's ViaVoice Gold, the voice control software included with SmartSuite.

Q&A

Q I'm apprehensive about creating a Web site; what's the best way to get started?

A Create a simple document in Word Pro, and save it in HTML format with File, Save As. Then open it in your Web browser (Netscape Navigator or Internet Explorer, perhaps?) and evaluate your work. (There should be some sort of File, Open command in your browser.) This will help demystify the process. Practice creating HTML documents in various SmartSuite applications, and opening them in your browser, until you become comfortable.

Q What is this jDoc thing, and how does it compare to HTML?

A jDoc is a Java-based formatting language for the Internet that enables you to more closely replicate the data's original formatting than HTML allows. All SmartSuite applications allow you to save your work in jDoc format as well as in HTML. The drawback to using jDoc is that only users with Web browser programs that support Java can see the data.

Q And what is Java?

A Java is a programming language designed specifically for use with Web browsers. Its uniqueness and value come from the fact that programs written in Java can be run on any kind of computer—Macintosh, Windows, UNIX, and so on.

Bonus Hour

Using ViaVoice

ViaVoice is a real boon for slow typists. With ViaVoice, you can dictate your text into Word Pro or 1-2-3 via a microphone attached to your system. In this bonus hour, we'll explore ViaVoice's setup and use in Word Pro.

Highlights of this hour include:

- Installing the ViaVoice Software
- Training ViaVoice to Recognize Your Speech
- Dictating Text in Word Pro

Why Use ViaVoice?

ViaVoice Gold is a product that recognizes your voice and converts it into typed text. The full version of ViaVoice Gold costs more than $100 in stores, and works with dozens of programs. The version you get with SmartSuite is free, but works only with Word Pro and 1-2-3.

ViaVoice is especially nice for people who type slowly, or for people who have a hard time typing. ViaVoice does make some errors, but you will probably find that correcting the errors is less trouble than typing everything from scratch. You will also encounter fewer errors over time, as ViaVoice learns from its mistakes.

What You Need to Use ViaVoice

In addition to the SmartSuite 98 CD, you need the following items to use ViaVoice:

- A SoundBlaster 16 (or 100 percent compatible) sound card. Beware; many sound cards purport to be 100 percent SoundBlaster compatible, but are not.
- A microphone. The best kind for speech recognition is a headset mike. The kind that you hold or sits on your desk do not work very well.
- Speakers, either built into the headset or separate units that sit on your desk.
- A fairly speedy computer. Processing your voice commands requires quite a bit of computing power. You must have at least a 150 MHz Pentium processor with at least 32 megabytes of RAM (or 48 megabytes if you are using Windows NT as your operating system).
- Plenty of hard disk space. You must have at least 125 megabytes free.

Installing ViaVoice

You can install ViaVoice immediately after you install the regular SmartSuite programs, or you can come back and do it later. Installing ViaVoice installs a limited ("runtime") version of ViaVoice Gold 4.3. It is limited in that it works only with Word Pro, not with other applications, but within Word Pro it is fully functional.

When you run the ViaVoice installation program, it also installs a special version of Word Pro that is integrated with ViaVoice.

> You must have already installed the regular version of Word Pro using the Install or Express Install options before you can install ViaVoice.

To Do: Installing ViaVoice

To Do ▼

1. Reinsert the SmartSuite CD in your drive. A menu of choices appears. (If you do not see it, use My Computer to browse the content of the CD and double-click the Autorun program in the Autorun folder of the CD.)

2. Click the Extras icon. A folder window showing the content of the Extras folder on the CD appears.

3. Double-click the ViaVoice folder.

4. Double-click the Setup icon (see Figure 25.1). The setup program runs.

FIGURE 25.1.

Locate the Setup icon within the Extras\ViaVoice folder on your SmartSuite CD.

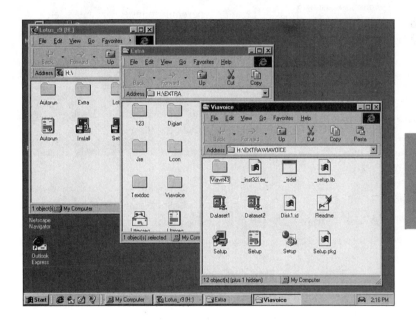

25

To keep the steps to a manageable length in this chapter, I won't belabor them in detail. For example, step 5 of these steps encompasses many individual actions, but each of the actions is clearly explained onscreen.

5. Complete the setup program, responding to its prompts as needed.

6. After the Setup program runs, the Microphone Setup Wizard opens (see Figure 25.2). Choose Set Up the Microphone (which is probably your only available choice) and follow the prompts onscreen to work through your microphone setup.

▼

The first time you use the Microphone Setup Wizard, you will not be able to choose Adjust the Audio Level until after you have chosen Set Up the Microphone and worked through those prompts.

FIGURE 25.2.

The Microphone Setup Wizard helps you configure your microphone to work with ViaVoice.

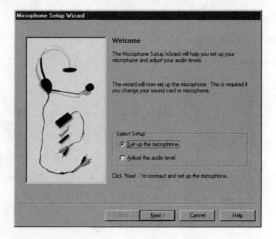

7. After the Microphone Setup Wizard is finished, the ViaVoice Enrollment program runs. Follow its instructions, speaking words into the microphone as directed, to train ViaVoice to work with your voice.

If you need more guidance in step 7, see "Enrolling a New ViaVoice User" later in this hour, which takes you through this same process in more detail.

When you are done training ViaVoice, you're ready to work in Word Pro! Go on to the next section, "Using Word Pro with ViaVoice."

If for any reason you had to abort any of the setup procedures (for the microphone or for ViaVoice Enrollment), you can complete them later. You can also re-run them at any time, or set up an enrollment for a new person, so that more than one person can use ViaVoice. If you need to do any of these things, see "Setting Up a Microphone" or "Enrolling a New ViaVoice User" at the end of this chapter.

Using Word Pro with ViaVoice

When you start Word Pro after you have installed ViaVoice, a special bar appears across the top of the screen. A ViaVoice icon also appears in the System Tray area of Windows (down by the clock). As these items load, a voice welcomes you to the ViaVoice program (see Figure 25.3).

FIGURE 25.3.

ViaVoice adds its own bar and an extra menu to Word Pro.

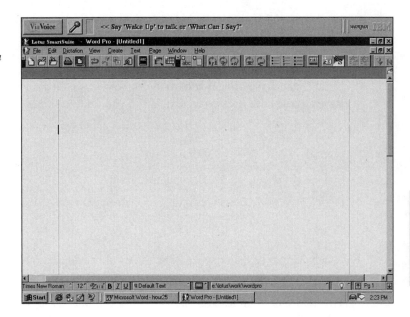

You can click the ViaVoice button on the bar to open a menu of ViaVoice commands for ViaVoice itself, such as Microphone Setup and User Settings. There is also a Dictation menu on the Word Pro menu bar, which contains commands for working with ViaVoice in Word Pro.

If you want to turn off ViaVoice for this Word Pro session, click the ViaVoice button and choose Exit from the menu that appears. ViaVoice will restart the next time you exit and reopen Word Pro. To permanently turn off ViaVoice, uninstall it (Start, Programs, IBM ViaVoice, Tools, Installation Tools, Uninstall ViaVoice Gold Runtime.)

25

Beginning Dictation

Ready to dictate? Strap on your microphone, and let's get started. Just say **Wake Up** into the microphone. The Microphone icon on the ViaVoice bar turns green, if it wasn't already, and the words Wake Up appear next to it, signifying that ViaVoice heard you.

If the microphone icon is gray, it means that the microphone is turned off. Click it to make it turn green, which means "on."

To begin dictation, say **Begin Dictation**. ViaVoice says "Begin Dictating." From then on, whatever you say becomes typed text. When you want to stop, say **Stop Dictation**.

As you are dictating, you can say these words and phrases to insert punctuation:

Comma	Semi-colon
End Paragraph	Exclamation Point
Dash	Period
Colon	

For example, to type the sentence "The names of my dogs are: Sheldon, Shasta, and Ashley" and then start a new paragraph you would say:

The names of my dogs are colon Sheldon comma Shasta comma and Ashley period end paragraph

Go ahead and try dictating a few paragraphs now—just the first things that occur to you to say.

Correcting Errors

Proofread the text that ViaVoice typed, and you will likely find at least a few errors. One way to correct them is to simply edit them normally, but if you plan on using ViaVoice in the future, it is better to correct the mistake through ViaVoice, as described in the following steps, to train ViaVoice to not make those mistakes in the future.

To Do: Correcting a ViaVoice Error

▼ To Do

1. Highlight the mistyped word or phrase.

2. Choose Dictation, Correct Error or press Alt+F2. ViaVoice plays your voice back to you, so you can hear exactly what you said, and a box pops up for you to type your correction (see Figure 25.4).

3. Type the correction, and then click OK. ViaVoice records the correction.

4. Repeat these steps for each error.

FIGURE 25.4.

Correct errors to help ViaVoice improve its accuracy in the future.

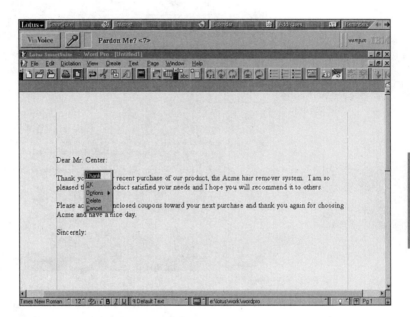

25

▲

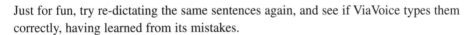

Just for fun, try re-dictating the same sentences again, and see if ViaVoice types them correctly, having learned from its mistakes.

Reading Text with ViaVoice

In addition to its recording capabilities, ViaVoice can also read typed text aloud for you. This is great for anybody who doesn't see very well, or for reading back a memo to you while you are up walking around the room doing something else.

To Do: Reading Text

1. If you don't want to hear the entire document, select the text you want to hear.

2. Choose Dictate, Begin Reading. A box appears below the ViaVoice button with a cartoon character in it, and the character reads to you (see Figure 25.5).

3. If you need to pause the reading, click Pause. To resume, click Resume.

FIGURE 25.5.

The character reads your text to you.

Click here to change the voice

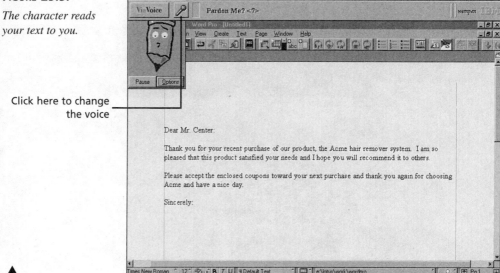

While the reading is occurring, you can click the Options button to set options for the reading. The coolest thing you can do here is change the character that is reading to you. There are a variety of voices, including adults, children, and elderly persons in both male and female. Choose who you want from the Selected Speaker drop-down list (see Figure 25.6).

FIGURE 25.6.

Set options for the reading voice, including choosing a speaker.

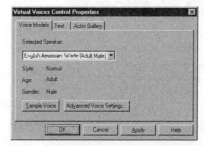

Setting Up a Microphone

You might need to set the microphone up again if you get a new mike, or if you are not happy with the recording levels. The Microphone Setup Wizard automatically sets appropriate recording levels, while it is setting up your hardware.

To re-run the microphone setup, choose Start, Programs, IBM ViaVoice, Tools, Microphone Setup. Then complete the Microphone Setup Wizard again.

Enrolling a New ViaVoice User

When you first installed ViaVoice, you were taken through the enrollment procedure. It is a somewhat lengthy process, however, and you may have had to abort it to take care of something else. You can complete the enrollment at any time, or enroll a totally new user.

To run the Enrollment Wizard, choose Start, Programs, IBM ViaVoice, Tools, Enrollment. Choose a person's name from the list and then click Enroll to pick up an already-started enrollment, or click the Create button to create a new user.

To Do: Setting up a New User

▼ To Do

1. In the IBM ViaVoice Enrollment window, click the Create button. The ViaVoice User Wizard window opens.

2. Enter the person's name in the Use Name field and then click Next.

3. Read the information about setting up the microphone, and click Next again. The Microphone Setup Wizard reruns.

4. Click the Adjust the Audio Level option button. (You do not need to run through the entire microphone setup again just because you are setting up a new user.) Then click Next.

5. Work through the audio level checks, following the prompts on the screen. (You already went through this once when you set up the microphone, so it should be old hat.) When the audio level checks are finished, you return to the ViaVoice User Wizard for Quick Training.

6. Follow the prompts onscreen, speaking the words into the microphone to train ViaVoice to recognize your voice (see Figure 25.7). When you are finished with this procedure, you have a voice of ending the wizard or doing the complete enrollment. (If you do the latter, see the next set of steps.)

▲

If you have time, I recommend you do the full enrollment right away. It will greatly improve ViaVoice's dictation accuracy. If you don't have time, you can come back and do this later, as described in the next set of steps.

25

FIGURE 25.7

Read each sentence in your normal speaking voice. ViaVoice learns from it, and improves its performance.

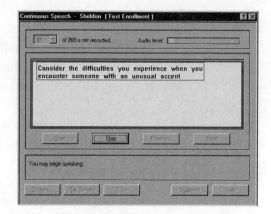

To Do: Completing a User Enrollment

1. In the IBM ViaVoice Enrollment window, click the user you want, and then the Enroll button. A statistics screen appears showing the progress that has been made in enrolling the user.

2. Click Start to pick up the enrollment wherever it left off.

3. Follow the instructions onscreen, reading the sentences that appear into the microphone.

4. When you are finished with the first 50 sentences, you have the option of choosing:

   Train to process the speech you have spoken so far.

   Suspend to delay the processing and come back later for more recording. I don't recommend this, because your first 50 sentences will not be processed yet, and you won't be able to benefit from having recorded them.

   Start to record a larger sample of your speech.

   If you are eager to get started, you can choose Train, but I recommend that you choose Start and record the full 250+ samples of your speech. This will save you editing time later.

Summary

In this bonus hour, you learned how to install and control ViaVoice, a voice-recognition program that lets you "type" with your voice in Word Pro. If you enjoy ViaVoice in Word Pro, you might be interested in upgrading to the full version of ViaVoice Gold, which works in a variety of other programs. See your local software retailer.

Thanks for reading this book! I hope you are leaving with a better knowledge of SmartSuite, and are feeling optimistic about tackling all your document creation and integration tasks. Good luck!

Q&A

Q I can't get past the Microphone Setup Wizard. It doesn't seem to hear anything from my microphone. It's as if the microphone is dead.

A Check the obvious things first—is your microphone plugged into the right socket on your sound card? Is there a mute switch on its cord, and if so, is it flipped to the right position? If you've eliminated all those factors, the problem may be that you have an off-brand sound card that is not 100 percent SoundBlaster Compatible. Sad to say, you may have to replace your sound card or give up on using ViaVoice. (Fortunately, a basic SoundBlaster 16 card is less than $50.)

25

Q ViaVoice isn't very good at recognizing my speech. What can I do to make it better?

A Have you run through the full Enrollment, all 265 sentences? It takes awhile, but it's worth it. See "Enrolling a New User" earlier in this chapter.

Q Is there a way I can add words to ViaVoice's list of recognized words?

A There are a couple of utilities installed with ViaVoice, and you'll find them on the Start, Programs, IBM ViaVoice, Tools menu. Vocabulary Expander lets you add words, and Vocabulary Manager manages your list of added words. (You can delete and change words from there.) You can also use Dictate, Vocabulary Expander from within Word Pro.

However, a simple way is to simply dictate a document that contains the words to add and then correct ViaVoice's errors (with Alt+F2).

Q There seem to be a lot of ViaVoice options and controls that we didn't cover in this hour. How can I find out more about them?

A A great place to start is the ViaVoice Help system. Click the ViaVoice button on the ViaVoice bar, and choose Help, Contents. You can also check out the Start, Programs, IBM ViaVoice, Dictation Runtime Readme file.

INDEX